Empowerment and Interconnectivity

Empowerment and Interconnectivity

Toward a Feminist History of Utilitarian Philosophy

CATHERINE VILLANUEVA GARDNER

The Pennsylvania State University Press
University Park, Pennsylvania

A portion of chapter 2 originally appeared in Catharine
Villanueva Gardner, "Heaven-Appointed Educators
of Mind: Catharine Beecher and the Moral Power of
Women," *Hypatia* 19, no. 2 (2004): 1–16.

LIBRARY OF CONGRESS CATALOGING-IN-PUBLICATION DATA

Gardner, Catherine Villanueva.
  Empowerment and interconnectivity : toward a
feminist history of utilitarian philosophy / Catherine
Villanueva Gardner.
    p. cm.
Summary: "Examines the work of three nineteenth-century
utilitarian feminist philosophers: Catharine Beecher,
Frances Wright, and Anna Doyle Wheeler. Focuses on
methodological questions in order to recover their
philosophy and categorize it as feminist"—Provided by
publisher.
Includes bibliographical references and index.
ISBN 978-0-271-05814-6 (cloth : alk. paper)
1. Feminist theory—United States—History—19th century.
2. Feminist theory—Great Britain—History—19th century.
3. Utilitarianism—United States—History—19th century.
4. Utilitarianism—Great Britain—History—19th century.
5. Beecher, Catharine Esther, 1800–1878.
6. Wright, Frances, 1795–1852.
7. Wheeler, Anna, b. ca. 1785.
I. Title.

HQ1191.U6G37 2013
305.42010973—dc23
2012029234

To LV

Contents

INTRODUCTION

Empowerment and Interconnectivity:
Toward a Feminist History of Utilitarian Philosophy

The central figures in this book are all nineteenth-century utilitarians of one stripe or another. They also have in common the fact that they have been seen as feminist, although they do not all share the same type of feminist views. Two of them—Jeremy Bentham and John Stuart Mill—are major figures in our Western philosophical canon. Others—Anna Doyle Wheeler, William Thompson, Frances Wright, and Catherine Beecher—are on the margins of our history of philosophy, their work neglected or their philosophical substance questioned or unrecognized.

What originally drew me to these philosophers was my study of the history of feminism, specifically British and American nineteenth-century feminism. The nineteenth century in these countries is often depicted as one of activism rather than theorizing. Much of the writing about the history of feminism at this time in the United States and the United Kingdom has focused on the activist work of figures such as Elizabeth Cady Stanton, Susan B. Anthony, and Emmeline Pankhurst.

Perhaps this is how it should be; after all, it was the political organizing of the nineteenth and twentieth centuries that lead to material changes in women's social, political, and economic lives.

Relatively speaking, compared to studies of the history of feminist activism, feminist *philosophical* work has been largely ignored. This neglect is unsurprising, given the tremendous achievements of the activists of this era. Similarly, general histories of nineteenth-century philosophy tend to be male dominated. Moreover, even though such general histories may discuss the feminist work of a canonical philosopher, such as John Stuart Mill, these histories tend to neglect the existence of feminist philosophers. However, as inheritors of the rights fought for by these activist foremothers, we now have the relative luxury to investigate the feminist philosophical work of the nineteenth century. Indeed, we can ask not just whether there were a few isolated philosophers who wrote on feminist issues, but whether there is an identifiable history of feminist philosophy. If such a feminist history of philosophy exists, we would need to determine its relation to "mainstream" or canonical history of philosophy. More important, we would need to ask about how we would decide who is to be included. In other words, we would need to ask how a history of feminist philosophy would be done.

This then is my focus: what can be said about nineteenth-century British and American *feminist philosophy*? This, however, is not an easy task. Twenty-first-century feminist philosophy is no one thing, moreover, to apply modern definitions to works that existed prior to the conceptualization of the subject area "feminist philosophy" (or even feminism itself) will strike many as inexcusably anachronistic. But I think it is worth the risk of such accusations to claim that feminist philosophical thinking has deep historical roots. Even with a limited focus on Anglo-American works, feminist philosophy is not a monolithic theory; however, it is possible to offer a working definition that is both applicable to contemporary thought and suitable for an examination of nineteenth-century works.

The fundamental distinction between contemporary feminist philosophy and mainstream philosophy in the Anglo-American tradition is that the former does not claim to search for knowledge solely for its own sake, but rather for the sake of a political goal: identification and elimination of the subordination of women. Here we are provided with our initial working definition for the examination of my chosen texts. As we shall see, the distinctive feature of nineteenth-century feminist philosophy will be what it has to offer its female contemporaries for their empowerment. We shall see that support for women's suffrage or critiques of the social injustices faced by women will not be enough to identify a particular text or texts as specifically *feminist* philosophical work or a particular philosopher as a specifically *feminist* philosopher. It is important to understand that my conception of feminist philosophy requires nuance; it is an initial working definition that will be developed as my overall argument progresses.

I recognize that there have been many valuable feminist readings of traditional texts that have sought understanding or clarification of the implications of these texts for women (either past or present) without any apparent goal of knowledge that will produce change (i.e., readings that do not reflect my working definition). Yet there is a sense in which the success of these readings seems more by accident than by design. My concern is that there is nothing common to all these individual readings that can be identified as an explicitly "feminist approach" to the reading of these texts: there is nothing that can provide a foundation for a distinctly feminist history of philosophy. What I want to do throughout this work is to draw attention to the need for self-consciousness about the political and ethical dimensions of our theorizing.[1] This is something we can also learn in different ways from the philosophers I study, and it is a worldview that is a corollary to the characterization of feminist philosophy with which I am working. It is this corollary about our ethical and political awareness—and thus accountability—that I claim is at the foundation of a feminist history of philosophy.

I aim to show how a feminist history of philosophy could carry out its political goal not just through canon revision and revaluation of neglected women philosophers, but through a consideration of its own methodology. I am not just interested in retrieving and evaluating the work of English and American nineteenth-century feminist philosophers; I am also interested in asking meta-questions about how this enterprise should be done. There appear to be two main questions here. First, what work has been done in what could be called the feminist history of philosophy, and are there already distinctively feminist approaches to the history of philosophy in place? Second, given the political goals of feminist philosophy, can we—and should we—employ what I am calling "standard" or "mainstream" Anglo-American approaches to doing the history of philosophy to these feminist historical texts? My concern is that the feminist content and politics of these texts makes it *harder* to use nonfeminist methodologies in an examination of them. In asking these questions the actual process of consideration of methodology *itself* becomes important. The approach—better yet, perspective or lens—I want to develop is less about overturning standard or mainstream approaches and then replacing them with a feminist approach, and more about reflecting on the process of interpretation itself and the political and ethical self-consciousness required for this reflection.

Philosophy has a very distinctive relationship to its history; as Jonathan Rée (1978, 1) points out, it "is much more concerned with its past than any other modern academic discipline." With other disciplines, their histories are typically seen as separate fields of study; more to the point, this separation is not contentious. Thus physicists may study historical cosmologies, but no physicist who wishes to be taken seriously would combine this historical study with his or her contemporary theoretical work. In the case of philosophy, however, the relationship—and the importance of this relationship—between its history and its contemporary study is far more complicated.

Like other fields of philosophical study, such as epistemology or ethics, there has been feminist work in history of philosophy. Feminist history of philosophy has focused, thus far, primarily on canon revision, canon critique, and the recovery of neglected or forgotten women philosophers. There has been some methodological work, but this has typically focused on discussions of the predominantly male canon.[2] Charlotte Witt (2007) places the feminist historical work done thus far into four main categories. The first category covers (a) work criticizing misogyny in the canon, (b) identification of gendered interpretations of philosophical concepts, and (c) "synoptic" interpretations. Of these three, the synoptic approach is the most radical, as it "considers the Western philosophical tradition as a whole, and argues that its core concepts are gendered male." Thus, Witt argues, "philosophy's self-image as universal and objective, rather than particular and biased, is mistaken."

The second category is revision of the history of philosophy. As Witt states, "Feminist canon revision is most distinctive, and most radical, in its retrieval of women philosophers for the historical record, and its placement of women in the canon of great philosophers. It is a distinctive project because there is no comparable activity undertaken by other contemporary philosophical movements, for whom canon creation has been largely a process of selection from an already established list of male philosophers." However, Witt points out that retrieving women philosophers—while it is a feminist project—has mainly found women philosophers who did not write feminist philosophy or philosophy in a feminine voice: "Newly recovered women philosophers suggest that there is little overlap among three groups: women philosophers, feminine philosophers and feminist philosophers." Witt says that the fact that there is no unified "voice" and that there is such diversity may raise the question of why recovery is an important project. She responds with two main reasons: first, it rights history by showing that there were women philosophers, and, second, it affects the image of philosophy in the present. In other words, philosophy is not male, and this is not justified by its history. The "us" of philosophy, as Witt puts it, is both male and female.

The third category is appropriation of canonical philosophers for feminist use; Annette Baier's work on Hume as a "women's" philosopher springs to mind here (e.g., her article on Hume as a women's moral theorist). There is little doubt that feminist history of philosophy, at least that done in these three categories, has been a successful enterprise. Compared to even just a decade ago, the project of the recovery and revaluation of historical women philosophers is well underway, historical women philosophers are slowly starting to be incorporated into the Anglo-American canon, and text books on the history of philosophy are becoming more inclusive of the work of female philosophers.

The fourth category identified by Witt is methodological reflections on the history of philosophy, and here it is important to note that Witt is focusing on the (male) canon. This methodological category remains under-explored compared to the other three. In the preface to their edited collection *Feminist Reflections on the History of Philosophy*, Lilli Alanen and Charlotte Witt (2004, xi) raise some central questions about methodology: "Is there a distinctively feminist approach to reading the history of philosophy? What makes it a feminist approach? Is it a matter of the questions that are brought to a philosophical text, or is the question of how to interpret the meaning of a historical text also at issue?" They suggest that "perhaps what unifies feminist approaches to the history of philosophy is not any particular methodological assumption about interpreting historical texts, but rather a commitment to emancipatory projects, and to finding a philosophical vocabulary that can contribute to those projects" (xiv).

These are the right questions to ask, but I think we should go further than just asking them about the (male) canon. We have unearthed previously forgotten or neglected women philosophers; the task is now to evaluate and analyze their work. We need also to understand that this task *itself* must be scrutinized; it must be open to self-reflective analysis. Doing feminist history of philosophy is not simply about canon revision, rediscovering women philosophers, and so forth, it is also about how this is done. What models of philosophy do we employ? What expectations do we bring to the texts that combine feminism and philosophy? How do we define the success or failure of a particular argument or text? How can we justify calling the work of a particular writer, such as Catharine Beecher, philosophy? On the other hand, how can we justify questioning the supposed feminism of canonical philosophers, such as Jeremy Bentham and John Stuart Mill? What is the overall goal in recovering or reexamining these writers? Is it merely to identify their historical existence? Or is it to include them somehow in our contemporary conversations about feminist philosophy and gender justice? Indeed, what is the relationship of feminist philosophy to its past?

Ultimately, therefore, we need to examine how the history of philosophy is done. More specifically, we need to ask whether mainstream Anglo-American history of philosophy is done in such a way that we can find suitably feminist answers to these questions. I have found that there are different—but inter-connected—barriers that make it difficult for me to "revalue" the work of the feminist philosophers I examine in this book. And by revalue I do not just mean that I find feminist philosophers where before there appeared to be none, but I also question standard attributions of feminism to canonical phi-losophers. I say that these barriers are interconnected because I think they are part—and I make no claims to exposing the whole—of a picture comprising doing philosophy and what philosophy is that is not particularly conducive to the study of the historical works of feminist philosophy. It would be rather harsh to claim that these historical works are deliberately excluded from this picture; rather, I want to claim that this picture is a bad "fit" for the retrieval of feminist philosophers and thereby functions to exclude them, or makes it hard to recover and include them. This claim is not equivalent to an outright rejection of Anglo-American mainstream history of philosophy; rather it is an invitation to consider whether alternative lenses or perspectives exist that may be more fruitful for the interpretation of early feminist philosophers, and I am going to offer one alternative lens or perspective.

Moreover, I need to consider the relationship of this alternative to main-stream approaches: is it completely new and separate, or do the two share certain elements? As I said earlier, my focus is to reflect on the actual process of interpretation and whether this reflection is in itself feminist. As I shall show, trying to overturn mainstream methodologies or replace them with a "new" feminist methodology is part of the mainstream picture of doing philosophy and thus a way of doing history of philosophy that I question. Given all these points, I shall typically use the terms "perspective" or "lens"— rather than "approach"—to refer to my positive thesis (a search for an alter-native to mainstream approaches), so as not to imply that I am overstating my claim and offering some new or replacement methodology, but also to indicate its signature characteristics that differentiate it from mainstream philosophizing.

"Mainstream" Ways of Doing the History of Philosophy

Within mainstream Anglo-American history of philosophy there are two dominant approaches, and my focus throughout is on Anglo-American philosophy. Obviously, like all aspects of our discipline, there is no complete consensus as to the delineation or existence of these mainstream approaches. However, the purpose of this work is not to focus on these mainstream approaches in themselves; I think there is enough agreement about their delineation and existence for my purposes, as I am less interested in discussions of their internal coherence and more interested in whether they are suitable for feminist philosophy and its goals.

The two dominant approaches are, essentially, history for its own sake and history for the sake of philosophical truths in the present. These are given different names by different philosophers—for example, Margaret Wilson (1992) calls them exegetical and philosophical, while Jorge Gracia (1991) calls them historical and polemicist. Gordon Graham (1982, 38) echoes R. G. Collingwood when he neatly—if perhaps a little simplistically—separates the two approaches by framing them as asking two different questions: "What did he say?" and "Is it true?"

The first approach, which I will call "historical," aims solely to examine historical texts as artifacts of a certain cultural–historical era. The historians who engage in this approach have no interest in philosophical theory as philosophy: philosophical answers or truths. As John Passmore (1964, 14) states, this may be simply because these historians are not interested in philosophy qua philosophy or because "of the conviction that philosophy is of such a character that to discuss it except in relation to its age is fundamentally to misunderstand it." This type of approach, according to Passmore, aims to "display philosophical theories in a cultural museum as representative expressions of a period" (18). A slightly looser definition of the historical approach is given by Wilson (1992, 5), who says it "is primarily concerned with interpreting (perhaps to some degree critically) the positions of philosophers of the past."

The second approach, which I will call "philosophical," treats historical texts as though they were the work of our contemporaries; the historical aspects of a particular philosopher's view are not seen as important. If we do not ground a philosopher's ideas against his or her particular historical background, then our reading of the history of philosophy becomes the categorizing of individuals into a particular school or the search for timeless philosophical questions—which rests on the assumption that all philosophers are concerned with answering the same questions—or the tracing of particular ideas through history and across disciplines—which rests on the assumption that ideas are "somehow atomic units . . . passed, either whole or in part, from author to author, without undergoing substantial changes in themselves" (Gracia 1991, 252).

On the philosophical approach, historical texts are not read because of what we can learn about the history of philosophy but because we can learn about philosophical truths in the present. These texts are important for our modern philosophical enterprise because we can "find insights or even solutions to today's problems—or at least to uncover mistakes and dead ends we should not emulate" (Freeland 2000, 370–71). Thus we read the history of philosophy with the goal of finding philosophical truths and answers to our current problems. Underpinning the philosophical approach are two assumptions: that philosophy is an autonomous enterprise and that philosophy comprises perennial, unchanging problems. It is only because philosophy can be seen as having a separate set of problems from, for example, those of scientists or theologians, and that these problems are timeless in some way, that the philosophical approach can treat historical texts ahistorically.

The problem for the recovery and interpretation of feminist philosophical work is that neither of these mainstream approaches is particularly well suited for this task. Feminist philosophy—as I am characterizing it—is a search for knowledge for the sake of political and social change, whereas the philosophical approach is better characterized as a search for knowledge for its own sake: a "pure" search. The historical approach could allow for the inclusion of political elements within the historical context of the work of a particular philosopher, but it does not have the theoretical space to allow for a discussion of political and social change itself.

Consideration of the Philosophical Approach

Both mainstream approaches have been subject to criticism within mainstream philosophy itself. Certainly, in their most extreme form, neither appears particularly useful. In the case of the philosophical approach, it leads—at best—to misunderstanding of historical texts as they are examined through the lens of the reader's own contemporary philosophical interests. At worst, there is no such thing as history of philosophy per se; for example, Collingwood (1939, 59) accuses those philosophers he calls "realists" for thinking that "the problems with which philosophy is unconcerned were unchanging. They thought that Plato, Aristotle, the Epicureans, the Stoics, the Schoolmen, the Cartesians, &c., had all asked themselves the same set of questions, and had given different answers to them." For Collingwood, these realists understand the "history" of philosophy only in the sense that these different answers had an identifiable chronological order.

Indeed, Collingwood argues that the philosophical approach is not actually possible, for it assumes that we can make a distinction between the historical (what x said) and the philosophical (whether x was correct). Collingwood argues that we cannot know what x thought about a particular—supposedly perennial—problem, as this assumes the existence of perennial problems in the first place; rather, we must first look at the text to see what problem x thought he or she was dealing with in the first place. We can then ask about x's solution, and thus both solution and problem are found in the same text or passage. In essence, there are not two sets of questions, but only one: the historical one.

Collingwood's ultimate position—that the philosophical approach is impossible—is radical; however, his concerns about the conceptualization of the philosophical enterprise as a series of perennial problems continues to have traction in more contemporary accounts of the history of philosophy. For example, Gordon Graham claims that the work of Jonathan Rée in *Philosophy and Its Past* (which Graham criticizes as extreme) originates in Collingwood. Whereas Collingwood denied that there are permanent problems in philosophy, Rée denies that there are permanent positions. Whereas Collingwood does not fully explore his position, Rée offers a thorough account of his own. It is in looking at Rée's critique of the notion of timeless positions in philosophy, therefore, that we can start to see how the philosophical approach might be a bad fit for feminist philosophy.

Rée argues, like Collingwood, that the history of philosophy is often done ahistorically: the thought is not placed within its historical context. He claims specifically that there is a tendency of historians of philosophy to "project into the past an idea of philosophy as a professional academic specialism—treating Aristotle and Descartes as though they were participants at a modern philosophy conference. . . . They do not explore historical sources other than explicitly philosophical writings. . . . They never consider general problems about the interpretation of philosophical texts; and they are so preoccupied with explicit controversies between philosophers that they fail to notice areas of agreement or of silence" (1978, 2). Rée locates the origins of this approach in the histories of philosophy that appeared in the eighteenth century; in particular, Rée points to the influence of Johann Jakob Brucker's *Critical History of Philosophy*. According to Rée, Brucker introduced the notion of philosophy as an explicit activity of "philosophers," separating it from religion, which had "sources deep in the wordless experiences of masses of non-intellectuals" (6).

Yet the history of philosophy is not something that occurs in isolation from contemporary philosophy. In identifying these "professional philosophers," their major works, and the trajectory from one thinker to another, the history of philosophy "provides an implicit definition of philosophy, indicating that being a philosopher means being a successor to Plato, Aristotle and the rest and perpetuating the practices which—according to the History of Philosophy—these Great Men have bequeathed" (Rée 1978, 2).[3]

From a feminist perspective, we can see how this conceptualization of philosophy depicted by Rée functions to exclude the participation of women in the philosophical enterprise. Although a few historical women intellectuals were regarded as philosophers (e.g., Damaris Masham), their lack of formal training and prohibitions (explicit or implicit) on women speaking publicly or publishing their ideas, mean that historians of philosophy looking for a trajectory of professional philosophers in the history of the discipline will be unlikely to notice the contributions of women philosophers.

Moreover, there is the question of subject matter and philosophical approach. These are aspects I shall examine more thoroughly in later chapters; suffice it to say at this juncture that studies of the work of historical women philosophers or feminist philosophers have shown that these figures often had philosophical interests (e.g., in the rights of women) that are not those of successors to the "Great Men," nor did these figures always practice philosophy in the "traditional" manner (e.g., they may have written philosophy in the form of fiction or poetry). Indeed, in Catharine Beecher's case, I shall argue that part of her philosophy can be found in her domestic advice manuals.

According to Rée (1978, 8), Brucker framed the history of philosophy as battles between schools of thought, and thus the form of philosophical discussion becomes framed as one of quarrels "with which an inward-looking elite filled their leisure." This meant that it was easy for eighteenth-century philosophes to dismiss the history of philosophy and instead concentrate on what could be discovered through natural reason; therefore, as Rée explains, accounts of history "became more and more like cautionary tales for the instruction of the young." This notion of the history of philosophy as a series of warring views remains with us in Anglo-American philosophy, and has meant that the study of the history of philosophy has not held much appeal.

This notion of the form of philosophical discussion as battles between competing "isms," with the history of philosophy a story of these quarrels, is something that should be questioned by feminist philosophers. This notion reflects, and may even reinforce, the dominant gender ideology, for we can see that the problem of the notion of battling philosophers is clearly connected to Janice Moulton's claims about aggression as a masculine value in her germinal article on methodology, "A Paradigm of Philosophy: The Adversary Method" (1983). Moulton argues that aggression, a trait that has a different social meaning and value for men and women, has been incorporated into the standard paradigm of philosophical technique: the adversary method. In essence, this method frames different philosophical viewpoints and arguments as being in opposition or competition. The aim is to defeat opponents' arguments through, among other things, challenging their foundational assumptions, exposing their inconsistencies, searching for argumentative fallacies, and showing how their premises lead to unintended conclusions that are untenable.

Moulton argues that this linking of aggression with philosophical ability serves to exclude women from philosophy, as it requires behavior that is not culturally constructed as feminine. Further, Moulton points out that the history of philosophy becomes both distorted and a limited resource, as it is read merely as a series of triumphs or failures among competing views (something I shall explore in the chapter on Wheeler and Thompson). I shall argue, moreover, that an approach that focuses solely on defeat of an opponent also serves to limit philosophy itself; for example, knowledge cannot be produced through dialogue, while subject matter that does not lend itself easily to an adversarial approach is ignored.

I identify another masculinist element in the construction of the history of philosophy as a set of battles over timeless positions: the notion of philosophical purity. According to Rée, Charles Renouvier in the nineteenth century took the notion of philosophers battling over timeless questions to its ultimate logical extension. Renouvier claimed that everyone's doctrine could be reduced to a small number of propositions. The doctrines themselves had no history: "The so-called history of philosophy was really only the story of individuals opting for different philosophical positions; the positions themselves were always there, eternally available and unchanging" (Rée 1978, 17). Bertrand Russell held a similar view: "The philosophies of the past belong to one or other of a few great types—types which in our own day are perpetually recurring." Russell in writing on Leibniz said that he was doing so with a "purely philosophical attitude"; in other words, "without regard to dates or influences, we seek simply to discover what are the great types of possible philosophies" (quoted in Rée 1978, 17–18).

In this—admittedly extreme—understanding of the history of philosophy, we can see the foundations of the more general philosophical approach to the history of philosophy: philosophy is a self-contained discipline with a fixed, timeless subject matter done by professional individuals (Rée 1978, 32). These individuals consider this subject matter in a disinterested manner; however, this approach is implicitly value laden, as we can see from its characterization as "pure" by philosophers such as Russell. Yet, if the philosophical approach to the history of philosophy is grounded on this conceptualization of philosophy, where does this leave feminist philosophy more generally, and the history of feminist philosophy more specifically?

Feminist philosophy is not self-contained, disinterested, or "pure"; it is about social and political change. Moreover, it also crosses disciplinary lines, connecting with, for example, literature. Strictly speaking, feminist philosophy as a field or identifiable pattern of work began only in the 1970s; indeed, its initial impetus was to uncover and critique the male bias in traditional philosophy. As to the specific eternal positions or questions of philosophy, while it has been argued that, for example, Plato talked about gender equality for the guardian class in his *Republic*, it is hard to claim that this is the same question or position as gender equality in the new millennium. Alternatively, if we try to squeeze gender equality into the box of a timeless question, we may lose sight of both the fact that it is women who have been targeted for prejudicial treatment and the need to ask why this is the case. This is something I will bring out in the next three chapters, on Anna Doyle Wheeler, Catherine Beecher, and Frances Wright.

Further, gender and gender justice have been typically left out of mainstream Anglo-American philosophical discourse. The reason why they have not been classified as problems in the way that issues of knowledge and metaphysics have been is because discussions of gender justice cannot be an independent intellectual pursuit in the way that philosophy—traditionally defined—needs to be. In order to discuss gender justice, as I shall demonstrate in the first three chapters, we need to introduce empirical elements to the discussion. We need to offer both an explanation of the causes—economic, social, cultural, historical, political—of the oppression of women and a description of their present situation. Finally, and most important, we must address the moral and political wrong of the oppression of women and engage the reader in such a way that he or she wants to end this oppression.

In other words, we start to push against the "purity" of the philosophical enterprise. On the dominant Anglo-American picture of philosophy, our discipline, while by no means completely separated as an intellectual enterprise, is an autonomous inquiry in that it has its own distinct set of problems and questions. Yet an exploration of issues of gender justice requires politicized questions and answers as well as historically and culturally contextualized empirical elements. This notion of purity is also at play in the picture of the history of philosophy as a set of battles over timeless positions; in order for these battles to take place and for these timeless positions to be identified, we must be able to clearly delineate philosophical positions. Further, framing the philosophical enterprise as one of eternal positions or problems, and as an intellectual enterprise that is self-contained, makes it hard to conceive how our new feminist issues and subject matter—whether theoretical, such as gender identity, or practical, such as reproductive rights—can be incorporated into this enterprise. Thus feminist philosophy, because of its dynamic and political nature, does not mesh well with the picture of philosophy as timeless.

The "Patrimonial" Picture of Philosophy

Feminist philosophers have already identified and critiqued the masculinist nature of the dominant Anglo-American picture of philosophy that underlies mainstream or traditional philosophy, in particular in the fields of epistemology and ethics. As we have seen, Moulton has also commented on the masculinist nature of dominant Anglo-American methodology: the adversarial method. However, less work has been done identifying and analyzing the masculinist elements of the picture of philosophy that underlies the two dominant Anglo-American approaches to the history of philosophy.

Underlying the philosophical approach to the history of philosophy is this dominant picture of philosophy that I am going to characterize as "patrimonial," and the elements of this patrimonial picture that are relevant to the study of the history of philosophy are something I shall explore throughout the work. While this characterization is not to be taken *too* literally, it can be an illuminating analogy for our understanding and critique of this picture. Jim Jose (2004) uses a similar term—"patrilineal"—to bring out the way

commentators have assumed that feminist thought originated in (male) political thought. However, the picture of the history of philosophy given above
invokes more than a descent that can be traced from one male philosopher
to another; rather than simply being the tracing of a male line (patrilineal),
the notion of patrimony is also one of male inheritance, legacy, and heritage.
With these latter concepts also come the notions of entitlement and dominance that are passed down from philosophical "fathers." Moreover, with
these concepts come the acceptance of the legitimacy of an inheritor's right to
fight for their inheritance and to protect this inheritance from others; battles
between opposing philosophical factions become normalized once we employ
this analogy.

The privilege that comes with patrimony means that an individual has no
need to justify why they should be allowed to write or to publish, and moreover there is already an established, legitimate—used in both senses of the
word—audience for this written and published work. Even if these philosophers are criticized or placed into the opposing camp, their right to philosophy itself and their right to be called philosophers is not questioned;
moreover, as we shall see in James Mill's case, modern interpretations of the
works of our intellectual fathers can at times be charitable to the point of
creativity. Historical feminist philosophers, on the other hand, have had to
justify their position as philosophers, the legitimacy of their subject matter,
and even the legitimacy of their audience if their target audience is women.

Inheritance laws historically gave economic and social power to men and
maintained women's subordination and exclusion from the public sphere. In
a similar way in the history of philosophy, there are (unwritten) rules about
what is inherited (and thus what is considered of philosophical value), who is
to inherit (who is to be a philosopher), and how inheritance happens (how
one comes to be considered a philosopher) that have functioned to exclude
women and feminist philosophers and to maintain male dominance of our
discipline.

Central to the patrimonial picture is the ideal of the purity or autonomy
of philosophy, and this ideal is bound up with a particular—traditional—
conceptualization of the knower, knowledge, and the way in which that
knowledge is gained. In essence, purity is an ideal of both true philosophy
and the true philosopher. The knowers on this picture are disinterested and
autonomous in that they are (supposedly) able to detach themselves and
remain separate from the objects of knowledge; these knowers are conceptually disembodied and disembedded. The truths these traditional knowers of

philosophy seek are those unencumbered by subjectivity or the trappings of the material world; indeed, philosophical knowledge is to be kept as free as possible from the external world.[4]

It is this ideal of purity or autonomy that is "inherited" on the patrimonial picture, an ideal that I claim is easier for men to inherit than women. Culturally, women have not been identified with the ability to think autonomously or disinterestedly.[5] This is not simply a case of sexist bias; women's traditional roles as caretaker and homemaker have kept them connected to the material and domestic world. Indeed, partialism toward and connectivity with others are seen as central characteristics for women to be able to fulfill these traditional roles properly. It is not as if there is an alternative space to include women's experiences, situations, and issues on the patrimonial picture of philosophy, however, for these things are subjective, embedded and, as such, devalued.

In this way we can see that what is inherited—what the discipline of philosophy is considered to be—and who is to inherit are tightly linked. How then does inheritance happen—or, more specifically, not happen? On a direct level, women have had, until recently, restricted access to education. I shall argue, however, throughout this work that there are more subtle ways that women are excluded from being counted as philosophers. We shall see, for example, that the notion of autonomy is at odds with the synthetic philosophy of Frances Wright, and that the ideal of the disinterested knower is in tension with much of Catharine Beecher's work.

This patrimonial picture of philosophy is clearly at play in Rée's characterization of the philosophical approach as one that projects into the past a notion of philosophy as a professional academic specialty, with an identifiable trajectory from one thinker to another, thus offering us an implicit definition of a philosopher as being a successor to the canonical greats and as maintaining the intellectual practices of these greats. More generally, on the philosophical approach to this history of philosophy, these professional individuals inherit the right to dispute a series of timeless questions that make up the subject matter and thus the delineation of the discipline of philosophy. This activity must be kept pure in that philosophical truths must be kept separate from historical particulars, while the philosopher studying timeless questions must preserve their individual autonomy and do philosophy from a disinterested standpoint.

What I wish to claim next is that—despite the fact that the historical approach to the history of philosophy is usually framed as being in opposition or in contrast to the philosophical approach—the patrimonial picture of philosophy lies behind both.

Consideration of the Historical Approach

Initially, it might seem that an obvious solution to the problems posed by the philosophical approach to the history of philosophy is to acknowledge that philosophical understanding is also historical understanding. As Rée (1978, 30) argues, simply because we are not always aware of our use of historical knowledge does not mean it is not there; indeed, he goes so far as to say that there is "no such thing as a really non-historical approach to philosophical ideas."

So how far should we embrace the apparent alternative to the philosophical approach, the one I am calling historical? In its most extreme form, for example, on Collingwood's account, the history of philosophy is basically the history of a certain age. It has no interest in philosophical theory qua philosophy; this may be simply because this type of historian is not interested or because this historian holds that philosophy can be understood only in its historical context.

Jorge Gracia (1991, 66) characterizes the practitioner of this extreme form of the historical approach as someone who holds "that conceptual translation has no role to play in history. The job of the historian is to present whatever concepts past philosophers held without trying to translate them into contemporary concepts." In other words, we are to understand the philosopher only on his or her own terms; anything else is anachronism. If this is the case, then we can report only what was said at a certain historical period. Anything more would involve interpretation that would be grounded on "contemporary concepts and ideas." The historian on this picture searches for historical, not philosophical, truth; he or she does not aim to make judgments about the truths of the claims made by historical figures: this is what Garber (2000, 15) calls a (philosophically) "disinterested" history. As Gracia points out, compelling arguments can be made for this position, in particular that our historical account is not distorted by a search for truth, and through learning about the different views of the past we may come to see what is missing in the present. As we shall see, however, this position shares much with its apparent "opposite"—the philosophical approach—in the way that purity and autonomy are framed as central to philosophy as a discipline.

The two main questions to be asked of the historical approach are what value it has, and whether a disinterested history is possible in this way. It can be argued that the historical approach ultimately gives us little more than description. We cannot do interpretation or evaluation, as these would be grounded on our contemporary philosophical knowledge and concepts; moreover, we cannot make connections between the past and the present. Gracia (1991, 66) asks what use this approach is if we cannot build connections between the past and the present; if the past stays just that, then what value is it to us moderns and why would we want to recover this past? Gracia also questions whether a disinterested history is possible. Even though we may not judge the truth of a philosopher's claims, we make other value judgments about him or her. Ultimately claiming that a philosopher, for example, contributed to epistemology, is saying that there were elements of truth in his or her philosophy. The problem with disinterested history is that no matter how hard we try to do "pure" or "objective" history, we still need to take a position if we want to assess another's historical thought.

What should feminist philosophers make of the historical approach? Cynthia Freeland in "Feminism and Ideology in Ancient Philosophy" (2000), considers the potential of what she calls the "exegetical" account for feminist historians of philosophy.[6] She claims that feminists can use it, even though it is not particularly feminist in itself.[7] The feminist could write about issues of interest to feminists without actually taking the viewpoint of a feminist. In this way the historical examination would be kept objective and disinterested (375). I would argue, however, that feminists have a political and philosophical agenda, and thus it would appear that adopting the historical approach will not ultimately be fruitful. In other words, we *want* an interested history and we will need to use contemporary concepts to produce such a history.

Freeland points out, moreover, that social contexts are not value neutral, which adds an additional layer to the question of whether we can actually set a philosopher's views in historical context. Further, Freeland claims that the ideal of a "true" history of philosophy is itself an ideology. Gender can be acknowledged as part of the broader social context of the history of philosophy, but it is not seen as part of "the integral, essential, ongoing set of issues and problems that are appropriately addressed by scholars in the field" (Freeland 2000, 377). In other words, gender can count as part of the broad social context that "may affect the nature of a philosopher's views," but it is not "part of philosophy proper." This is an important point and connects to my

criticisms of the patrimonial picture of philosophy and the purity and autonomy of philosophy that is foundational to this picture.

However, despite the (different) difficulties that both Gracia and Freeland
identify with the historical approach, I intend to argue that historical context
is vital for any feminist examination of a philosophical text. The question
then for feminist historians of philosophy is whether a requirement that we
read texts within their historical context need necessarily bring with it the
other aspects of the historical approach: disinterestedness and the autonomy
and purity of philosophy as a discipline.

The Patrimonial Picture and the Historical Approach

Despite the fact that these two mainstream approaches to the history of philosophy are typically framed as being in tension or contrast to each other, I
maintain that they have shared elements, specifically, elements that are part
of what I call the patrimonial picture of philosophy. Unlike the practitioner
of the philosophical approach, the practitioner of the historical approach does
not participate in a shared inheritance of philosophy or a trajectory of thinkers, but this practitioner is an inheritor nonetheless. Texts are objects in the
care of historians to be jealously guarded from distortion by contemporary
concepts or interested use. While this does not mean that women or feminists
are actually excluded from the historical approach, it does mean that feminists
may not be interested or may find little of value in this approach.

Both approaches inherit a surprisingly similar object of study. The historical approach is in agreement with the philosophical approach over the autonomy of philosophy as a discipline, and, as such, does not have the potential
to dovetail with the feminist philosophical project. Both approaches share a
similar inheritance in their ideal of the disinterestedness of knowledge that
we gain from the study of the history of philosophy. In the case of the historical approach, the knowledge we gain from the examination of texts is value-
free in the sense that we aim not to distort this knowledge by interpreting it
through our own historically situated position or by using our contemporary
philosophical concepts. In the case of the philosophical approach, we search
for timeless truths: knowledge that is free of our historically situated position.
Both approaches strive for purity in their own separate way, whereas feminist
philosophy, by its very nature, is not pure in the sense that both the historical
and philosophical approaches share.

Both approaches aim for autonomy or purity of their subject matter, whether it is keeping philosophical truths separate from historical particulars or keeping textual analysis free of anachronistic interpretation. Both approaches also value the autonomy of the individual knower. The connection between the philosopher studying timeless questions and their individual autonomy is obvious, but perhaps the connection is not so clear in the case of the historical scholar. This connection becomes more evident when we look at, for example, the claims of Collingwood (1939, 274–75), who argues that the historical scholar needs to be autonomous—free of his or her own historical particulars—in order to be able to "reenact" the experience of the past. As I shall show, however, the feminist interpreter/knower of historical texts can draw on their own ethical and political consciousness and a reflection on this consciousness in order to produce an interpretation of historical works of feminist philosophy.

This notion of purity does not simply function as an ideal, it also functions both literally and metaphorically to maintain philosophical inheritance. In the case of the mainstream philosophical approach, if we want to trace philosophical lineage or assign philosophers to sects or groups (e.g., the British Empiricists), we need to smooth away difference and separate "philosophical truths" in a disinterested manner from their historical and cultural contexts. In the case of the mainstream historical approach, the commentator inherits the right to analyze and interpret texts through their own purity—their disinterestedness—and through guarding the purity of the texts they study from distortion from modern concepts of a search for timeless truth.

At present, the claim that the patrimonial picture underlies both approaches is—not surprisingly—skeletal; I shall explore and develop this picture and the shared elements of the two approaches as I study the work of my chosen nineteenth-century feminist philosophers.

Considerations for a More Feminist History of Philosophy

Thus far it would seem that neither the philosophical nor the historical approach is a particularly good match for the goals and requirements of the feminist philosophical enterprise, especially if our particular interest is examining feminist historical works, which aim to describe not abstract truths but the real-life truths of the oppressions of women, and to argue for practical change through the subjective change (empowerment) on a real audience.

As Alasdair MacIntyre (1984, 31) points out, however, it is easy to "imprison oneself within the following dilemma": to believe we must *either* translate past philosophies to make them relevant to our present concerns and ignore what cannot be translated, *or* read them in their own terms so that they end up as a historical artifacts and nothing more. So let us now consider two examples of approaches to the history of philosophy that avoid the extremes of the philosophical and historical viewpoints and aim to combine them in some way.

John Passmore, for example, advocates for what he calls a "problematic" approach. He argues that the problem with the historical approach is that it misconceives the philosophical enterprise. Philosophy is more than a historical feature of a certain era; Passmore holds instead that it is "an independent—although not *wholly* independent—intellectual pursuit." However, he says that it is possible to bring out the historical and cultural context of a thinker while also demonstrating his or her importance to contemporary philosophy. He is able to hold this position because he sees philosophy as "an autonomous inquiry, in the sense that it has its own problems; but it by no means follows that those problems arise for it in isolation from the problems of scientists, theologians, poets, or independently of social and economic changes" (Passmore 1965, 16). While Passmore does not maintain that there are such things as "the problems of philosophy," he claims we can "speak of certain types of problems as continuously recurring in philosophy, although in different shapes" (28). Even if these problems are not "solved," there is little doubt that we make advances in understanding them. Thus, for Passmore, we should be both a historian and a philosopher. We see the inner history of the development of philosophy, but this is not done in isolation from historical and cultural context.

Jorge Gracia (1991, 68), a more modern example than Passmore, holds that we can examine and understand some elements of our history without the distortion of our contemporary lenses. This is because he sees some problems as fundamental to "all thinking beings." Gracia states that a "proper understanding and account of history entails in a sense becoming part of it, becoming a contemporary, and that involves judgment, since contemporaries engaged in the philosophical enterprise are in the business of judging truth value" (79). In other words, Gracia is promoting what could be called an "interested" history. This approach requires the assumption that there are some shared standards within the discipline of philosophy that are at play both today and historically, and Gracia claims that "there is a sufficiently solid core of standards, based on the most fundamental requirements for communication and the overall aims of the discipline, to ensure that evaluations can take place" (80).

While these more moderate approaches to the *history* of philosophy may be more suitable for feminist historical enterprise, they are—ultimately—still not a good fit. The problem is the understanding of *philosophy itself* at play in these more moderate approaches. The identification of philosophy as an autonomous intellectual enterprise with identifiable problems and aims—rather unfortunately—is the foundation for the potential agreement between the philosophical and historical approaches. Yet it is this very notion of autonomy, as we have seen, that makes it hard for feminist philosophy to incorporate its "new" issues—drawn from the material lives of women—into the mainstream philosophical enterprise.

In addition, women have rarely been allowed to participate in discussions of what Passmore sees as recurring problems or what Gracia calls the overall aims of philosophy, either discussions of the problems themselves or discussions where these problems are identified as such. Yet both the philosophical and the historical approaches are grounded on the assumption that the goals and processes of their separate enterprises are objective or unbiased. Feminist philosophers have shown us that this is not the case. Simply put, the construction, whether literally or metaphorically, of what we call the discipline of philosophy has been male dominated and has functioned to exclude women. We want to ask "*Whose* problems?" and "*Whose* standards and aims?" To claim that these are "human" problems or aims is dangerous, given our cultural history of misidentifying human with male or men. In other words, we are left with the sense that the revised approaches of Gracia and Passmore are framed against the background of the patrimonial picture of philosophy and thus a patrimonial history of philosophy.

Cynthia Freeland (2000, 380) suggests that it is possible to offer a feminist version of a combined philosophical–historical approach. She calls this the "inheritance approach" and gives the work of Charlotte Witt on the history of philosophy as an example. On the mainstream approach, we read the history of philosophy for truths and the answers to current problems; the feminist version of this is, according to Freeland, that "we can and should make use of our canonical tradition as a resource in developing our own feminist views" (379). This claim can then be combined with a historical study of why a particular philosopher said what he or she did. A central question Freeland asks is whether this approach is feminist enough. Drawing on the work of

Luce Irigaray, she argues that this approach requires the acceptance of the notion of "history as roughly continuous and its current goal as problem-solving," and she questions whether feminists want to become part of a canon that has excluded them (384).

I would agree that the general goals of the inheritance view are important; in reading the history of philosophy as feminists, we want, among other things, to find our intellectual foremothers and offer "historical justification for the importance of 'our' theoretical issues and 'our' philosophical perspective" (Freeland 2000, 380–81). A feminist approach to the history of philosophy that begins with the canon as a resource is valuable for the feminist enterprise, but I am uncertain that it encompasses the entire enterprise. Surely we should also allow for the possibility of beginning with figures who are potentially feminist philosophers, even though they will typically be noncanonical or even forgotten. Moreover, Freeland's concerns about whether the inheritance view is feminist enough would appear to share common ground with my more general concerns about the patrimonial picture of philosophy and the history of philosophy.

What then do I want for what I am calling a feminist lens or perspective for the history of philosophy? I have argued that neither the historical nor the philosophical approach is well suited for examining the work of early feminist philosophers. This is not to say that these approaches *cannot* be used to interpret the work of these philosophers; rather, I am claiming that using these approaches does not ultimately contribute to the feminist philosophical enterprise as a whole. I hold that we should look for another approach (or approaches) that will result in more fruitful interpretations of specific texts and philosophies and the retrieval of previously neglected forbearers, while at the same time—due to both its conceptualization and its actual results—this approach will participate in and develop the feminist philosophical enterprise. I want to avoid another false dilemma. Just as MacIntyre claims that we do not necessarily have to reject one of the mainstream approaches and keep the other, so I want to claim that we may not necessarily have to mount a whole-sale rejection of both mainstream approaches in order to produce an alternative feminist perspective. To do so would be to buy into the picture of philosophy as a series of battles or opposing positions with one viewpoint as the winner and the other as the loser.

A new—feminist—lens or perspective should certainly place early feminist philosophers within their historical and cultural context; indeed, as I argued above, this context is central to a feminist history of philosophy. Whereas the mainstream philosophical approach aims to search for truth for its own sake, a feminist approach—simply put—should search for truths about the subordination of women and the knowledge that will end this subordination. In the same way that the two mainstream approaches can be simplified as asking the questions (respectively) of "What did x say?" and "Is it true?" a feminist interpreter should ask "Does it empower women?"

It may be asked where the significant differences lie between the question I have just outlined and the mainstream historical and philosophical approaches I have argued are not a good fit for interpreting feminist philosophical texts. Initially, it may appear that the empowerment question is simply a version of the philosophical approach in that I am asking of historical texts a transhistorical question: "Does it empower women?"

On a strict interpretation of the philosophical approach an interested question, such as the empowerment of women, would be forbidden. But conceived more loosely, it might seem that the philosophical approach allows for such interested questions. Indeed, there have been many valuable feminist readings of traditional texts that have sought understanding or clarification of the implications of these texts for women (either past or present), which means they have employed an "interested" philosophical approach or question.

I would argue that the empowerment question is more than an interested question. It is not simply that we are making value judgments about a particular text or philosophy or taking up a particular position from which to examine a text or philosophy; rather, the empowerment question brings with it the need for self-consciousness about the political and ethical dimensions of our theorizing. Feminist philosophy is not an intellectual game; we theorize about lived oppressions and hope to remove them. This self-conscious interpreter must hold him- or herself accountable, and be held accountable, to the overall goals of the feminist philosophical enterprise. The interpreter is thus a member of and accountable to a community of knowers. This community is one that comprises their contemporaries, but it also contains the historical philosophers and their contemporaries in the much looser sense that the interpreter—through his or her analysis of historical theorizing—is "speaking for" these philosophers and their contemporaries. It is here that I think it makes sense—both conceptually and for the sake of clarity—to shift to talking of a feminist perspective or lens rather than an approach. To call the empowerment question an approach may indicate that I am offering some new or replacement methodology, whereas to call it a perspective or lens points to these signature characteristics that differentiate it from mainstream philosophizing.

As I shall show, the empowerment question is asked against a background of a different picture of philosophy from the patrimonial one. As I said, the knower is a self-conscious knower, who is held accountable to a community of knowers with common goals. These knowers do not just search for philosophical or historical truths; both the end of the search and their understanding of the search are different. Their search is "impure" not only because they are searching for truths that produce the political goal of alleviating the oppression of women, but also because the search is turned on themselves as individuals, both in an examination of their personal motivations and biases and as a way of maintaining their awareness of their political and ethical accountability to the greater community of knowers.

This stands in contrast to the patrimonial picture of the knower as a disinterested, autonomous knower who is supposedly able to detach him- or herself and remain separate from the objects of knowledge, where the truths sought after are unencumbered by subjectivity or the needs of the material world. I have argued that this position is harder for women to inherit than it is for men. Being able to take up the position of the knower on the empowerment picture, on the other hand, is about wishing to join a community because of one's common political goals with that community; it is not about inheritance, legacy, or privilege.

The self-conscious knower of the empowerment picture hopes to find truths that will produce political change, did produce political change, or could have produced political change, truths about women's experiences, situations, and issues under interlocking systems of oppression. Even if it were to appear that the empowerment question is simply a version of the philosophical approach, there does not seem to be a theoretical space for the answers to this question on the patrimonial picture of philosophy that lies behind the philosophical approach.

Thus the approaches *themselves* are not at issue here; rather, it is the patrimonial picture of philosophy that lies behind them. The approaches themselves are potentially neutral; it is how they are used or can be used and the picture of philosophy that informs them that are my concerns. Certainly, it may be possible to have feminist variants of the two approaches, but while the patrimonial picture of philosophy lies behind these two approaches, these variants will not easily accommodate historical feminist texts. With a shift in how we are constructing the enterprise of the history of philosophy will—

obviously—come a shift in what counts as the success or failure of a particular view or theory. I shall argue that success within a feminist perspective for the history of philosophy is less about having an unbeatable argument or a highly original theory, or being remembered a century later, but is rather about empowerment—both as a product, if the theory and its prescriptions are followed, and, potentially, as individual empowerment in its intended audience. In addition, and connected to the feminist philosophical enterprise, I shall also consider how we are to identify historical texts for the feminist project, specifically, what is to count as a philosophical text.

I am not offering an alternative full-blown methodology per se, but I am going beyond offering either some kind of amalgam of the two approaches or the philosophical approach with an added "interested" element. Ultimately, offering an alternative methodology to replace the two traditional methodologies may be self-defeating, as I said above, for to do so would be to buy into a masculinist picture of philosophy as a series of competing positions. Moreover, to attempt to do so would be to run into a central question for contemporary feminist philosophy: how much do we want to break with the—or is it our?—philosophical tradition? There is always something of a balancing act with feminist philosophy. Too radical a break with tradition means that we fight to be recognized and taken seriously; not radical enough and we are subsumed or ignored, albeit for different reasons.

Ultimately, then, I am offering what might best be described as a "politicized synthesis," a perspective that I will justify using the work of Frances Wright. Calling on Wright is not problematically circular but instead reflects the concept of connectivity at play in both Wright's work and my interpretive perspective. I aim to offer a working hypothesis as to how history of philosophy should be done for feminist purposes. I will read different philosophical texts using this hypothesis to see what can be learned about these texts. Obviously, I am not doing science so I cannot prove my hypothesis per se; however, I believe that I can demonstrate its plausibility by the explanatory richness it produces and the interest of its results for both contemporary feminist philosophy and feminist history of philosophy.

Throughout the work, I shall demonstrate the problems with using the two mainstream approaches of the history of philosophy for reading the works of early feminist or proto-feminist philosophy; however, as I have said, I will not reject outright both mainstream approaches. Elements of both approaches clearly remain in the "empowerment question" I employ to interpret these texts. Underlying this politicized synthesis perspective is a picture of philosophy and philosophical interpretation that differs from the traditional patrimonial picture; it is a picture of ethical and political consciousness and a responsibility—and thus connectivity—to both to a community of knowers and to the author of a text. This politicized synthesis perhaps could be described as a new methodology for feminist history of philosophy, but only in the loosest of senses; certainly it does not fit traditional definitions of a methodology.

English and American Utilitarian Philosophers of the Nineteenth Century

Examining all the texts that may be works of feminist philosophy would be a massive enterprise and I can show only one facet of the history of feminist philosophy. Thus I decided to look at one small group of works: English and American utilitarian philosophy on the subject of women from the nineteenth century. Each chapter examines a different utilitarian philosopher or connected group of philosophers. Some of these philosophers are well-known, some forgotten or barely recognized; some are clearly feminist, others less so. I examine the canonical philosophers Jeremy Bentham and John Stuart Mill, as well as James Mill, who, if he is not strictly speaking canonical, is certainly a well-known historical figure. I recover the more politically radical work of Frances Wright and coauthors Anna Doyle Wheeler and William Thompson. I also analyze the work of Catharine Beecher, who—despite the fact that she may have been America's first female philosopher—remains better known for her work on home economics.

There are two other figures from this era who have been recognized for their feminist thought: Harriet Taylor Mill and Henry Sidgwick. I decided that critical and expository secondary literature on Harriet Taylor has been thorough enough that I had little to add, whereas in Sidgwick's case it is clear that there are nothing more than a few pro-women or pro-feminist elements in his work, certainly nothing that could even justify a claim that he was in some way an early feminist philosopher.

Focusing on this utilitarian group alone appeared to make sense. Not only was there a variety of work to examine, but there were interconnections between the writers. Moreover, it seemed that looking at a more closely knit group of writers would make it easier to raise meta-questions about doing the history of philosophy than would be the case if looking at a more disparate group connected simply by a time period or some other more contingent factor. This stance in itself, I would argue, is part of doing a feminist history of philosophy. Rather than offering a sweeping history, a series of canonical figures, or answers to the supposedly timeless questions of philosophy (feminist or otherwise), I want to examine philosophy at a particular historical cultural moment. However, I do not want to fall into Brucker's "sect" trap; while all the figures I examine fit under the general rubric of utilitarian, they are often more differences than similarities in their philosophies.

Another reason for my choice of figures is that, on the surface at least, utilitarianism and feminism are a comfortable match. Giving women equal rights, education, and so forth would seem automatically to bring about the best states of affairs, or in classical utilitarian terms, the greatest happiness overall. However, the relationship between the moral and political theory of utilitarianism and the goals of feminism ultimately proved more complex than I anticipated, and an examination of this relationship forms a secondary, minor element to this book. In particular, I explore whether utilitarianism can truly connect with feminism only when it is not "theoretically" pure, as in the case of Catharine Beecher and Frances Wright.

In the first chapter I examine Anna Doyle Wheeler and William Thompson's coauthored 1825 work, *Appeal of One Half the Human Race, Women, Against the Pretensions of the Other Half, Men, to Retain Them in Political, and thence in Civil and Domestic Slavery*. Both Thompson and Wheeler were originally from Ireland and were part of the intellectual circles of their time, including that of the English utilitarians. The chapter begins with an introduction to this neglected radical work on the rights and equality of women. I demonstrate that neither of the two mainstream approaches can allow for a proper examination of the *Appeal*. The historical approach cannot allow for an interpretive space within which to evaluate the arguments of Wheeler and Thompson relative to the feminist project of social justice; however, a search for our feminist foremothers is one of the reasons feminists engage in the history of philosophy. The philosophical approach does not appear to have the theoretical space within which we can examine the truths of the *Appeal*. Wheeler and Thompson are not just producing knowledge or presenting truths for their own sake; rather, they are producing knowledge and presenting truths for a specific political end, one that, moreover, has a particular historical and cultural context.

In examining the *Appeal* through the lens of the empowerment question, we come to see that the problem ultimately rests with the picture of philosophy itself that underlies mainstream approaches to the history of philosophy. This picture struggles to allow for Wheeler and Thompson's impure and non-autonomous philosophy of gender justice, with its political, empirical, and historically contextualized elements. Thus an examination of the *Appeal* allows us to begin building a picture of the features an interpretive lens for feminist history of philosophy might contain. An examination of the *Appeal* also raises the question of philosophical authorship. Even though Thompson explicitly acknowledges both Wheeler as coauthor and her epistemic authority for the work, commentators have struggled to recognize her role as an *equal* intellectual contributor. This, I show, is part of what I am calling the patrimonial picture of philosophy.

Despite their best efforts, Wheeler and Thompson fail to offer a theory that truly empowers women. While Wheeler and Thompson's utopian socialist community would liberate women in many ways, the philosophers remain stuck in traditional female roles and rely on men to provide the necessary impetus for social change. This failure is ultimately due to Wheeler and Thompson's utilitarianism serving as the theoretical foundation of their call for women's liberation.

The second chapter, an examination of the philosophy of Catharine Beecher, helps us to see that any proposed feminist approach for the history of philosophy will require a broadening or reconceptualization of both how we define philosophical texts and our notion of philosophical authorship. Despite the fact that Catherine Beecher was one of the most productive female philosophers of the nineteenth century—and it could be reasonably claimed that she was the first female American philosopher with a properly worked out philosophical system—she is best known as domestic economist. This is perhaps not surprising once we consider the dominant Anglo-American model of the "philosophical" and its corollary, the "philosophical author" (this model is at play in both mainstream approaches to the history of philosophy). This author retains a certain level of impersonal detachment and writes on abstract or universal topics for a "general" audience, which in the nineteenth century would have been educated males for the most part. Beecher's domestic advice manuals and letters of counsel, however, are intimately written and are based on personal experience; moreover, their target audience was women.

On the standard Anglo-American picture of what philosophy "is," much of Beecher's work is not philosophy. Accordingly, neither of the two mainstream approaches to the history of philosophy is well suited for an examination of her work. Yet Beecher explicitly chose these particular forms of writing and the type of knowledge she was trying to convey as part of her philosophical approach. Beecher's primary audience was women, for they are to be the moral leaders in Beecher's utilitarian plan for the increased happiness of humanity. Domestic advice manuals and letters were acceptable "feminine" genres for women to read; moreover, they would have learned how to "read" these forms, unlike the specialized training needed for reading philosophical treatises. As I shall argue, Beecher in her domestic advice manuals and letters is writing *philosophy for women*.

Reading Beecher through the lens of the empowerment question requires us to ask about the practical, projected results of her work for an actual, historically situated group of women; indeed, the empowerment question will always require us to place historical works within their historical and cultural context. However, reading Beecher as historically located in this way need not prevent us from asking about Beecher's philosophical or political connections to the "us" of modern readers, but the empowerment question goes beyond being an interested question that could be part of the mainstream historical approach. As I shall show, drawing from Beecher's own work on reading philosophy, the interpreters themselves are involved in the search (and its subsequent answers), as they must hold themselves accountable, and be held accountable, to the overall goals of the feminist philosophical enterprise. While there may be room for interested questions on the philosophical approach, there is no room for this politically and ethically self-conscious interpreter, one who will be personally and politically involved with his or her chosen texts and theories, on what I am calling the patrimonial picture of philosophy.

The argument for the interpretive fruitfulness of asking the empowerment question and a closer examination of the features or characteristics of a possible feminist history of philosophy come together in the chapter on Frances Wright. Wright was Scottish, but her important philosophical and activist work was done in the United States. Wright's central work of philosophy is her *Course of Popular Lectures*, in which she argues for the equality of both American women and African Americans. While Wright's focus is primarily on offering a social and moral philosophy, she produces a complete philosophical system in that she offers an epistemology and metaphysics that ground her arguments for social justice. Wright's epistemology is distinctive, in particular for her claim that we are to work together collaboratively to find knowledge. Indeed, we cannot do otherwise, according to Wright, because we are all (humans and the natural world alike) interconnected. However, the rest of her philosophy has been criticized because it is a synthesis of—often "competing"—canonical and radical philosophies, among them Benthamite utilitarianism, moral sense theory, Owenite socialism, and Enlightenment rationalism.

It is these notions of synthesis and collaboration that make Wright unsuitable for the dominant Anglo-American picture of philosophy and thus the history of philosophy. As I have already discussed, this picture is often one of competing schools and an adversarial methodology. Moreover, philosophical truths or knowledge are typically the preserve of the solitary (male) knower, who demonstrates the mistakes of previous theorizing and produces his own distinct system that furthers philosophical knowledge. I would argue, however, that this expectation of "originality" and theoretical purity is part of a patrimonial picture of the history of philosophy.

I argue that Wright's philosophy does truly offer empowerment for her contemporaries, but, given the differences in our social and political situation, this then raises the question of how we "moderns" can relate to her work. Here we have to leave aside the binary thinking that characterizes mainstream history of philosophy and move toward a different model of the relationship between the interpreter/knower and the text/philosophy. The interpreter/knower does not just read for historical or philosophical knowledge, he or she also searches for political connections with historical texts or philosophers, a search that is grounded on a political and ethical self-consciousness of our role as interpreters and intellectual grandchildren of these early feminists.

This notion of the interpreter/knower requires an alternative picture of philosophy to the patrimonial one, and Wright's philosophy can offer a way this alternative might look, although I am by no means claiming that this is the only alternative. Wright's philosophy offers us a picture of the (constantly) ethically and politically self-aware knower who collaborates with a community of like-minded others to produce political change. This knower is linked to others by shared political goals and a common sense of responsibility to one another, those goals, and those whose lives he or she wishes to change. On this picture, commitment and responsibility are "inherited" as much as ideas, positions, or texts, and the analogy becomes one of shared traits among a family rather than patrimonial inheritance.

In the final chapter I turn to canonical nineteenth-century (male) philosophers who have written on the subject of women, and this time I will show how the "empowerment question" can be used not to recapture but to critique. I briefly discuss James Mill and Jeremy Bentham, but focus primarily on John Stuart Mill, specifically his work *The Subjection of Women*. Mill has been praised for his feminism, and *The Subjection* has been seen as a (the?) major work of nineteenth-century philosophical feminism. I argue that commentators have misunderstood Mill's work, in part because Mill's work has been interpreted utilizing the philosophical approach to the history of philosophy. Asking the admittedly still skeletal empowerment question of Mill's *Subjection*, we find some interesting results: I am able to resolve the tensions modern-day feminist commentators have seen in *The Subjection*, and I also demonstrate that the work is not about the empowerment of women. Somewhat more controversially, I argue that, ultimately, *The Subjection of Women* is as much a work about the moral requirements for the English in their role as "civilizing" colonialists as it is a work about the liberation of women; indeed, it may have been mistakenly placed in the feminist canon.

In the concluding chapter I consider the empowerment question itself. Neither of the two mainstream methodologies on its own is adequate for the recovery and examination of historical works of feminist philosophy; however, this does not imply an outright rejection of these two methodologies. Clearly, the empowerment question shares elements with the two mainstream approaches; however, the question is asked within a different picture of philosophy and philosophical knowledge from the dominant Anglo-American picture, which I am calling patrimonial. Given that the alternative philosophical background I am proposing is open to synthesis and collaboration, I do not see the inclusion of elements from the philosophical and historical approaches in the empowerment question as necessarily being a weakness.

The empowerment question, as it stands, is not a new feminist methodology; it is better understood as an interpretive lens or perspective. Indeed, it may even be the case that a new feminist methodology, defined in the mainstream philosophical sense, should not be a goal for feminist historians of philosophy. Instead, feminist historians of philosophy may perhaps be more fruitfully engaged in a search for features or characteristics of a feminist approach to the history of philosophy rather than in the construction of a new or alternative methodology. The empowerment question allows us to see some of these features, including—but not limited to—the recognition of the importance of making women's experiences central to our interpretive investigation, the ethical and political responsibility of the interpreter, and questions associated with the authority to speak for ourselves or for others. Simply put, these features show us that feminist history of philosophy is a politicized inquiry undertaken by a politically and ethically responsible inter-preter/knower who acknowledges their own historical and cultural location.

Put so simply, it may seem that there is nothing I am saying that has not already been said by feminist philosophers working in the fields of epistemol-ogy and ethics. But surely this is the point. While our feminist "foremothers" and "forefathers" are valued, the binary historical/philosophical thinking of mainstream philosophy still seems to play out in the way that feminist history of philosophy is not integrated into the feminist philosophical project more generally. Early feminist philosophers are valued either for their historical significance or for their potential, ahistorical use for a specific disciplinary discussion or field, such as ethics. If we can move beyond this binary thinking about our own history of philosophy, then we perhaps we will come to see the different fields of the feminist philosophical project as interconnected rather than comprising disciplinary silos like traditional philosophy. We can-not do history without an understanding of epistemology, ethics, politics, and so forth, nor can we do epistemology, ethics, or politics without an under-standing of our feminist history.

Notes

1. Rorty, Schneewind, and Skinner (1984, 11) state that the history of philosophy should be written as "self-consciously as one can—in as full awareness as possible of the *variety* of contemporary concerns to which a past figure may be relevant."

2. See, for example, Jose 2004; Witt 2007.

3. Rée (1978, 2) points out that even disagreements about what philosophy is simply reinforce this, as these rival definitions are meant to be about the "same thing; and the identification of this 'same thing' is performed by the History of Philosophy."

4. See, for example, Descartes or Locke. Despite the fact that they are often depicted as being "opposite" philosophically, their philosophical knower shares much.

5. See, for example, Code 1991, 9–10.

6. Freeland (2000) offers one of the few accounts that addresses the approaches to the history of philosophy from a feminist perspective, and deserves recognition as such. Her focus is on dominance and exclusion, while mine is on the masculinist nature of the two approaches. However, reading her work has been helpful to me in solidifying my own ideas.

7. A discussion of feminist elements of a historical text need not be anachronistic on the historical approach if the concepts at play are historically appropriate.

1 WHEELER AND THOMPSON

....

The Appeal *and the Problem of Empowerment*

Anna Doyle Wheeler and William Thompson's 1825 work, *Appeal of One Half the Human Race, Women, Against the Pretensions of the Other Half, Men, to Retain Them in Political, and thence in Civil and Domestic Slavery*, is a radical argument that starts with a rebuttal of James Mill's claim that women's interests are "covered" by those of their husbands and fathers, and ends with a call for a new form of cooperative living as the only way for there to be true equality—understood as equal happiness—for women. The *Appeal* begins with an introductory letter from Thompson to Wheeler describing the genesis of the work. It is then divided into two parts: the first, shorter part examines Mill's argument in general; the second is the critique of Mill and finishes with a "Concluding Address to Women."

Despite the fact that the *Appeal* resonates far more with the modern reader due to its insightful analysis of the oppression of women and the interconnections of capitalism with patriarchy, it remains overshadowed by two other main nineteenth-century works of philosophical feminism: John Stuart Mill's *The Subjection of Women* (which is discussed in another chapter in this book) and Harriet Taylor Mill's *The Enfranchisement of Women*. This is unfortunate, as the feminist thought of the *Appeal* is far more provocative and progressive than the thought found in either of these two other works. Moreover, as Richard Pankhurst (1954, 135) claims in his biography of Thompson, it was the "first book ever written with the express purpose of advocating the grant of the parliamentary vote to women." It is not clear why the *Appeal* has all but disappeared; Dolores Dooley (1996) argues that it is this radical nature of the *Appeal* that has contributed to its invisibility, and this would seem to be the most logical explanation.

My focus in this chapter, however, is less on why the *Appeal* disappeared and more on how we are to go about recapturing the work. Specifically, I will ask whether the two mainstream approaches to the history of philosophy discussed in the introduction to this book are adequate to recapture historical philosophical work that is also feminist. I will demonstrate that these two approaches are not a good fit, and thus that we should consider exploring the possibility of whether we can develop a third—more feminist—interpretive lens or perspective, and if so, how that lens or perspective might look.

Given that the *Appeal* is not well-known, the first part of this chapter will necessarily be an overview of its central arguments. In analyzing the content of the *Appeal*, I will be able to bring out elements that could underpin a feminist perspective for the history of philosophy, and the later part of the chapter will examine three of the questions raised in the introductory chapter: How well do mainstream approaches to the history of philosophy fit historical texts that are both philosophical and feminist? What should we look for as feminists in these historical texts? What counts as success or failure through a feminist lens? In addition, underlying these questions is the further question of what counts as a philosophical text. This question will come out only indirectly with the discussion of Wheeler and Thompson and will be developed more fully with the later chapters on Catharine Beecher and Frances Wright.

The Authorship Question

There are currently only two book-length studies of Wheeler and Thompson: Richard Pankhurst's *William Thompson* (1954) and Dolores Dooley's *Equality in Community* (1996).[1] Of these two works, Dooley's is of the most interest to the modern feminist commentator because of her discussions of gender equality. Of central interest for Dooley is demonstrating how the radical nature of the *Appeal*—both its philosophical and practical content—contributed to its invisibility. For Dooley, the *Appeal* is both a critique and a revision of the utilitarian canon, as it aimed to show the invisibility of women in this canon. In order to examine these issues, she places the *Appeal* within a wide-ranging assessment of Thompson's philosophy. Indeed, most of Dooley's *Equality in Community* is an examination of the philosophical theories of Thompson.

This is a difficult line to draw. On the one hand, philosophical thorough-ness requires using texts that will shed light on a particular thinker, but on the other, it is not clear how they should be used in the case of this text, the *Appeal*, which Thompson himself says he would never have dared write alone, and which he describes as his and Wheeler's intellectual "joint property." Dooley's approach then—somewhat paradoxically—has the potential to make the *Appeal*'s coauthor, Wheeler, invisible herself, as an examination of Wheel-er's contributions become subsumed under an examination of Thompson's philosophy, even though Dooley aims to critique the invisibility of women in the utilitarian canon.

Given the way that women philosophers have remained so invisible in the history of philosophy, this is unfortunate. Moreover, Dooley's approach appears to be mistaken, as Thompson is clear that the work is a collaborative venture. He states in his introductory letter to Wheeler, "Though long accustomed to reflect on this subject, to you am I indebted for those bolder and more comprehensive views. . . . To separate your thoughts from mine were now to me impossible, so amalgamated are they with my own" (Thompson and Wheeler 1825, vi). Thompson further states that he has been waiting for Wheeler to write herself. Realizing that "leisure and resolu-tion to undertake the drudgery of the task [on the part of Wheeler] were wanting," he says that he has decided to write down these shared ideas himself. This then means, he says, that only a few pages are Wheeler's exclu-sive work: "The remainder are our joint property, I being your interpreter and the scribe of your sentiments" (vii).

Pankhurst was writing in the 1950s, before feminist academics had begun to question the easy attribution of work to men and the neglect of the work of women. Thus we should not be surprised when he assumes that Thompson is the sole author. What is curious is that Pankhurst spends time repeating Thompson's claims about being the "scribe" of the work and that the work is "joint property," and yet he offers no conjectures about Wheeler's role and does not include Thompson's comment that some of the pages are Wheeler's own work. Further, Pankhurst (1954, 137) states that Wheeler was encouraged by the success of "Thompson's book" to write more frequently. Unfortu-nately, Pankhurst does not speculate as to whether Wheeler's earlier writings could have influenced the *Appeal*.

It would seem that attributions of authorship by both Dooley and Pank-hurst have been affected by the gender of the two potential authors. In Pank-hurst's case, Wheeler's potential contributions are simply ignored despite

Pankhurst's apparent recognition of Thompson's claim that Wheeler was coauthor and that she was a writer in her own right. Dooley's interpretive approach of placing the *Appeal* against the background of Thompson's philosophy means that Wheeler's contributions are framed in a certain way: inspiration or muse. Dooley (1996, 57) argues that "Wheeler's contribution is uniquely that of a woman's consciousness for Thompson's ideas, for his emphases in the agenda of philosophy and for his style of doing philosophy." Placing Wheeler in the role of muse or inspiration undercuts the possibility that Wheeler had *intellectual or argumentative* contributions to make to the work. Moreover, the muse role means that Dooley is problematically framing their collaboration as a dualistic one of (male) reason and (female) emotion or insight; as Dooley states, "Thompson became the voice of precise argument for Wheeler and she provided a keen insight and woman's consciousness for Thompson" (31).

Why has it apparently been so difficult to acknowledge the contributions of the female half of the partnership, especially as her contemporaries, including John Stuart Mill, recognized Wheeler's intellectual abilities? Even the pro-feminist commentator Dooley does not allow for an equal *intellectual* contribution by Wheeler. I would claim that what I call the "patrimonial" picture of philosophy or intellectual thought at play in mainstream Anglo-American history of philosophy is at the root of the apparent difficulty in acknowledging the contribution of Wheeler.

In mainstream Anglo-American history of philosophy, the philosophical approach, as we have seen, is characterized by Rée as a trajectory of professional thinkers, each one an heir or successor to previous "great" thinkers. Looking more closely, this narrative of a chain of philosophers in relationship to one another would appear to have two main forms—either master–pupil relationships or relationships of intellectual influence (e.g., Jeremy Bentham and John Stuart Mill), or opponent relationships (e.g., Hume and Kant)—that can lead to a traceable trajectory of the development of philosophical theories and ideas. While it may seem on the surface that these two sets of relationships are not connected, we can see that they are two sides of the same coin once we recognize that they are both part of the same type of narrative of philosophical inheritance.

Unfortunately, women do not belong on either version of this picture. As I discussed in the introduction, taking on the "opponent" role would require women to step outside culturally prescribed roles and boundaries of their behavior. What is in fact the other side of the coin to the opponent picture, the master–pupil picture, potentially excludes women *literally*, because it is unlikely that women would ever have the education to take on the "master" role; further, taking on this role would require the breaking of social boundaries and set gender roles. The master–pupil picture also excludes women *metaphorically* in that it assumes a set of masculine-identified psychological and cognitive characteristics, such as rationality and objectivity, possessed by the master that can be transferred to the pupil. Interestingly, in the best-known case where a female philosopher—Harriet Taylor Mill—was seen as having a strong intellectual influence on a male philosopher—John Stuart Mill—she is often castigated by biographers for her emasculating control of him, while descriptions of *his* character are sometimes, unflatteringly, feminized.[2]

Women, however, can fulfill the pupil role, although the story of Héloïse and Abélard functions as a cautionary tale for male philosophers thinking of embarking on a male/master–female/pupil relationship. The muse role of the kind attributed to Wheeler, on the other hand, is not sexualized in any way and has the weight of historical/mythical precedent behind it; the allegorical figure of philosophy in Boethius's *Consolation of Philosophy* would be a classic example here. As such, the muse role can fit comfortably into what I am calling the patrimonial picture of Anglo-American history of philosophy: great men can have their inspiration as long as it remains at an intellectualized level. However, the problem is, of course, that a place in history is made for Wheeler at the expense of allowing her any real intellectual contribution to that history.

The conceptualization of coauthorship fares somewhat better on the historical approach to the history of philosophy, as this would entail examining the text as a historical–cultural artifact that is part of a certain era. Using a historical approach to reading the *Appeal*, however, would appear to lead to an attempt to work out who wrote what; for example, it may seem that the comments on utilitarianism are most likely Thompson's, while the comments on the life of women would seem to be Wheeler's. However, identifying who wrote what ultimately means that we would miss the entire point of Wheeler and Thompson's coauthorship. They are deliberately modeling for their readers a central point of the *Appeal*: that the two sexes must work together and that men will benefit from the intellectual companionship of women.

Perhaps it may seem that the problematic nature of Wheeler and Thompson's coauthorship is simply an issue for modern commentators (from either approach) and that there is nothing problematic in itself with coauthorship as such for mainstream history of philosophy, regardless of the gender of the authors. I shall explore this question more fully with the chapter on Frances Wright. There is certainly nothing in mainstream Anglo-American philosophy that disallows coauthorship, but there does seem to be some difficulty with its actual conceptualization. Two examples should indicate this: Marx and Engels collaborated on *The Communist Manifesto*, but it is often casually attributed to Marx, and we certainly see him as the dominant figure; and we want to identify at what point the works of Plato are no longer an account of the thought of the historical Socrates.

The problem is not with two or more people actually writing a philosophical work, but rather that a philosophical work, at least on the philosophical approach to the history of philosophy, is a work of knowledge. Prominent in mainstream epistemology is the picture that can be traced back to René Descartes, of the knower as solitary individual. The notion of a solitary knower is not exclusive to the rationalist tradition; even though the knower of the empiricist tradition gains knowledge through reason in conjunction with the senses, the empiricist knower is often conceived of as independently attaining knowledge. Even though the practitioners of the historical approach do not seek philosophical knowledge from the texts they examine, their goal of understanding the philosopher on their own terms (gaining historical truth) would seem to imply a solitary knower—or at the very least, a solitary knower will reach this goal more easily.

So who should be credited with authorship of the *Appeal?* I think that we must quite simply take Thompson at his word: the *Appeal* is a joint venture. We have to ask ourselves why he would have claimed it were this not true. It would certainly not have helped the book; female authorship would have been far more likely to both diminish sales and attract criticism. While it is tempting to decide who wrote what, it is probably not that helpful to an analysis of the *Appeal*. We should instead look carefully at Thompson's introductory letter to Wheeler. Thompson says that the book is about the condition of women, about which he has learned so much from Wheeler. He says he cannot *feel* what she does, as he is a man, nor does he have the same personal interest in alleviating the condition of women; however, he can *understand* how she feels and her interests, to the point where they have come to think the same way. Thus Wheeler is bringing to the work an understanding of the condition of women based on her experiences, an understanding that can be shared with others.[3] In other words, she is the epistemic authority for the work.

We can learn with Thompson the ethical and political importance of giving Wheeler her proper due. The words on the page will be the same no matter who is credited as author, but its overall message would fail if Thompson had taken the credit (or had patronized Wheeler by giving her all the credit). Thompson has recognized—and this is part of his frustration with James Mill—that we are accountable for the ethical and political results of our theorizing: "I love not literary any more than any other series of piracy: I wish to give everything to its rightful owner" (vi).

Obviously, the issue of coauthorship is a very minor point on which to judge the fit of the two mainstream approaches of the history of philosophy for an analysis of the *Appeal*, and I would not want to allow too much to rest on it; however, it provides a good starting point for the work I wish to do in this chapter examining mainstream approaches to the history of philosophy in relation to historical feminist philosophical work. Specifically, I want to demonstrate that neither of the two mainstream approaches to the history of philosophy—the philosophical and the historical—can offer a fully adequate reading of the *Appeal*. I find instead that we should explore the possibility of an interpretive perspective or lens that better fits the political and practical elements of feminist philosophy. Our goal is not simply knowledge for its own sake, whether this be historical knowledge or the timeless truths of the philosophical approach, but knowledge that will lead to the alleviation of the oppression of women. In brief, I will argue that we need to ask whether the *Appeal* would lead to the empowerment of women.

Given that the *Appeal* is not a well-known work, it is best to begin with a fairly lengthy examination of its arguments, followed by an analysis of the broader issues about utilitarianism and feminism and the history of philosophy raised by the text. As a way into the arguments of the *Appeal*, and with an eye to the fact that both Wheeler and Thompson are unlikely to be known to the modern reader, I begin with a brief introduction to their lives and works.

Anna Doyle Wheeler, Her Life and Works

Given Dooley's view of Wheeler's contributions to the *Appeal*, it is unsurprising that her account of Wheeler's life focuses on bringing out the life experiences that could have been used as "data" for the *Appeal*. While Dooley may indeed be correct that there were certain formative experiences that under-pinned Wheeler's philosophical and political views, it is always questionable to let biography explain philosophy. Speculation about the psychological fac-tors that caused an individual to hold certain ideas is certainly interesting, but these factors cannot explain the *philosophical* reasons for these ideas, nor does knowledge of these causes aid us in any attempt to make a judgment about those ideas.[4]

In the case of Mary Wollstonecraft, for example, the brutality of her father toward her mother, and Wollstonecraft's role as a child in protecting her mother, are often cited as causal factors for Wollstonecraft's feminism as an adult, in that she had directly experienced the private and public oppressions of women. Wollstonecraft's feminism is not simply a reactive state of mind, however, it is also a carefully thought through system of political beliefs and ideas. We want to examine the philosophical reasons for this system—for example, other philosophers she claims as influences and the arguments she uses as evidence—and we make judgments about the relative strengths or weaknesses of her philosophical system both overall and for its supporting reasons. Looking to psychological factors to explain Wollstonecraft's philo-sophical system will lead us, at best, to ask general questions about, for exam-ple, the relation between childhood experiences and adult belief systems and, at worst, to unsubstantiated intuitions about Wollstonecraft's subconscious.

What is fascinating here for the feminist philosopher is how often this "biographical" approach is used in interpretations of the work of female phi-losophers. Rarely do we read accounts of how marriage or family life affected the philosophical thought of *male* philosophers, and thus there is no reason why we should treat the lives and work of female philosophers differently. I am not arguing that we cannot or should not interpret someone's philosophy within the context of the concrete experiences of their lives. However, I am concerned that the fact that this is done primarily for women and not for men reinforces the masculinist dimensions of the dominant Anglo-American model of philosophy: traditionally, the abstract and the universal have been associated with men/masculinity, while women/femininity have been associ-ated with the concrete and the experiences of everyday life. This is another way in which the need to be politically and ethically self-conscious in our theorizing—in this case, our approach to interpretation—plays out.

Thus, although I am indebted to Dooley for her research for my account of their lives, my focus is on the intellectual biographies of both Wheeler and

Thompson, and indeed, throughout this work I shall focus as much as possible on the intellectual biographies of the figures I have chosen to interpret.

Wheeler was born Anna Doyle in Clonberg Parish, County Tipperary, Ireland, in 1785, and died in 1848. She was married in 1800 to Frances Massey Wheeler, but left him twelve years later to go to live with her uncle, the governor of the Isle of Guernsey. Little is known about Wheeler's early education, but as a young woman she read philosophy and Mary Wollstonecraft's *Vindication of the Rights of Woman*. In 1812 Wheeler began to move between Caen, London, Dublin, and Paris, and it is through the philosophers and political activists she met there that she became immersed in reformist philosophies.

In Caen she began a lifelong association with the Saint-Simonians. She then met followers of Robert Owen's cooperative movement. When Wheeler went to Paris in 1823 she met Francois Fourier, the French utopian socialist. According to Margaret McFadden (1996, 206), Wheeler saw the socialist systems of Fourier, Owen, and Saint-Simon as fundamentally the same: "Cooperation is central; men and women are entitled to both equal education and employment opportunities; and marriage and divorce law changes eliminate the double standard and give women equal rights." Wheeler worked to bring together the three different groups through, among other things, translating their work and arranging meetings between them. During the 1820s Wheeler also became friends with Jeremy Bentham, and it was through him that she met William Thompson. Aside from the *Appeal*, Wheeler's central writings are her letter in *The Crisis* of August 1833 and her 1829 lecture at Finsbury Square on the "Rights of Women."

William Thompson, His Life and Works

William Thompson was also born in Ireland, but ten years earlier than Wheeler, in 1775. Dooley (1996, 3) describes him as a man of his era. He was concerned both intellectually and politically with "poverty, developing industrialization and exploitations of labour . . . chasms of abused power between many wealthy landed and the poor . . . degradation of women through poor labour conditions, specious marriage contracts, multiple childbirths and forced prostitution." The subject matter of his work ranges "from legal codes of practice to church tithes, inheritance, agriculture, heating, plumbing, marriage, child-bearing, romance, sexuality and architecture" (4).

Thompson's works are works *of* utilitarianism; they are not works *about* utilitarianism. It is easy for the modern reader in our age of analytic meta-ethics to forget that the early utilitarians were practical reformers.

In 1824 Thompson published his major work, *An Inquiry into the Principles of the Distribution of Wealth*. Although this has been seen as primarily a work of interest to economists and political scientists, it does contain comments on sexual equality.[5] Dooley (1996, 28) shows how, just as with Thompson's other works, the *Inquiry* offers a study of "human nature *and* society with its multiple influences (economic, social and legal) affecting the potential happiness of individuals through specific institutions in diverse cultures."

Central to Thompson's reformist philosophical beliefs was the establishment of cooperative communities. These were small communal societies of workers "based completely on voluntary association of workers and their families and designed to promote security in labour and equality in all its forms" (Dooley 1996, 43). In 1830 he published a work on these communities, *Practical Directions for the Speedy and Economical Establishment of Communities*. Unfortunately, he died before he was able to implement a community of this kind.

The Utilitarianism of Wheeler and Thompson

Wheeler and Thompson held what we would nowadays call a form of "rule utilitarianism": social and political institutions—rather than individual actions—are judged on the amount of happiness they produce. Wheeler and Thompson say that such happiness can be judged only on of the effects on the individual. They reject the notion of a general public good, as this may justify the promotion of the happiness of one group over another, for at the core of their theory lies the belief that all individuals are equal and must be given equal opportunity to experience happiness: "When every individual is made happy, the happiness of the whole is promoted. The mountebank jargon of 'public good,' distinct from the good of the individual members of society will lead astray the human mind no more" (Thompson and Wheeler 1825, 119).

Wheeler and Thompson hold that the desire for happiness and aversion to misery for one's own self is "the original principle of human nature" (13). Happiness is understood as "the aggregate; of which pleasures are the items" (76). Wheeler and Thompson include all forms of pleasure, which they place into four categories: sensual, intellectual, social, and sympathetic. The sensual pleasures, which are to be experienced only in moderation, include food, drink, wealth, and sex.[6] The pleasures of the intellect are those experienced from the gathering and using of knowledge. The intellectual pleasures are portrayed as those that come out of interactions with others, of belonging to a community. Worse still, those who cannot participate in intellectual interaction with others are the objects of contempt, and this further takes away from the potential happiness of the individual: "The happiness of every human being [is] necessarily increased by the respect of those by whom it is surrounded" (121).

At times Wheeler and Thompson seem to run together the social and sympathetic pleasures. This is not surprising as both sets of pleasures are those of interaction with others, but there are fundamental distinctions between the two that are important for the philosophical enterprise of the *Appeal*. The social pleasures are—in essence—the enjoyment we receive from friendship and the company of others. The pleasures of sympathy go beyond this, and are those of feeling the pleasure (or pain) of others because of our connection with them. This connection need not necessarily be one of intimates such as parent and child; in its highest form it is a connection between one human and another.

The pleasure of sympathy is the cornerstone of Wheeler and Thompson's utilitarianism because it is the basis for their central moral principle of benevolence. In contrast to James Mill, they do not hold that it is human nature to use power over others to produce one's own happiness; however, they do not hold that humans naturally promote the happiness of others. Rather, our acts toward others—whether we promote or take away their happiness—are dependent on our knowledge and level of civilization. The benevolent person is one of enlarged sympathies whose attention goes beyond themselves "to matters in which numbers of their fellow creatures, to an indefinite extent beside themselves, are interested" (121).[7] The benevolent person demonstrates what can be called enlightened self-interest. People cannot promote their own genuine happiness with actions that result in the unhappiness of others. Those who attempt to achieve happiness, even though it produces the unhappiness of others, will be shown by others how it will be outweighed by the reactions of the injured parties and the sympathies of others with them:

> It will be found that no person or persons can promote their real happiness, looking comprehensively into all the results of their actions, by

any line of conduct which is incompatible with the happiness of others; that is to say, which detracts more from their happiness than to it adds to that of the agent or agents. It is incumbent on those disapproving of any given line of conduct in others, to show, not only that such line of conduct is absolutely indifferent to them, that it does *not add* to their happiness,—but to point out how it interferes with, how it *lessens*, their happiness: that demonstrated, it will cease to be the interest of the agent to pursue such injurious conduct, because the necessary reactions of selfishness of others and of their sympathy with the injured will more than counterbalance the apparent individual immediate gain. (119)

While their theory has much in common with Bentham's, it is more complex. One of the common criticisms aimed at Benthamite utilitarianism is how it would deal with the possibility that someone's pleasure at the pain of another could be more than—and thus outweigh—that felt pain of the other person. Wheeler and Thompson avoid this problem while maintaining the important Benthamite emphasis on the equality of the individual in deciding which courses of actions will bring about the greatest happiness overall. For Wheeler and Thompson, the greatest pleasure that an individual can feel is sympathy toward others, a pleasure that will increase the happiness of others. The happiness of the whole is not merely an oversimplistic Benthamite sum of the relative happiness of each isolated individual; the happiness of each individual is interrelated with that of others. Indeed, one of the central thrusts of the *Appeal* is to show men that keeping women oppressed is not simply wrong because of the loss of happiness of one half of society, but also because it takes away the potential pleasures men can gain from the liberation of women. Men will gain far more pleasure from a willing, equal sexual partner, from the intellectual and social companionship of women, and from attention to women's interests and welfare, than from the "lower" or "negative" pleasure of power over women.

But Wheeler and Thompson now seem to incur another standard criticism made of classical utilitarianism: how are we to judge between pleasures? Bentham famously judged between pleasures based only on their quantity, claiming that a game of pushpin was of equal value with music and poetry, and if pushpin produced more pleasure then it was more valuable. Wheeler and Thompson clearly make distinctions between the pleasures, however, with the pleasures of the senses having the lowest value and the pleasures of sympathy having the highest. In this way they are closer to the utilitarianism of John

Stuart Mill in his categorizing of pleasures into the "higher" (intellectual) and the "lower" (bodily).

Unfortunately, this distinction between pleasures seems to mean that Wheeler and Thompson's utilitarianism is open to the classic criticism made of Mill concerning how this valuation between the two categories is made. To argue that the higher pleasures are a more refined or elevated type of pleasure easily collapses into claims that such pleasures last longer, and this is ultimately to argue that these pleasures just bring a greater quantity of pleasure. A standard example is to compare reading a book and eating food. In trying to explain why the former is higher than the latter, one is eventually forced to say something along the lines of how education aids our future development or pleasures, while the taste of good food can linger on the palate for only a comparatively brief amount of time. In other words, distinctions of quality collapse into distinctions of quantity.

Does Wheeler and Thompson's categorization of pleasures avoid a similar fate? Their pleasures of sympathy are valued the most because they are the pleasures of the most enlightened people. Wheeler and Thompson do not explain this evaluation. However, Wheeler and Thompson value sympathetic pleasures not just based on what they give to the individual but how they contribute to the overall happiness of society. This allows the placing of sensual pleasures at the bottom of the ladder, sympathetic at the top, and intellectual and social pleasures as roughly even. Thus it may seem that Wheeler and Thompson are relying on quantity of pleasure to distinguish quality of pleasure.

But Wheeler and Thompson's categorization of pleasures, unlike that of Mill, is to be taken as a working definition based on their notions of human nature. Mill's account is aimed at shoring up utilitarianism against the critiques of Bentham's theory. Wheeler and Thompson, on the other hand, have a purely practical need to value some types of pleasure over others, for, as we shall see, women's liberation is conceptualized as—at its core—equal opportunity for pleasures. While Mill is anxious to make distinctions of quality (and fails to do so), Wheeler and Thompson's theory can function even if those distinctions of quality are ultimately little more than distinctions of quantity.

The real problem for Wheeler and Thompson's utilitarian theory is where it intersects with their feminist goals: how are other men to be brought to understand that the equality of women will bring about happiness for *both* sexes? Other men do not have the experiences Wheeler brings to the discussion, nor have they had the advantages, like Thompson, of long discussions with Wheeler. This question lies at the foundations of the *Appeal* and its resolution of the inequality of women. Wheeler and Thompson identify the problem in the following way: how can men be convinced to sympathize enough that they will allow women equality? It is not enough to give women equal civil and political rights, as this would not entail that women have equal happiness. To wish for true equality for women, men must understand the intellectual and sympathetic pleasures of equal interaction with women. Yet, as Thompson acknowledges—and he says Wheeler would agree—many men have not yet achieved that level of intellectual and sympathetic development. The question Wheeler and Thompson are then asking is "How can men come to see that women's equality will bring about more happiness or pleasure for men as well?"

As I shall demonstrate, the troubling aspects of Wheeler and Thompson's utilitarian theory have less to do with its theoretical structure and far more to do with its ultimate failure to support their feminist project. This is not to dismiss the philosophical foundation of their work as useless for their feminist project. What is interesting about their utilitarianism is the way that it underpins the *Appeal*, providing the basis of their critique of Mill and the unequal civil and political rights of women, as well as the justification for a radical overhaul of the social arrangements of society to produce a "more comprehensive system, founded on equal benevolence, on the true development of the principle of Utility," and one that produces gender equality (xiv). As we shall see later in this chapter, this new system will be the socialist system of "Mutual Co-operation."

The Response to Mill

The impetus for the *Appeal* was the comments in James Mill's 1820 essay on government, his theoretical account of a representative government grounded on utilitarian principles. Based on the introductory letter to the *Appeal*, it would seem that two events spurred Wheeler and Thompson into writing their rebuttal of Mill's discussion of the political and civil rights of women in the essay. First, the essay on government had been reprinted in the popular press rather than remaining in the more obscure venue of the Supplement of the *Encyclopaedia Britannica*. Second, Mill appears to have refused to remove the problematic section about women even though he had been asked by "one whose lightest suggestion on such a subject ought to have been a command," presumably Bentham (Thompson and Wheeler 1825, viii).

The troubling section is where Mill (1820, 500) discusses who should vote: "One thing is pretty clear, that all those individuals whose interests are indisputably included in those of other individuals may be struck off without inconvenience. In this light may be viewed children, up to a certain age, whose interests are involved in those of their parents. In this light, also, women may be regarded, the interest of almost all of whom is involved either in that of their fathers or in that of their husbands." As Wheeler and Thompson observe, the notion of "involvement of interest" is vague. What Mill means is that women's happiness is included with that of men and thus there is no reason to consider the happiness of women (or children) separately. What infuriates Wheeler and Thompson is that Mill chose to exclude women as a group expressly when he could have left women's position in doubt by talking about the rights of "man." Further, women are dismissed in a single sentence without any justification.

Wheeler and Thompson therefore set themselves the task of considering whether it is in fact the case that women's interests are involved in that of their fathers or husbands. What they find is that far from women's happiness being involved with that of men, women are made unhappy by their oppressive relationships with husbands and fathers, who—in their turn—gain pleasures from the oppression of women.

In essence, Wheeler and Thompson show that the identity of interest between men and women simply does not exist, and—even if it were to exist—it is not a sufficient reason to deprive women of rights. What is interesting is that Thompson and Wheeler also use their critique of Mill to engage in a more general discussion about the equality of women, specifically through their depictions of the oppressions faced by their contemporaries and their vision of a better society where women will achieve true equality. In addition, running throughout Wheeler and Thompson's work is their desire to "retrieve" utilitarianism as a moral and political philosophy and demonstrate its consistency with the equality of women (and all humans). For Wheeler and Thompson, Mill has put forward a doctrine "which disgrace[s] the principle of utility" (ix).

The response to Mill comes in the form of three questions in part 2:

> Does an identity, or an involving, of interest in point of fact and of necessity, exist between women and men? (21)

If this involving of the interests in those of men do exist, is it a sufficient cause, or any reason at all, why either of the parties, men or women, with interests so identified, should therefore be deprived of civil or political rights? (116)

Is there in the nature of things, any security for equality of enjoyments, proportioned to exertion and capabilities, but by means of equal civil rights? Or any security for equal civil, but by means of equal political rights? (152)

To answer the first question, Wheeler and Thompson divide women into three classes: women without husbands or fathers; adult daughters living in their fathers' homes; and wives. In discussing the first class, Wheeler and Thompson take clear pleasure in showing Mill's lack of logical thinking. On the one hand, Mill says that *all* those whose interests are not involved with others who can represent them politically ought to have votes; on the other, Mill says that *almost* all women have their interests involved in that of their fathers or husbands and thus *all* women should be excluded from political rights. Despite this latter claim, Wheeler and Thompson argue that, by Mill's own measure of identity of interest, this first group of women—those without husbands or fathers—must have political rights. Wheeler and Thompson are not particularly interested in examining why Mill would think this way; their focus is simply to undercut his arguments.

Wheeler and Thompson then turn to adult daughters and wives. Their argument in both instances takes the form of showing just how far from the case it is that these women's happiness or interests are identified with men's, and thus that these women must be given political rights. In demonstrating the truths of their contemporaries' lives, Wheeler and Thompson's argument also becomes a call for a life free of oppression for these women.

In the case of adult daughters, Wheeler and Thompson divide the class into two subdivisions: illegitimate and legitimate offspring. In the case of the former, their fathers often neglect them or are ashamed of them; thus, Wheeler and Thompson argue, it cannot be claimed that their interests are involved with those of their fathers. In the case of legitimate daughters, Wheeler and Thompson claim that the lives of fathers and daughters are so different that the former can have little connection with the latter, as women are restricted from the pleasures and occupations of men. For example, sons can discuss the affairs of the world and their activities within it with their fathers, whereas women's only conversational offerings are the humdrum affairs of the home. It is instead with their mothers that daughters share an involvement of interests, but their mothers cannot represent them as they themselves do not have political rights.

Young women have been taught that their happiness will come through sexual/romantic love alone; moreover, they hope that they can use their romantic/sexual power over their partners as a way of obtaining a measure of freedom of actions. In the course of their argument for political rights, Wheeler and Thompson show that this is a delusion. They liken marriage to slavery and see it as an institution that makes the woman "in the minutest incidents of life, *obedient* to his will [her husband's], be it wise or capricious" (65). They scoff at the notion that women are free not to marry, for men have created society in such a way that women have been excluded from learning economically useful knowledge or skills and from possessing property. While the comparison of marriage to slavery is frequent throughout the *Appeal*, there is little further discussion of women's feelings of love, although Wheeler took up this issue in her later writings.

Wives are more oppressed than are adult daughters, as they are no longer seen as their own persons. The interests and enjoyments of two married beings become one: the husband's. The focus of Wheeler and Thompson's argument in part 2 is the lives of married women, and it is here that they become their most impassioned, detailing the miserable circumstances of their contemporaries. Women are made slaves by men's superior physical strength, by public (male) opinion, by the marital contract, and by their own lack of skills, knowledge, and money. Indeed, Wheeler and Thompson hold that there is something worse about European (white) women's situation than that of the slaves of the West Indies, in that the latter are not made to pretend to surrender voluntarily to their masters.

What sets Wheeler and Thompson's claim that marriage is a form of slavery apart from similar claims—for example, those of Mary Astell or John Stuart Mill—is their detailed account of how women are oppressed in every facet of human life. Thus Wheeler and Thompson ground their opposition to Mill on a foundation of the specific context in which their female contemporaries lived. This means that the *Appeal* needs to be read—at least in part—as a particular historical artifact, and therefore that it will be hard to read using the mainstream philosophical approach to the history of philosophy: as containing timeless questions about social justice. I shall return to the question of the best interpretive tools to examine the *Appeal* at the end of the chapter.

As true utilitarians, Wheeler and Thompson see that the wrong of marital slavery is that women are deprived of the "pleasures of freedom" (69). Even if the wife is allowed other pleasures by her husband, the fact that these are controlled by another means that she will not achieve the amount of happiness that she could experience. Men also have their pleasures reduced by the institution of marriage. They surrender "the delights of equality, namely those of esteem, of friendship, of intellectual and sympathetic intercourse, for the vulgar pleasure of command" (70). As we have seen, within Wheeler and Thompson's utilitarian framework these are significant pleasures to forego, as the sympathetic and social pleasures are the highest a human can experience.

The measure used to identify whether there is an identity of interest is whether "wives enjoy as many pleasures of all sorts as their husbands" (76). On Wheeler and Thompson's utilitarian account, identity of interest is defined as the involvement of the *happiness* of the wife with the husband. They consider the different pleasures humans can feel and compare the experiences of husbands and wives. In the case of the sensual pleasures, men are allowed to indulge freely in eating and drinking, while public opinion restricts women by labeling such behavior as unfeminine. Further, her husband dictates the amounts of food or drink she is allowed. In the case of sexual pleasures, women are restricted by the double standard. Again, public opinion and the will of her husband produce inequality of pleasures. It should be noted that Wheeler and Thompson are not arguing for excessive eating and drinking or adultery; they believe that pleasures should be pursued in moderation. Their goal is to show inequalities in pleasure due to the fact that the husband has control over the pleasures of his wife while he is free to indulge himself.

Men deprive their wives of the pleasures of knowledge because they need to keep them obedient. They deprive their wives of the pleasures of sympathy and socializing by restricting their interactions with the outside world; women cannot form associations or friendships with others without the permission of their husbands. Wheeler and Thompson see this deprivation not simply as the absence of happiness, but as "a state of positive torment" (81). Indeed, they say that those women who do not recognize what they are losing are better off than those who do.

Even if men were to permit women equal enjoyment of these pleasures, there would not be equal happiness, as women would still be deprived of the pleasure of what Wheeler and Thompson call "voluntariness." This is not only a pleasure in itself but a prerequisite to the use of our mental powers and our ability to perform moral actions. What is interesting here is that these concepts are framed in terms of pleasures: "Voluntariness is requisite for morality. That self-approbation which accompanies and follows the performance of a virtuous act, arising from the consciousness of the successful exertion of our mental powers in producing a result of preponderant good; that peculiar zest of sympathy which arises from the contemplation of the happiness which we have *voluntarily*, and not as machines, co-operated to produce . . . these are the pleasures, which, above all others, are requisite to real, to exalted happiness" (89–90).

In demonstrating that there is not an identity of interests between spouses, Wheeler and Thompson show that the power relations between the sexes prevent the possibility of women's happiness. While women are still under the power of their husbands they may have certain pleasures, but they can never be happy. Even if the husband is well intentioned in the use of his power, he will not be able to promote her happiness as much as she can promote her own.

Even though Wheeler and Thompson do not expressly state this, it is also clear that the wielding of power is a pleasure, albeit a crass and perverted one, and thus it is unlikely that men will give up their power over women willingly. A few enlightened men will recognize that they lose higher pleasures by this use of power, but most do not. The question is then how gendered power roles could ever be dismantled—and thus the oppression of women alleviated—unless men can be brought to see how they themselves will not lose from it and, indeed, would gain from it.

It is their utilitarianism—their focus on pleasures—that leads Wheeler and Thompson to these insights and to a resolution of these questions that, as we shall see, is part of a far more progressive feminist theory than that of their predecessors or their contemporaries. Unfortunately, however, Wheeler and Thompson's utilitarianism also means that, rather than aiming to empower women, they focus on changing men and the prevailing economic and political system. The issue of the empowerment of women is something I will begin to develop throughout the rest of the overview of the *Appeal*, and it will be central to my final analysis of the work at the end of the chapter.

In conclusion, according to Wheeler and Thompson, there is no identity of interest between daughters and fathers or wives and husbands. If this is the case, it then follows that—on Mill's own account—women must be given the vote.

Political Rights and Women's Capabilities

Wheeler and Thompson next ask whether, if it were indeed true, as Mill claims, that there is an identity of interests between men and women, this would be a sufficient reason for excluding women from political rights. Wheeler and Thompson see political rights to be important for two reasons. First, because political rights are the preconditions of civil rights, and because they keep these latter rights—once obtained—secure. Second, because "the exercise of political rights affords the best opportunity for the exercise of the intellectual powers and enlargement of the sympathies of human beings, leading their attention out of themselves, to matters in which numbers of their fellow creatures, to an indefinite extent besides themselves, are interested" (121). Clearly, then, we can see that the person with political rights is the person who has the opportunity to become the benevolent utilitarian. This is important, as we must not forget that Wheeler and Thompson's argument for women is based on their argument *for* utilitarianism. They are not just saving utilitarianism from its corruption by Mill, they are also interested in producing "a new science . . . the science of promoting human happiness" (xiv). If it were true that women's interests were involved in men's, then women would not lose the first benefit, but they would not have the second. Wheeler and Thompson believe that the exercise of political rights requires someone to consider others outside their immediate circle and to become knowledgeable about the political and social world outside their own homes. Thus women are prevented from equal participation in happiness with men by their lack of political rights, and are also prevented through this lack of rights from enlarging their minds and developing their characters. This is a crucial point, as Wheeler and Thompson claim that this development of mind and character is necessary to enjoy pleasures of the highest kind and in the highest possible degree.

Here again the argument for political rights is a utilitarian one. Political rights provide the best opportunity for individual happiness and will also, according to Wheeler and Thompson's version of utilitarianism, lead to the happiness of society. Clearly, then, men should be able to see that equal political rights will benefit both sexes. For those who do not see this, Wheeler and Thompson point out that giving political rights to women will cause no harm. These rights are described as "innocent" and "improving" pleasures, and they say that it would cost nothing to give these rights (148). Thus giving women equal political rights will lead to increased overall happiness at nobody's expense. Here Wheeler and Thompson are partially addressing the question, asked earlier, of how men can be persuaded to support women's equality.

This question is also addressed when they ask who would it please to deprive women of these rights. Their answer is that only those who take pleasure in the misery of others would take pleasure in this. Faced with this claim, it is easy to imagine the *Appeal*'s readers who were against women's suffrage being stumped about how to respond. This is one of the strengths of Wheeler and Thompson's utilitarian framework for their feminism: it can circumvent the typical reasons to reject political equality, such as tradition (women have never voted), women's capabilities (they are not rational enough to vote), unfairness to other groups (not all men have the franchise), or potentially disastrous consequences (women would make bad choices or, worse, demand further rights or become like men). The focus on pleasure—and pleasure alone—as the grounding for political choice means that those who resist women's political equality must face what lies behind their arguments: they must examine their own moral character.

Continuing with their assumption (which they make for the sake of argument) that it is true that there is an identity of interests between the sexes to the point that only one needs political power, Wheeler and Thompson perform what we would nowadays call a "thought experiment." As we shall see later, this is a curious piece with some significant repercussions for Wheeler and Thompson's overall argument.

Although they do *not* think that either sex (or any one group) should have political power, Wheeler and Thompson ask what if women were to be the ones in power, and compare how this would look to men's exclusive power in making laws. Ultimately, they argue that a "community of rational beings, desirous of promoting equally the happiness of all," who were in the position where they *had* to choose to give political rights only to one sex, would need to choose to give these rights to women (147).

Wheeler and Thompson reach this surprising conclusion based on a number of arguments about women's physical and mental qualities. They argue that women could never overlook the interests of men or rule by force, as men have the physical strength to resist injustice. Moreover, women, due to their lack of physical strength, are inclined more to "intellectual and sympathetic pursuits than those of brute force," and therefore they would be more likely to "to cultivate the arts of persuasion and peace, and to avoid offensive wars, one of the greatest scourges of humanity" (128). For Wheeler and Thompson, the most useful quality for a legislator is the ability to sympathize with the pains and pleasures—and thus to promote the happiness—of those for whom they are making laws. They hold that the inferior physical strength of women means that they would be more sympathetic toward the interests of the whole of the human race. It is important to notice that Wheeler and Thompson see the relationship between women's intellectual and psychological capacities and their physical strength as one of cause and effect: the development of one capacity as a response to the lack of another. This is clearly distinct from the problematic claim of biological determinism, which holds that physiological differences between the sexes determine their perceived psychological differences as well as their different social and cultural roles.

Wheeler and Thompson even suggest that this lack of physical strength would ultimately mean that women would make better laws than would men. Their argument is rather strange at this point. The idea is that physical power is generally cultivated over intellectual power. If women were allowed to develop their intellectual power, they would focus on this (as they would still remain at a disadvantage due to their lack of physical power) and thus would "excel as much in intelligence as men in strength, and would therefore be better adapted than men to the making of wise laws" (127).

There are two other qualities for a good legislator identified by Wheeler and Thompson: intellectual ability and "active talent," by which we should understand physical energy (128). In the case of the first, they say that women would appear to be equal to men in this capacity. Regarding the physical element of active talent, women will be inferior to men; however, regarding the mental element (perseverance) women possess more of this than do men. This is a quality their gender roles and their oppression have actually produced in them (140–41). Wheeler and Thompson argue that this latter capacity—that of the "nurse" rather than the "warrior"—makes for a better legislator (141). Having said this, however, they point out that men are at an advantage in the amount of active talent they possess, in that they are not incapacitated by childbirth. Moreover, they argue that men are excused from performing their duties if they are ill, even if the illness is self-induced, whereas women are "ridiculed" for ignoring their other duties. Here Wheeler and Thompson appear to be referring to contemporary arguments other than Mill's for keeping women out of political life. Thus they argue that, in the case of active talent, men have a slight advantage over women.

Wheeler and Thompson's account here of how—in theory—women would make superior legislators is unusual. It may help to see it as a response to arguments that would have been prevalent among their contemporaries that women's weaker physique (and thus weaker mental capacities) meant they were unqualified to take on public roles or even vote. However, Wheeler and Thompson take their response further than is necessary. Instead of merely denying that this is the case, they argue that women's physical weakness is potentially an *advantage* for producing a happier (better) society. It is here that we see the first sign of tension in Wheeler and Thompson's argument between their feminism and their utilitarianism, a tension that will lead us to ask about the ultimate success of the argument of the *Appeal*. The crucial point to notice at this stage is that Wheeler and Thompson's form of utilitarianism cannot allow them to take the next step and argue for women to be the dominant political group. For one group to have political power over the other—even if the power was used to good ends—is to subsume the happiness of individuals to the greater good. Yet, if women as a group do possess the abilities to be better legislators, it may be that women's potential is being restricted because Wheeler and Thompson's utilitarianism will not allow women to be in a dominant position in society.

Civil Rights and Political Rights

In the final part of the *Appeal*, Wheeler and Thompson argue that equality of enjoyments can be secured only by equal civil rights, and equal civil rights can be secured only by equal political rights. Their use of a distinction between the two sets of rights, with political rights as foundational, is what makes the *Appeal* such a compelling and sophisticated argument for women's suffrage. Wheeler and Thompson equate civil rights with rights covered by civil and criminal laws; in particular, they criticize laws that do not allow women ownership of inherited property or their own wages, laws that are barriers to women becoming educated or entering into lucrative occupations in the workplace, and criminal laws that treat the sexes unequally, such as the fact that women are not protected from domestic violence. Political rights, as we have seen, are the rights to elect or be elected to legislative and administrative offices.

Wheeler and Thompson recognize that equality cannot be guaranteed through the goodwill of individuals or a change in public opinion. They argue that there would be no security in gender equality when it is conferred from individuals who remain in power; further, the laws that exclude women from education or owning property would remain in place. They then ask whether equality of civil and criminal laws is enough for the happiness of women. Would being without political rights make them happier or their rights more secure? The answer to this will clearly be no. They argue that there is an added pleasure to possessing these rights in knowing that such rights are secure. Civil rights on their own cannot give as much happiness as civil rights and political rights together. Here, then, their utilitarianism supports a full-fledged claim for women's rights.

There is a shift in Wheeler and Thompson's argument for political rights for women in the final part of the *Appeal* from a moral approach to one based on factual, physical circumstances. Child bearing and child rearing mean that women will be more confined to the homes while men have more chance of associating with others and gaining knowledge and influence. Wheeler and Thompson do not argue that there is anything "natural" about women's tendency to see the private sphere as more important than the public; rather, they say that this is produced by women's physical circumstances. According to Wheeler and Thompson, the physical disadvantages of child bearing and rearing would be counteracted by political rights in the same way that the invention of gunpowder placed weak men on level with the stronger in the area of combat.

It is important to notice that Wheeler and Thompson take a decidedly unsentimental view of child bearing and rearing. They see political rights as providing a sort of "check" to prevent women from slipping back into what they see as the intellectual torpor of the domestic sphere. Here again it is not that such a slippage is the result of "natural" maternal feelings, but rather the result of women's capacity for reproduction. The intellectual stimulation provided by political involvement would mean that women would become less childlike and more intellectual and they would enter into the social world.

This view is radical, and Wheeler and Thompson acknowledge that change will be slow. Women have been oppressed for so long that it will take time for them to assert their rights. Moreover, even with changes in women's rights, men still remain the stronger and, under the system of individual competition, will always consider themselves superior.

It is at this point that Wheeler and Thompson speak directly to their readers, and the *Appeal* ends with an "Address to Women." This section is a combination of a call to arms and a discussion of a societal system that would produce equality of happiness for the two sexes. It is here that we are told how equality of happiness can be achieved. There is an important shift here in the direction of the *Appeal* from arguments *that* women should have political rights to *how* equal rights and happiness could be achieved.

The Call to Women

Wheeler and Thompson call on women to take responsibility for their own liberation. To be free, they say, women must demand it and respect themselves; indeed, it is only when women respect themselves that men will respect them: "To be free, women . . . have only to desire it . . . and fearlessly to advocate it. . . . Demand with mild but unshrinking firmness, perfect equality with men. . . . To obtain equal rights, the basis of equal happiness with men, you must be *respected* by them. . . . To be respected by them, you must be respectable in your own eyes; you must exert more power, you must be more useful" (195–97). But this call for change appears to be in tension with the constant emphasis throughout the *Appeal* on the tyranny of men. It is hard to imagine how women could make the change to equality from their state of near helpless subjection and slavery merely by respecting themselves and calling for equality. It may be possible that Wheeler and Thompson have made a shift. Throughout the *Appeal* when they talk about the tyranny of men, they usually are referring to the individual in the home. Individual women are unlikely to be able to fight against individual men, given the control and physical superiority these men have. Instead, Wheeler and Thompson seem to be talking about women as a group working against the male system. It may make sense then for Wheeler and Thompson to be seen as making one of the earliest calls (perhaps the earliest) for an actual women's movement. If so, then this is a watershed moment in European feminism that has been neglected.

Overall, however, women's role in this part of the *Appeal* remains vague; Wheeler and Thompson are far more specific about the changes in men that need to be made in order to bring about equality for women.[8] We are told in the introductory letter to the *Appeal* that Wheeler would not want equality with men as things stood. Quite simply, their male contemporaries would be unable to appreciate liberated women. The only pleasures such men look for in relation to women are sexual pleasure and the pleasure of power and control. It is only, Thompson says, through knowledge given by education that men will understand the higher pleasures of equality with women. Men need to be convinced that these lower pleasures are far outweighed by the higher pleasures of the companionship of equals, and by the pleasures of seeing the happiness of another human.

But we can see that the actual mechanism by which this is to happen is unclear. A simple appeal to men's self-interest is not a strong foundation for the equality of women. The relative certainty or uncertainty of the consequences of actions or systems of rules has always been a weakness of utilitarian theory. Moreover, it is not just an appeal to men's rationality that lies at the heart of Wheeler and Thompson's call for a change of heart, it is an appeal to their benevolence.[9]

The notion of benevolence is at the core of their utilitarian theory and binds it together, but is it able to take the theoretical weight that Wheeler and Thompson place on it? On an immediate level, how men will learn to become benevolent is left vague on Wheeler and Thompson's account. Women's sympathies will apparently become enlarged by entering the public sphere, but men are already there and it does not appear to have had much of an effect on them! This is problematic, as Wheeler and Thompson need to demonstrate how men will learn to understand that women's equality will benefit both sexes. It would seem that it is only in Wheeler and Thompson's proposed new society, which will be discussed shortly, that such education can take place.

Even assuming that men develop the necessary utilitarian-grounded benevolence to wish to give equal happiness to women, this will not accomplish all of Wheeler and Thompson's feminist goals. Wheeler and Thompson do not just wish for women to be treated equally, they also want women to be treated with respect and dignity. Indeed, this is what makes their feminism so appealing. They understand that the liberation of women goes beyond the formalities of rights and requires opportunities for self-actualization and self-respect. Now, certainly respect and equality are what we want for others—it would be odd if we did not. It could be argued that the possession of rights gives dignity and self-respect, but this is not what Wheeler and Thompson need as part of their specific argument. Treating someone benevolently— paying concern to their interests—is not interchangeable with treating someone with dignity and respect. The benevolent man will understand the need for women to have rights and will understand the pleasure that self-actualization or self-respect can give to women, but there is no guarantee that a concern for the pleasures or happiness of others actually produces a respect for those others or allows them to develop self-respect.

It is here that we can start to see more signs of tension between their feminism and their utilitarianism. The principle of benevolence can be used to argue for basic political and civil rights for women; however, Wheeler and Thompson want for women—and rightly so—what their utilitarian framework cannot guarantee: autonomy, a thoroughgoing moral agency, dignity, respect, and *self*-respect. In short, they want empowerment for women.

Justice for Women

The further problem is that Wheeler and Thompson not only want equal political and civil rights to be given to women, they also want men to *understand* that the subjection of women is wrong and to acknowledge the rightness of claims for the equality of women: they are calling for justice. Unfortunately, it is here that we begin to see how their form of utilitarianism cannot fully satisfy their feminist goals. In other words, the *Appeal* may have theoretical failures. The second problem, external to the *Appeal*'s textual or argumentative consistencies, is how we, as modern readers, are to interpret Wheeler and Thompson's call for justice for women.

Neither of the mainstream approaches to the history of philosophy suffices to bring out what Wheeler and Thompson are trying to do here. To employ the historical approach to reading Wheeler and Thompson's call for justice is to miss out on a passionate argument for righting the wrongs women suffered; moreover, it is to disallow the possibility that we moderns may have something to learn from reading the *Appeal*.

Interesting enough, Wheeler and Thompson's utilitarian framework, in the final analysis, makes gender justice an ahistorical issue; however, this is problematic. Certainly Wheeler and Thompson recognize that the injustices their female contemporaries suffer are far worse than the effects of the institution of gender on men, and that it is important for men to become a part of the removal of sexist oppression. As we shall see, however, once Wheeler and Thompson stop theorizing within their specific historical and cultural context and begin theorizing within a more timeless utilitarian perspective, they begin to lose something important about the goal of gender justice.

The descriptions in the *Appeal* of the treatment of women are so stirring and the rhetoric they use is so much the rhetoric of justice, that it is easy to "feel" that justice will be done when the situation has been righted. Wheeler and Thompson clearly believe that they are arguing for social justice; for example, this is the purpose of their thought experiment of placing women in power: "If from the analysis we have gone through, there is a strong probability that the moral aptitude would be greater on the side of the weaker, it will show more strongly the odiousness of the injustice which, without inquiry, gives to the stronger as a matter of course those exclusive powers, which superior strength necessarily impels any thing short of comprehensive and benevolent wisdom to abuse" (147–48).

But their actual argument for the rights of women is grounded in their utilitarian theory. Here we see the first problem: they cannot provide a fully developed argument for justice. Within their utilitarian theory there is certainly room for some kind of notion of justice: everyone is given an equal opportunity to achieve happiness or to experience pleasures, and the prevention of women having such opportunity is unjust. However, this is a notion of justice framed within the utilitarian theoretical framework of the production of happiness. Indeed, it is significant to notice that women will not be moved to "feminist" action by a sense of justice, but by a "love of happiness" (188).

It is certainly possible to argue that benevolent men will *want* justice for women. It is even possible to argue—as Wheeler and Thompson do later in the *Appeal*—that their utilitarian society will be a just society, but one must be hesitant to make the claim that the *Appeal* is a full-blown argument for justice for women. The goal of happiness is an important one, and allowing women equal opportunities for individual happiness is part of achieving gender justice, but it is not the equivalent of gender justice. There is no theoretical space in Wheeler and Thompson's theory for a demand for women's justice, either because they are women or because justice is the right course to follow. There can be only a theoretical space to argue that justice is the equal opportunity for happiness. Just as with their call for respect and dignity for women, Wheeler and Thompson's call for justice for women points to a tension between their feminist ideals and their utilitarian theory. As feminists, Wheeler and Thompson want to appeal to a stand-alone principle of justice, yet on a utilitarian framework justice is—at best—a secondary principle framed in terms of the greatest happiness of the greatest number.

This leads to the second and more important problem of whether Wheeler and Thompson's utilitarian framework has the theoretical space to allow for a call for gender justice. Wheeler and Thompson offer—and cannot do otherwise—a notion of justice that comes out of their utilitarianism, a notion that is part of utilitarian theory regardless of historical context. To argue that gender justice for their female contemporaries is included under this general umbrella would be to miss the specific reasons why justice is required for these women and why it has been denied them. Talk of equality of happiness makes us lose sight of the important fact that women have been targeted for prejudicial treatment. The notion of justice that comes out of utilitarianism simply rights the balance for the sake of overall happiness; it is not motivated by the political goal of gender justice, nor is it historically or culturally contextualized.

This is one of the consequences of trying to treat "gender justice" as a problem of philosophy in the same way that the philosophical approach to the history of philosophy conceptualizes philosophy as comprising a series of timeless or universal problems. We lose sight of the fact that there are issues specific to women, issues that are historically and culturally specific, and gender injustice becomes "lost" as another variant of the general "human" problem of injustice.

While there is certainly something to be said politically or pragmatically for making a call for gender justice part of general social justice, we lose something important philosophically. If gender justice becomes subsumed under the general rubric of the "problem of justice," then it automatically becomes both an abstract notion and part of a general concept (justice) that has historically ignored the material needs of women. Moreover, the concept of justice has historically been associated with reason and therefore has metaphorically excluded women from being receivers or givers of justice because of their association with the "opposite" of reason: emotion. Surely, we want "our" justice, not this abstract, male justice, and in order to achieve this we need to be able to include the concrete elements of women's lives and have the flexibility to introduce new issues as we identify them. Historical calls for gender justice, therefore, need to be examined within their particular historical and cultural context. Whether this means historical texts have nothing to say to modern readers is an issue I will discuss in later chapters. For the present, I simply want to claim that we should be cautious of reading feminist historical texts for "the [ahistorical] problems of philosophy," even if on the surface these appear to be feminist problems.

A New Society

As Wheeler and Thompson recognize, even if women are granted equal rights they will still be at a disadvantage in their measure of happiness due to the physical differences between the sexes, and Wheeler and Thompson hold that this will continue as long as the system of individual competition exists. Moreover, they claim that not only will men be resistant to increased competition (from women), they will also have more individual wealth since they do not leave the workforce to bear and rear children. Even with equal rights, women will remain financially dependent on men. Their happiness will therefore always be tenuous; their providers could die or their lives could be made miserable in hundreds of small ways that the laws cannot cover.

Wheeler and Thompson then offer an alternative scheme of social arrangements, which they say is "the only one which will complete and for ever insure the perfect equality and entire reciprocity of happiness between men and women." This is the system of "Association, or of Labor by Mutual Co-operation" (199).[10] In this community there will be no individual property or happiness; men and women will work together cooperatively instead for mutual happiness. There is no expectation that everyone can contribute equal amounts of work, as people have varied talents and capabilities. The goal is for people to contribute what they can. Under this scheme, women will not need to marry or prostitute themselves for survival, nor need they fear being left an unsupported widow.

Wheeler and Thompson claim that this scheme removes the motivations for men to be unjust and the motivations of women to submit to injustice. As long as individual competition is the motivating factor in human life, men will always have the natural advantage of strength and "uninterrupted" exertion, which they will use to indirectly through their economic and legislative power to dominate women (203). Wheeler and Thompson say that we cannot expect human beings, in a system of individual competition, who have power and means, not to exercise it. The system of Mutual Co-operation takes away this power and its means.

Even though Wheeler and Thompson are talking about human nature in general, it is clear that they must mean men. It is men who have power due to their physical strength. The system of Mutual Co-operation will place a check on this, both literally and psychologically. There are no motivations for women to be in oppressive relationships. The community takes care of their health and well-being, and they share equally in the benefits of the community; in return, they work for the common good in whatever way for which they are best suited. In this community, women will have equality in rights, duties, and enjoyments.

It is here that we can see that Wheeler and Thompson are offering their complete answer to how men will be persuaded to want gender equality: society itself needs to undergo a radical transformation. With their physical power in check and the opportunity to see women flourish, men will learn to see how women's equality brings happiness to everyone in the community—or at the very least, that men will not lose from it. Unfortunately, the actual psychological process through which both sexes will develop the benevolence that is central to Wheeler and Thompson's utilitarianism is still not explained. However, it is possible to believe that—without a system of individual competition and within a system of Mutual Co-operation—such a feeling could easily be produced.

There are difficulties, however, in the structure of this new society. Wheeler and Thompson state that in order to "enjoy equal happiness with men, to associate with them in terms of perfect equality, you [women] must be equally useful to the common good by an equal improvement and equally useful application of all your faculties of mind and body" (204). The contributions of men and women to the community are not the same. Men's contribution to the happiness of the community is greater because their physical strength allows them to produce more. Women contribute through "the peculiar pains, privations and cares" of child bearing and rearing (205). Physical strength and the capacity to bear children are seen as the particular "faculty or talent" of each of the sexes (204).

This division of labor is clearly problematic. Men's contributions are at least neutral when measured by the amount of pleasure or pain they bring to the individual, while women's contributions are considered painful. This raises the question of what is meant by the equality of happiness in this community. Wheeler and Thompson's solution is interesting: they suggest that there should be compensation for these "punishments of nature" (206). They state that reproduction is far more useful for the community than the levels of productivity of men; however, they do not explain what this compensation might be. Is it possible that Wheeler and Thompson think that being more socially valuable than men would be compensation enough for women? Thinking within their utilitarian framework this may well be the case: benevolent women gain pleasure from working for the good of others.

What Wheeler and Thompson gloss over is the fact that most women will be spending a lot of time reproducing. This is not simply due to the fact that available contraceptive measures were minimal at this time, but—more important—the community needs to grow. Wheeler and Thompson explicitly state that "the race itself should be every year increased." They do not specify in the *Appeal* whether the biological mothers will rear their own children or whether there will be a communal system for that task. It is worth noting, however, that either way it is likely that women will be primarily responsible for child rearing, at least of children too young to be in school; indeed, in discussing the different contributions of men and women to the community, the other contribution of women (besides reproduction) is that children will be "kindly and skillfully nurtured" (206).

Thus we can see that, even if reproduction is socially valued more than men's physical productivity, and even if women are given equal opportunities to develop their intellect and capabilities, women's lives, as women, will be filled with far more pain than men's, pain that is, unfortunately, a necessary part of the functioning of this community. Moreover, men will have different choices as to how they contribute to the community, whereas most women will remain restricted to their traditional gender roles. Thus it would seem from a modern perspective that women will not be equal in terms of happiness in this new community. Wheeler and Thompson do not offer any explicit argumentative support for the fact that most women are to remain in the traditional gender role of mother and nurturer; all they say is that the role of women in this new community is better than the present state of things, where women are looked on as inferior because of their capacity for reproduction.

This role of women in the community is in tension with their earlier comments in the *Appeal* about women's legislative abilities. Why do Wheeler and Thompson focus on women's contributions as mothers and not even raise the possibility of their contributions in organizer or leader roles? Surely the community would benefit greatly from having the best qualified to lead or organize the community and its different sectors taking the reins. If so, it would make sense to have as many women as possible in leadership roles. It is this type of change that would be a real step forward for women in the new community. A truly progressive, feminist society would allow women the opportunity to break away from their traditional roles and assume leadership positions.

Wheeler and Thompson's Utilitarian Feminism

Unfortunately, it is Wheeler and Thompson's own particular version of utilitarianism that would prevent the development of a progressive community that would give women opportunities to emerge as leaders. Wheeler and Thompson would need to engage in a discussion of which role—mother versus leader—would produce the general or overall good, and they criticize this kind of discourse. Moreover, we have already seen that considerations of justice will not provide a strong enough argument for women to take on leadership roles.

Wheeler and Thompson argue throughout the *Appeal* that equality will come through removing restrictions on opportunities to experience pleasure. In the new community, men are restricted (through the lack of individual competition and women's economic independence) from using their physical power over women to gain pleasures (and will learn to appreciate higher pleasures), while women are freed from the oppression of men and compensated for the pains associated with being both female and a productive member of the community. This, they believe, creates an equality in opportunities for happiness in the two sexes.

What is concerning is that in an effort to level the playing field for all the individuals in the community, it is not clear that individual women will be given maximum opportunity to develop their capacities. Even though Wheeler and Thompson have offered happiness for women, have they truly offered liberation and individual empowerment? Wheeler and Thompson are clearly satisfied with what their community will offer women, but it may seem that they have ultimately failed womankind. More accurately, it may be that their utilitarianism has ultimately failed their feminism.

At the heart of this failure is the fact that the *Appeal* does not offer empowerment to women. While women are called on to make the changes to their situation, it is clear that women's subordination will be alleviated only through social changes aimed at restricting men's power and persuading men of the pleasures connected with association with women as equals. Even though Wheeler and Thompson open the window to the possibility that women could be in charge in their new society and have different roles to play, they revert to offering women little more than the traditional gender roles of child bearing and rearing.

Why does the *Appeal* not offer empowerment when its authors so clearly understand women's lack of power? The problem may be that the moral philosophy of the *Appeal* is fundamentally masculinist. The true moral—utilitarian—agent of the *Appeal* is the person who is free to enjoy all levels of pleasure, in particular, the benevolent person who is able to understand and promote the happiness of others. This model is based on male experience, as

Wheeler and Thompson are quite clear that women are not free to experience different types of pleasure and that the domestic sphere prevents women from developing their intellects and characters in the way needed to achieve the highest pleasure of sympathy: to become the benevolent person.

Wheeler and Thompson argue that both sexes need to achieve this goal of moral agency. Women need to be this way in order to be truly equal, and men need to be this way in order to understand the need for women to be truly equal. The asymmetry is problematic, as women's equality is ultimately contingent on changes in men (which will be produced through the system of Mutual Co-operation). Moreover, men need to develop the enlightened self-interest of the benevolent person. Women also need to do this; however, the structure that will lead to benevolence in men—the society for Mutual Co-operation—does not seem to require the same level or type of benevolence in women. Women's role of child bearing and rearing for the society may mean that they are more useful than men, but surely the sort of enlightened self-interest required to recognize the dignity and interests of another human being is very different from the enlightened self-interest required to breed for the good of society. The former is intellectual and—even if it cannot be proved—would appear to be a good for its possessor, whereas it is quite hard to even place the role of women within the framework of enlightened self-interest.

It is likely these are *not* the sorts of conclusions Wheeler and Thompson would have wanted drawn from the arguments of the *Appeal.* There is little doubt that their goal of women's equality was something genuinely and passionately felt by both of them, yet ultimately there is something about their theory that does not have women or women's empowerment as its central focus. They do well to understand the importance of bringing men into the discussion of women's equality, yet somehow their theory ends up being dominated by men's experiences. Despite their good intentions, Wheeler and Thompson's version of utilitarianism means that they cannot avoid these conclusions.

This is disappointing, as Wheeler and Thompson clearly want to provide a theory that achieves sound ethical and political goals; however, ultimately, they do not or cannot allow for all the political and ethical dimensions and conclusions of their theorizing. Thus we can learn from Wheeler and Thompson that if we wish to use utilitarian theorizing as a foundation for feminist theorizing, it must be "politicized" in some way. The possibility of what I shall call an "empowerment utilitarianism" is a theme I will explore in the next two chapters, on Catharine Beecher and Frances Wright.[11] Wheeler and Thompson also show us that "pure" utilitarian theory will ultimately fail their feminist enterprise, and I shall further explore the issue of the purity of philosophy and philosophical theory in the following chapters on Beecher and Wright.

Analysis

Throughout I have been aiming to explicate Wheeler and Thompson's utilitarian feminism and to show how their utilitarian theory can both aid and prevent their feminism. Even though I may not have explicitly employed any particular approach to the history of philosophy in my examination of the *Appeal*, it would be naive to believe that my examination has been neutral; I employ modern concepts in my analysis that would not have been available in the nineteenth century, and I also place the *Appeal* within its historical and cultural context. What I need to do now is to consider what interpretive perspective or lens I *should* take; to consider, in particular, whether the two dominant mainstream approaches of Anglo-American philosophy are a good fit for the feminist philosophy of the *Appeal*.

In the introductory chapter I discussed the two mainstream approaches to historical texts—the historical and the philosophical—which can be put, somewhat oversimplistically, as "What did *x* say?" and "Is it true?" (Graham 1982, 38). There is a sense that a discussion of whether we need historical and cultural context in order to understand what Wheeler and Thompson said would be pointless, as it carries with it an implication that textual analysis can actually be treated separately of this context. Wheeler and Thompson may have a theoretical disagreement with Mill over the interpretation of utilitarianism, but they ground their opposition to his view of the rights of women on a foundation of the specific historical and cultural context in which their female contemporaries lived. For the moment, I claim that that this *specific* text cannot be separated from its historical and cultural context; I will return to the general question of whether this holds true for all historical feminist philosophical texts in the conclusion to this book.

However, I would argue that merely seeing the *Appeal* as a historical artifact is not conducive to the feminist enterprise. This is not simply the question of whether a disinterested and value-free approach to history is conceptually possible, it is the question of whether such an approach is of any use or interest to philosophers engaged in the feminist project of political change, both change within our discipline and a more general social change. Part of the project of feminist philosophy is the retrieval of forgotten or neglected texts, and we want to be able to find our philosophical "foremothers" as a way of counterbalancing the male domination of our philosophical canons and histories. Moreover, we may also want to look to these foremothers for ideas for and connections to our own modern theorizing.

Thus it would seem that if we are to employ a mainstream approach to reading the *Appeal*, we would be better served by the philosophical approach or some combination of the two approaches. Yet the second question—"Is it true?"—also needs to be considered carefully. We are not asking whether Wheeler and Thompson's theory is true in the same sense as asking whether Locke's epistemological theory is true. Surely, we want to know whether it is true that Wheeler and Thompson's theory would have produced practical results for an oppressed group. In other words, we are not just asking whether Wheeler and Thompson produced knowledge for its own sake, but rather whether this knowledge would produce a specific political end.

What is the significance of the difference in understanding this second question? The "Is it true?" question has at its foundation the assumption that philosophy is an independent intellectual pursuit, one with its own problems and processes. This assumption need not be the hard-line position I discussed in the introductory chapter, where these problems are seen as wholly atemporal. We can take the more nuanced approach of Passmore (1965, 28), who does not hold that we can talk of the problems of philosophy, but rather that we can "speak of certain types of problems as continuously recurring in philosophy, although in different shapes." Moreover, Passmore does not see the problems of philosophy as occurring in complete isolation; he argues that philosophy is "an autonomous inquiry, in the sense that it has its own problems; but it by no means follows that those problems arise for it in isolation from the problems of scientists, theologians, poets, or independently of social and economic changes" (16).

Yet is even this more nuanced approach the way we should examine the work of Wheeler and Thompson? We can argue that justice is a problem that can be traced throughout Western philosophy, albeit in a variety of forms. In other words, it is a human problem. Thus it could be claimed that gender justice is simply one of those variety of forms. As I argued above, however, to see gender justice as just one form of social justice means that women's oppression may appear to be random, and we lose sight of the related question of why women are a targeted group for prejudicial treatment. Moreover, I have argued that the general concept of justice has historically and conceptually excluded women.

Is gender justice a philosophical problem in the same way that the construction of the ideal state is a philosophical problem? This is something that Cynthia Freeland (2000) points to: mainstream philosophy has typically left out questions of gender and gender justice. But we must not consider just the fact that gender and gender justice have been typically left out of mainstream Anglo-American philosophical discourse—we must ask why they have been left out. The reason is that discussions of gender justice cannot be an independent intellectual pursuit in the way that philosophy—traditionally defined—needs to be. In order to discuss gender justice we need—as Wheeler and Thompson recognize, even though they cannot fully follow through—to introduce empirical elements to the discussion. We need to offer both an explanation of the causes—economic, social, cultural, historical, political—of the oppression of women and a description of their present situation. Lastly, and most importantly, we must address the moral and political wrong of the oppression of women.

In other words, we start to push against the "purity" of the philosophical enterprise. On the dominant Anglo-American picture of philosophy, what I am calling the patrimonial picture, our discipline, while by no means completely separated as an intellectual enterprise, is an autonomous inquiry in that it has its own distinct set of problems and questions. Yet issues of gender justice require politicized questions and answers and historically and culturally contextualized empirical elements in order to explore these issues. In other words, the autonomy of philosophical inquiry is challenged. Moreover, the contextualized and empirical nature of issues of gender justice means that it is hard to frame them as timeless questions or problems, which then makes them a bad fit for one of the dominant pictures of philosophy within Anglo-American philosophy and history of philosophy.

Here I think is at least part of our answer as to why Wheeler and Thompson remain neglected. Wheeler and Thompson do not offer a pure or autonomous political or moral philosophy, and they are fully conscious that a philosophy with the goal of relieving the oppression of women requires practical political elements as well. Their work simply does not correspond well with the dominant Anglo-American picture of what philosophy is, and thus remains neglected in dominant narratives of the history of philosophy. As I claimed in the introductory chapter, this notion of a pure or autonomous philosophy is a central part of the patrimonial picture. It functions as an ideal—albeit in different ways—for both mainstream approaches: the historical approach aims for a disinterested interpretation free of value claims about the truth of a particular text or theory, whereas the philosophical approach aims to keep philosophical truths pure by keeping them separate from historical particulars or the subjective interests of the interpreter.

Thus Wheeler and Thompson's *Appeal* is an important text for any discussion of how to take a specifically feminist approach to the history of philosophy. Their text is grounded in its historical and cultural context. The fact that they aim to change this context—and thus the situation of women—demonstrates that they are fully conscious of it. Wheeler and Thompson do not offer a pure or autonomous political philosophy, and—again—they are fully conscious that a philosophy of gender justice requires practical political elements as well.

In this way, however, the *Appeal* is not a good match for the philosophical approach of mainstream philosophy. This is one of the central lessons we can learn from Wheeler and Thompson: that the philosophy of gender justice does not fit the standard understanding of what philosophy is, and thus the mainstream approaches to the history of philosophy may not also be appropriate for an examination of Wheeler and Thompson's philosophy. It would seem that we should look for a different—feminist—perspective to reading a text like the *Appeal*, and in so doing I must also address the accompanying question of just how different this perspective is, ultimately, from mainstream approaches. Here I am deliberately using the term "perspective" instead of approach, as I want to be careful not to imply that I offering a full-blown methodology.

What question might then identify a feminist perspective? Neither the value-neutral, disinterested question of "What did *x* say?" nor the ahistorical question of "Is it true?" is a good fit for the *Appeal*. However, I do not want to replace these questions with the question "Will this text/philosophy/theory produce gender justice?" Instead, the question I want to ask is "Will it empower women?" This is something we can learn from Wheeler and Thompson, despite the fact that there may be potential circularity in my claiming this, since I want to turn the question back onto their work, for Wheeler and Thompson recognize the importance of self-actualization and self-respect—in other words, empowerment—as well as the formalities of equal rights. Even though I have claimed that, ultimately, Wheeler and

Thompson fail to empower women, it is clear that they wish to do so; they recognize that gender justice and equal rights can never take place without changes in the gendered power structure. Asking about empowerment is therefore a broader question than asking about gender justice, which is a more formal concept. Moreover, a shift away from using a variant of the traditional philosophical concept of justice may help to keep us wary about the use of mainstream approaches to the history of philosophy for historical feminist texts.

The empowerment question allows us to examine the *Appeal* for both its philosophical strengths *and* its political content. It also gives us a different way of evaluating a text, theory, or philosophy for its relative successes and failures. Surely, it would seem to make sense that just as feminist philosophy differs from mainstream philosophy, so should our evaluative criteria of historical work also differ.

On the historical approach to the history of philosophy, the historian of philosophy does not evaluate the arguments or views under examination. Perhaps, at most, this historian can comment on the consistency or clarity of a philosopher and his or her work. For the philosophical approach, the success or failure of a philosophical argument is implied by the question "Is it true?" The goal is to get the answer to a problem right and to show that your opponents are wrong. Even the more extreme ahistorical positions I discussed in the introductory chapter, such as Brucker's picture of philosophy as a series of sectarian battles or Renouvier's picture of philosophy as merely choosing which eternal position to take, are still about picking the "right" side. Wheeler and Thompson would appear to be failures if read in this way. To invoke the patrimonial picture, they have lost the fight for inheritance, as they are not part of the canon; indeed, they are pretty much forgotten. Moreover, they were not even particularly good at being utilitarians. Further, while their inclusion of a critique of capitalism is something we should recognize as progressive, modern feminists will find little in the content of the *Appeal* to use for our own theorizing.

What instead do we achieve if we ask the empowerment question of Wheeler and Thompson's philosophy? First, the question allows for more nuanced categories of evaluation beyond success or failure or "getting it right." It can allow for such evaluations as praiseworthy attempts, novel approaches, or insightful analyses. Perhaps it can even allow for an evaluation like audience empowerment. In the introduction—following Janice Moulton—I questioned seeing the history of philosophy solely constructed as a series of winners and losers. Not only does this mean that philosophy becomes a masculinist enterprise, but, as Moulton points out, the history of philosophy becomes both distorted and limited, as it is read merely as a series of triumphs or failures among competing views.

The empowerment question also shifts our expectations away from trying to establish some sort of direct lineage in feminist theoretical thinking; we are no longer looking for a series of truths, successful arguments, or defeats of the false notions of our opponents. As I said earlier, the paradigms of master–pupil and opposing sects in mainstream history of philosophy are part of a bigger picture of the history of philosophy as containing traceable trajectories of the development of philosophical theories and ideas. Perhaps we should stop trying to expect a direct lineage—a patrimony—in theoretical thinking, and instead aim for something closer to a Wittgensteinian family resemblance among texts and thinkers, connected by their goal of empowerment of women.

What does a philosophy that empowers women look like? This is something I will develop throughout this work. As the analogy with Wittgensteinian family resemblance indicates, it will be no one thing. Other nineteenth-century utilitarian philosophers like James Bentham or James Mill emphasized the vulnerability of women or focused on paternalist concerns for their well-being, but they did not argue for the empowerment of women. To write on the empowerment of women is to write with passion, to take risks, and to remain committed to justice in the face of prejudice and critique; it is to place women—and a commitment to their liberation and fulfillment—at the center of one's argument, and not to sell them out for the sake of the unity of one's philosophical theory or pragmatic political or social concerns. Moreover, as I shall argue in a later chapter, to write for the empowerment of women is also to stir the appropriate political emotions in the reader—it is not simply to appeal to the intellect. Thus to ask the empowerment question is not simply to ask a value-free, disinterested question about a text; however, it need not be an ahistorical question about a timeless issue either.

The question is then whether Wheeler and Thompson offer empowerment for women. As I argued above, despite their best efforts, Wheeler and Thompson do not offer a theory that is fully focused on female empowerment or that has female empowerment integrated within their theory; rather, they employ utilitarianism to argue for feminism. Their theory is problematic when they are unable or unwilling to be flexible in the employment of the mainstream political and ethical theory—rule utilitarianism—to fit their practical and political needs for the liberation of women. As I said earlier, Wheeler and Thompson want to provide a feminist utilitarian theory that achieves sound ethical and political goals; however, in the end, they do not or cannot allow for all the political and ethical dimensions and conclusions of their theorizing. While Wheeler and Thompson clearly call for women's rights, autonomy, moral agency, respect, dignity, fulfillment, and self-respect, these central aspects of women's empowerment cannot be guaranteed within their utilitarian framework. Indeed, it may even be that their utilitarian framework will ultimately restrict women.

Even though I am hesitant to claim that Wheeler and Thompson have "successfully" argued for the empowerment of women, we must recognize that there is a shift in the sort of evaluation I am doing in assessing their "success" from the way that success or failure is done in mainstream evaluations of texts and arguments. Mainstream success is connected to a picture of battles between individuals and their views, a picture that I have already suggested is masculinist. Wheeler and Thompson, on the other hand, can be praised for their political beliefs and commitments, even though they were let down by their own theory.

Yet reading Wheeler and Thompson is important both for building a history of feminist philosophy and for coming to see the problems with mainstream approaches to the history of philosophy. In analyzing the *Appeal*, we can come to see the centrality of women's empowerment for arguments for the equality of women, because we see where Wheeler and Thompson recognize the need for that empowerment even though their arguments cannot provide it. It is not so much that we learn from their "mistakes," as with the mainstream philosophical approach to the history of philosophy I described in the introduction to this book; rather, we have come to identify a guiding question for examining historical feminist texts.

I think this is an important claim, but I want to be careful at this stage not to overstate it. I want to argue that neither of the two mainstream approaches on their own is a particularly good fit for reading historical feminist texts, whereas reading these texts through a lens of empowerment offers a more philosophically and politically interesting interpretation. This is simply a first step. I need to explore further just how different the empowerment question is from the two mainstream approaches and in what ways. As I stated in the introductory chapter, the interpretive lens I want to develop is less about overturning standard or mainstream approaches, and then replacing them

with a feminist approach, and more about reflecting on the process of interpretation itself and the political and ethical self-consciousness required for
this reflection. Indeed, albeit in a very minor way, I have also been able to
use my analysis of the *Appeal*—specifically, my concerns about Wheeler and
Thompson's ultimate inability to offer empowerment to their female contemporaries—to start a discussion of this need to be self-conscious of the political
and ethical foundations and implications of our theorizing.

In the next chapter, on Catharine Beecher, I shall develop how the empowerment question can be used to understand her work—specifically, to identify
it as feminist philosophical work even though she has been recognized primarily as a domestic economist, not as a philosopher or even a feminist. I will
also show that the empowerment question does not simply allow for a
broader understanding of the content of texts and arguments, but it also
allows for a more flexible discussion of how modern readers can interact with
historical texts and philosophies than that offered by the two mainstream
approaches.

Notes

1. Scholarly articles are scarce as well.

2. See, for example, St. John 1954; Hayek 1951; Borchard 1957.

3. I do not mean here that this knowledge is available only to women or that she has
accessed this knowledge through a particular "women's" way of knowing.

4. Reading Gracia (1991) helped me articulate this type of explanation.

5. For a fuller account of these comments and an overview of Thompson's other
works, see Dooley 1996.

6. Wheeler and Thompson are progressive in their recognition of women's sexuality.
However, we must also recognize the fact that their utilitarian beliefs would have required
this progressiveness. Given that they believe that sexual activity is a pleasure, and they wish
to argue for equality of pleasures, consistency dictates that women's sexual pleasures be
recognized.

7. Dooley (1996, 121) demonstrates the importance of the principle of benevolence for
impartiality.

8. Wheeler and Thompson share this problem with other feminist arguments of this
era: how are men to be made to listen, give up their privileges, and give women rights (or
whatever the specifics the author is calling for). There is, however, a strength in their
argument compared to, for example, Mary Wollstonecraft's appeal to reason, in that men
will get something: an increase in happiness.

9. I found Dooley's work (1996) to be of great help in understanding the importance
of benevolence for Wheeler and Thompson.

10. See Dooley 1996 for a full discussion of Thompson's ideas for these communities.

11. Unfortunately, the term "feminized utilitarianism" has already been coined.

2 CATHARINE BEECHER AND WRITING PHILOSOPHY FOR WOMEN

The next philosopher I wish to examine, Catharine Beecher, is an interesting case. Despite the fact that she was one of the most productive female philosophers of the nineteenth century, and it could be reasonably claimed that she was the first female American philosopher with a fully worked out philosophical system, Beecher is best known as domestic economist.

Claiming Beecher as a utilitarian feminist philosopher may at first seem a stretch to those who know her only as a domestic economist. Beecher is certainly a utilitarian, but not in the strict classical mode. Her commitment to women has also been questioned; she has been seen—at best—as a relational feminist, while she has also been critiqued for her stance against suffrage and women's rights.[1] However, I think that this critique misinterprets what Beecher had to say about women. We need to recognize her as a philosopher with a complete moral system that leads to a robust form of empowerment for women. Relational feminism may offer moral empowerment—indeed, it may even offer social influence—but neither moral empowerment nor social influence is what most feminists mean by real power.

I am going to argue that Beecher offers a level of mental, moral, and economic independence that constitutes a real form of empowerment for nineteenth-century women, albeit white middle-class American women, relative to their historical and cultural context. In so doing, I will also continue the discussion initiated in the previous chapter on Wheeler and Thompson about the use of the notion of empowerment as a guiding concept for analyses of feminist or potentially feminist historical texts and philosophies.

Beecher's arguments for the empowerment of women are part of an identifiable philosophical system, yet, as I have said, Beecher has been ignored as a philosopher. Beecher was one of the few historical women philosophers who were "professional" philosophers, meaning that she had formal training and both spoke publicly and published her ideas. Yet she is not part of the "trajectory" of the history of the discipline, not even in specialized American, nineteenth-century, or utilitarian histories.

In Catharine Beecher's case, her neglect as a philosopher can be attributed to both the content and the apparently "nonphilosophical" forms of some of her work, in particular, her domestic advice manuals and collections of advice letters. I specifically argue, however, that to separate these works from her more traditionally philosophical works would be a mistake; Beecher chose these particular genres because they fit the goals of her *philosophical* system: educating and empowering women. Moreover, as we shall see, women—more specifically, empowered women—are a central component of Beecher's philosophical system, which is exceedingly rare in historical philosophies.

By extension, I will also indicate that traditional philosophical genres were aimed at men. Moreover, I will show how traditional genres reinforce a picture of philosophy that is "masculinist" and has historically excluded women. Thus I will also argue that a feminist reading of historical texts will need to allow for nontraditional genres like those employed by Beecher. In this way, then, the meta-questions I examine in this chapter focus on the concepts of philosophical authorship and philosophical texts that are wrapped up with the two mainstream approaches to this history of philosophy; and as with my analysis of the work of Wheeler and Thompson, I shall again show that these two approaches are not well suited for the examination of feminist philosophical texts.

Catharine Beecher's Biography

Born in East Hampton in 1800, Catharine Ward Beecher was the daughter of the Calvinist theologian and evangelist Lyman Beecher and an older sister of Harriet Beecher Stowe, the novelist. Beecher was well educated; she studied literature, mathematics, and science as well as the more traditionally "feminine" subjects of religion and what we nowadays call domestic science (Waithe 1991, 235). In 1823 Beecher opened what became a highly successful school, the Hartford Female Seminary. According to Beecher's main biographer, Kathryn Kish Sklar (1973, 59), Beecher's "contemporaries believed and historians have since held that Catharine Beecher's school constituted one of the most significant advances made in early nineteenth-century education for women." Beecher remained with the school for eight years. She began to teach moral philosophy to the students and in her final year there started training the students to be teachers. At that time, teaching was not considered to be a woman's profession, but Beecher thought that making it into one could mean that unmarried women need not be dependent on their families, giving them a socially respectable alternative to marriage. Beecher left the school in 1831 to accompany her father to Cincinnati. According to Sklar, Beecher felt that she could go no further at the school with her broader educational goal of reforming the moral character of women, who in their turn would reform society.

Beecher established the Western Female Institute in 1833 in Cincinnati, a school that was to be directed not only at learning suitable for young women of the time but also at their moral development. The school, however, was a failure. Beecher then turned to other avenues for financial support and to achieve her goals for women and societal reform, specifically, through writing and giving lectures. Even though Beecher had published since the 1820s, it was her *Treatise on Domestic Economy* in 1841 that brought her public attention and success. According to Sklar (1973, 151), the *Treatise* "established her as a national authority on the psychological state and the physical well-being of the American home."

Buoyed by the success of her *Treatise*, Beecher gave lectures intended both to produce converts to her vision of a society ameliorated by the moral power of women and to raise money for what she hoped would be a national benevolent movement to found schools and train teachers. Not only would women be teachers of national morality in the home, but they would also become a new breed of missionary teachers in the rapidly developing West. Sklar (1973, 203) claims that Beecher's earlier vision for women had an evangelical emphasis that had disappeared by the late 1840s, to leave "a single focus upon women—a more secular, distinctively urban perspective that envisioned special professional roles for women." Here Beecher was thinking of professions, such as nurse or teacher, that grew out of what she saw as women's domestic "profession."

Beecher's last major project was the establishment of a female college in Milwaukee in the 1850s. Part of her motivation for this project—according to Sklar—was that it would provide a place for her to retire; unfortunately, the board of trustees was not prepared to contribute to the financing of this retirement project, and Beecher parted ways with the college and moved to live with her sister Harriet. Beecher continued to lecture and write from the official end of her career as an educator in 1856 until her death in 1878.

Beecher's Philosophy

The recognition Beecher has gained for her involvement in the actual teaching of women and in her campaigning for female education—and especially the fact that she has been identified as a domestic economist—has tended to overshadow the fact that she was also a philosopher. Indeed, as Sarah A. Leavitt rather bizarrely states in her otherwise well-researched work on domestic advice manuals, *From Catharine Beecher to Martha Stewart: A Cultural History of Domestic Advice* (2002, 16), "Catharine Beecher's . . . writing [career] focused exclusively on the role of women in the household." Mary Ellen Waithe in *Modern Women Philosophers* (1991, 242) puts this syndrome best when she states, "Despite the comprehensiveness of her philosophical views, Catharine Ward Beecher is not remembered as a philosopher, nor as a theologian, nor as a social reformer. Rather, she is best known as the founder of a field of study which grew from her views of the central social importance of women as homemakers and educators: the discipline of home economics."

Even commentators who have discussed Beecher's philosophical thought have tended not to focus on offering a philosophical analysis of this work. For example, Sklar explores Beecher's philosophical and religious thought in her definitive account of Beecher's life and work, *Catharine Beecher: A Study in American Domesticity*, but Sklar's concern is to place it chronologically within the historical context of the evolving social structure of nineteenth-century America.

Likewise, Mark David Hall, in "Catharine Beecher: America's First Female Philosopher and Theologian" (2000, 65), decries the lack of attention paid by commentators to Beecher's philosophical thought, something he considers to be particularly egregious in light of the fact that he holds her to be "America's first female philosopher and theologian to publish her work in a systematic form." But while Hall includes a discussion of Beecher's central philosophical work, *The Elements of Mental and Moral Philosophy*, his main goal is to elaborate Beecher's theological beliefs and their interconnection with her philosophical views.

For the best philosophical analysis of Beecher's work, we must then turn—perhaps not surprisingly—to Mary Ellen Waithe's account in the third volume of *A History of Women Philosophers*. From Waithe (1991, 236–37) we learn that we can admire Beecher as a philosopher for the way she intertwined Calvinist thought—particularly the notions of submission, self-denial, and self-sacrifice—with Common Sense philosophy and utilitarianism. According to Waithe, Beecher developed her philosophy through several philosophical writings, as follows.

Letters on the Difficulties of Religion (1836), *An Address to the Protestant Clergy of the United States* (1846), and "An Essay on Cause and Effect in Connection with the Difference of Fatalism and Free Will" (1839) are three of Beecher's works on the philosophy of religion.[2] The *Letters* are focused on replying to the difficulties raised by the nonbeliever, such as the existence of God or how to explain the fact that many so-called Christians behave in immoral ways. The *Address* is a discussion of the moral education of children, and is also a critique of the fact that the Protestant Church—unlike the Catholic Church—does not use women to promote its aims and educate its children.

The "Essay" aims to show that we can differentiate between mind and matter if the concept of causation is properly defined. According to Waithe (1991, 236), these writings are evidence of Beecher's dissatisfaction with the Calvinism of Beecher's father, mainly because of its "spiritual and social limitations" on women; however, Waithe also sees this dissatisfaction as leading to Beecher's adoption of Common Sense philosophy.

The Elements of Mental and Moral Philosophy (1831) is primarily a work of metaphysics and epistemology. It is here that Waithe (1991, 237) sees Beecher supplementing "Common Sense rationalism with communitarian and utilitarian perspectives: minds exist in a social system in which each mind is dependent on other minds as sources of happiness"; by promoting social virtue in others, one contributed to the development of the "greatest social happiness." As we shall see, this promotion of social virtue will require self-denial for the sake of others and a submission to this goal of the greater good. In *Common Sense Applied to Religion; or, The Bible and the People* (1846), Beecher's central theme is that the real moral challenge is "to overcome temptations through suffering, self-sacrifice, and self-denial and to lead others through education and example to a life of social and spiritual virtue" (Waithe 1991, 238).

Waithe (1991, 238) identifies *An Appeal to the People on Behalf of Their Rights as Authorized Interpreters of the Bible* (1860) as a central pillar for Beecher's philosophy. In this work Beecher maintains the Calvinist notion that our "base desires must be controlled and denied"; however, this negative moral duty is supplemented by a positive moral duty to sacrifice one's own good for the greater good of society: "a principle of benevolent utility." According to Waithe (238), Beecher places a constraint on this principle of utility in that it must accord with principles of justice: "Principles of religious benevolence and utility were subject to a principle she called 'rectitude.' Rectitude meant that personal sacrifice and self-denial for the good of others must be motivated by a desire to right social wrongs and by a commitment to principles of social justice."

Waithe argues that Beecher further develops this notion of a morally praiseworthy act—the self-sacrificial act that brings about the greatest good to the greatest number, done for the sake of bringing about this good—in *An Essay on Slavery and Abolitionism, with Reference to the Duty of American Females* (1837). Here Beecher claims that the morally praiseworthy act is one that shows moral leadership—it brings about an increase in virtue in others— and treats those who are not virtuous with care (Waithe 1991, 239). More important for any study of a utilitarian philosophy, Beecher argues that both the means and the ends must be virtuous: she does not accept any variant of a claim that the ends can justify the means. The *Essay* also demonstrates that women play a central role in Beecher's philosophy: they are to "educate and to provide moral example through acts of benevolent utility involving personal sacrifice and self-denial" (Waithe 1991, 241).

Waithe (1991, 241) identifies two other philosophical works by Beecher on women's nature that discuss this role: *The Duty of American Women to Their Country* (1845), and *The Evils Suffered by American Women and American Children: The Causes and the Remedy* (1846). Unfortunately, Waithe does not fully explain why these two works, out of the many by Beecher on women, are "philosophical" (this is an issue we shall return to later). In essence, Waithe holds that Beecher saw women as having a role as moral educators not just within the home, but also by making their children virtuous citizens: "The logical conclusion, drawn from Common Sense as much as from Calvinism, is that women must make the world a virtuous place by populating it with virtuous children and also be instilling virtue in others through teaching, persuasion, and example" (241).

Based on this brief account of Waithe's analysis, we can see how Beecher developed her own social ethics from these philosophical and theological foundations, and thus we can add her to our expanding history of women philosophers. No doubt readers are hesitant, however, to categorize her as a specifically *feminist* philosopher. Even within the myriad developments of feminist thought, there does not seem to be much room for a moral philosophy that demands the self-sacrifice and submission of women as the way to a greater good, while offering them in return nothing but a saccharine moral power.

How to Read Beecher's Philosophy

Yet despite these initial obstacles, I believe that it is important to read Beecher not simply as a philosopher but as a feminist philosopher. I believe this is important for two interconnected reasons. The first is that Beecher herself thought she was working toward the raising up of women. As we shall see, while Waithe is essentially correct in her assessment of Beecher's view of the role of women, Beecher's view is far more complex and, ultimately, far more empowering to women than may at first appear. We must not forget that it is *women alone* whom she calls on to be these leaders in self-sacrifice for the general good.

It is certainly troubling for a modern feminist reader that women are apparently expected to lead from a subordinate position within the confinement of the domestic sphere, while it is men who will inhabit the world of business and politics. Yet even though Beecher does not consider it appropriate for women to enter these traditionally male spheres, she does claim for them a potential for moral influence—and a corresponding duty to exercise that influence—over the men who occupy them. This moral power is to be exercised in the domestic and social circle. Here women can exert an influence by making themselves so respected and loved, and their motives can be seen to be pure because they are so lacking in ambition and self-interest, that "the fathers, the husbands, and the sons, will find an influence thrown around them, to which they will yield not only willingly but proudly" (Beecher 1837, 101).

Women as moral and social leaders are not restricted to this indirect political influence; they are also, in their role as child rearers, more directly

involved in the proper moral and social education of future voters and legislators. It is in this role as a "heaven-appointed educator of mind" that Beecher
(1857, dedication) sees women as making their central contribution to moral
and social progress.

This moral power of women, according to Beecher, means that they
play a vital role in the moral and social progress of nineteenth-century
America. Problematically, this power can be obtained only through their self-
subordination to the greatest social happiness; however, as I shall show, this
notion of subordination, properly framed within Beecher's ethico-religious
system, can in fact lead to economic independence for women and a surprisingly robust conception of moral power.

The second reason why I hold that it is important to read Beecher not
simply as a philosopher but as a feminist philosopher, stems from my more
general interest in how we are to approach historical women philosophers.
From within our mainstream philosophical tradition, we naturally place Beecher's work against its background of Common Sense philosophy and Calvinist theology. Beecher's philosophical works can certainly be placed within the
canonical tradition, although she will never occupy a major place there, and
in so doing, we gain another female philosopher to add to our heritage. If we
allow the focus of our examination of Beecher's philosophy to be mainly
comparative work with the predominantly male canon, however, we lose the
opportunity to mark the boundaries of our own "feminist" tradition and
to expand our understanding of our nineteenth-century American feminist
intellectual heritage. Moreover, and most important, Beecher's entrance into
the mainstream tradition comes at the price of ignoring the significance of
the role of women in her philosophy for our feminist heritage and neglecting
her "nonphilosophical" works: her domestic advice manuals and letters.

I do not want merely to repeat or add to a discussion of the Calvinist or
Common Sense underpinnings of Beecher's explicitly philosophical thought.
I take these as given. Instead I want to show how *all* of Beecher's works—both
her "philosophical" and her "domestic" works—fit together to form a coherent whole, glued together by her utilitarian thought. As we shall see, Beecher's
version of utilitarianism is available for feminist (or proto-feminist) use;
indeed, there is a sense in which her utilitarianism—or more strictly speaking,
her whole moral philosophical system—leads to the mental, moral, social,
and economic empowerment of women.

I want to argue that Beecher's writings on home economics are not simply
the offshoot of her views regarding the role of women, nor are they domestic

advice books designed to gild the domestic cage of nineteenth-century middle- and upper-class women. Beecher offers a picture of a moral world that is thoroughly systematized and ordered. Just as her work on moral philosophy offers a theoretical understanding of this world for educators, so her work on home economics and female education provides the practical moral advice and teaching that both reinforces this system for those who labor in the home and offers an explanation of and justification for this labor.[3] Once we understand Beecher's moral world, we shall be in a position to understand in what ways she did in fact offer the potential for social change and a type of power for women.

In order to read Beecher in this way as a feminist philosopher, I am going to need to show how and why her works on domestic economy would not be included in mainstream accounts of the "philosophical," and how and why they should be considered philosophy. Moreover, I am going to need to develop the notion of empowerment from the previous chapter to use as a hallmark for the identification and evaluation of historical feminist philosophy, in this case, Beecher's philosophy.

Beecher's "Nonphilosophical" Works

Given the central role that women play in Beecher's social ethics, it can come as no surprise that much of Beecher's writing is aimed at training women for their moral and social roles and exhorting them to fulfill these roles. Yet for Waithe, as for most other commentators, many of Beecher's works do not properly fit into the category of the "philosophical."[4] Waithe (1991, 241) characterizes Beecher's writings—other than those already identified as philosophical—as "practical" and aimed at assisting "women in meeting their responsibilities," whether these are moral or domestic. Waithe, however, does recognize the link between Beecher's work on home economics and her philosophy: "Catharine Beecher's work on the subject of home economics must be understood as an essential, pragmatic consequence of her philosophical views. . . . Although many of Beecher's writings, including those on home economics, are not philosophical . . . they are firmly grounded in her . . . social, moral, political, and educational philosophy" (242).[5]

Beecher's main nonphilosophical works can be roughly classified into three different categories—education, women's role, and domestic economy—although, as I shall show, these are all interconnected in ways that help to make a coherent whole of Beecher's thought. *An Essay on the Education of Female Teachers* (1835); *The Moral Instructor* (1838); an article, "Female Education" (1827), published in the *American Journal of Education*; *Suggestions Respecting Improvements in Education, Presented to the Trustees of the Hartford Female Seminary, and Published at Their Request* (1829); *Religious Training of Children in the School, the Family, and the Church* (1864); and *Educational Reminiscences and Suggestions* (1874) are all works with a primary focus on education. *The True Remedy for the Wrongs of Woman; with a History of an Enterprise Having That for Its Object* (1851); *Something for Women Better Than the Ballot* (1869); and *Woman's Profession as Mother and Educator with Views in Opposition to Woman Suffrage* (1872) are all discussions of women's role; however, as Beecher sees this role as specifically a domestic and educational one, this set of works also intersects with those on education and domestic economy. *A Treatise on Domestic Economy* (1841); *Miss Beecher's Housekeeper and Healthkeeper* (1873); *American Woman's Home: or, Principles of Domestic Science*, coauthored with Harriet Beecher Stowe (1869); *Principles of Domestic Science: As Applied to the Duties and Pleasures of Home: A Text-Book for the Use of Young Ladies in Schools, Seminaries, and Colleges* (1871), which is a version of *American Woman's Home*; and *Miss Beecher's Domestic Receipt-Book: Designed as a Supplement to Her Treatise on Domestic Economy* (1850a) are her works on domestic economy.[6] The final two of Beecher's works, one on health, *Letters to the People on Health and Happiness* (1855), and one addressed to (female) servants, *Letters to Persons Who Are Engaged in Domestic Service* (1842), do not fit clearly into any one category but span all three. Interesting enough, these latter two works are frequently neglected but are surprisingly important for an understanding of Beecher's philosophy.

The problem is that a division of Beecher's works into philosophical and nonphilosophical will, ultimately, prevent us from recognizing that Beecher's nonphilosophical works have an important role to play in our understanding of her thought, specifically, her feminist thought. Moreover, I want to show that her work on domestic economy and human health is not so much a consequence of her philosophy; rather, it must be read as *part* of her philosophy. We can understand what I am calling her "moral world" only by reading all her works together; and we can understand how Beecher can be seen as an early feminist philosopher only by placing what she has to say about women against the background of this utilitarian moral world. Waithe is correct that Beecher addresses the theoretical structure of her version of utilitarianism in her philosophical works, but we need to turn to Beecher's nonphilosophical works in order to understand the moral and political significance *for Beecher* of her utilitarian views.

This point about the use of Beecher's nonphilosophical texts in an interpretation of her thought should not be underestimated. It raises general questions about the particular forms of writing that are considered properly philosophical; it raises questions about what types of issues are considered the domain of philosophy; and it asks us to consider for whom philosophy traditionally was written. I would argue that all these points are taken as a given—and are thus unquestioned—in the dominant model at play in mainstream approaches to the history of philosophy. Indeed, it is only because there is agreement at some fundamental level about what philosophy "is" that there can be disagreement about how we are to read historical texts of philosophy and how we are to do the history of philosophy. As we shall see, if we are to read Beecher's philosophy properly we must push against notions of the purity of philosophy, the disinterested or autonomous knower, and how philosophical knowledge is "inherited" or passed on.

Reading Beecher

In Beecher's case, we find that the majority of her work that has been identified as philosophical is written using the traditional genres of the treatise or the essay, and this fits with our expectations of the philosophical genres of the nineteenth century; whereas her nonphilosophical work is often in the form of letters or domestic advice manuals. This is not the case for all of Beecher's nonphilosophical work; it applies primarily to Beecher's work on women and women's roles, but it does not fit Beecher's work on education. This latter point is perhaps not surprising. Works on education at the time Beecher was writing had a long history (unlike the "new" topics for the nineteenth century of women's suffrage and domestic advice) and thus had developed a standard form. Beecher's works on education typically conform to these conventions, namely, plain, informative writing.

Letter writing has historically been a "mixed" genre for philosophical writing. We find that even as far back as ancient Greek and Roman philosophy, the question of whether a letter is an appropriate vehicle for philosophical thought has been a subject for discussion. Demetrius, for example, in *On Style*, argues that letters convey warmth and friendship, and that their moral or philosophical teachings can only be in the form of proverbs. Anything else becomes impersonal and sermonizing and, as such, is no longer a letter. Seneca, on the other hand, shows us that a letter can be an appropriate form for a certain type of reflective moral philosophy (Harrison 1995). By the nineteenth century, letters had two basic forms: the disguised essay or treatise, and personal communication. The latter had become strongly identified with women, and the ability to write good letters was seen as an important feminine skill. Given how distinct the former "essay" letter form was from "feminine" letter writing, it was—by implication—masculine, or at least nonfeminine.

Four of Beecher's main works are in the form of letters: *The True Remedy*; *Letters to the People on Health and Happiness*; *Letters to Persons Who Are Engaged in Domestic Service*; and *Difficulties of Religion*. We find that these works reflect the two basic forms that letter writing took during Beecher's era. *Difficulties of Religion*, as we have seen, is a work on philosophy of religion, and it is therefore unsurprising to find it didactic, with Beecher taking on the role of an authoritative teacher to someone, perhaps a younger man, who is raising standard questions about religious belief. In many ways it is just a rehearsal of Beecher's version of the standard answers to those questions.

The True Remedy, on the other hand, is a series of letters written to Beecher's sister, Harriet Beecher Stowe, and shows Beecher's understanding of the power of the intimate nature of the "feminine" letter. Not only does Beecher say that an illusion of intimacy helps her to write, but it is this intimacy that is the best way to transmit what she has to say:

> This little volume, which you know, I have been planning, I designed to put in the form of letters addressed to American Women. But I find it difficult to write letters to nobody in particular. And when I place myself, in imagination, before so large and respectable an audience, I lose that flow of thought and language which I wish to command. For I seek that kind of access to those whom I would address, which I might gain if admitted to the private boudoir of each, and privileged to sit by her side in unrestrained and earnest conversation.
>
> Let me then compromise the difficulty, and address *you* [Harriet Beecher Stowe] as the representative of that large class of intelligent and benevolent ladies, whose attention I would ask to the pages that follow. (1851, 1–2)

The letters on health and happiness and those addressed to servants both follow the same form and are addressed to "my friends" (in the former) and "my countrywomen" (in the latter), with Beecher speaking directly to the reader throughout (1855, 7; 1842, 5). Indeed, despite her class status, Beecher places herself rhetorically in the latter work with servants—rather than employers—by stating that Christian ladies should buy the book for their servants so that "there will be many who will be joined, in the best of all fellowship, with their friend and countrywoman [meaning Beecher herself]" (1842, 6). These two sets of letters contain personal reminiscences, observations about her own family, stories, and reflections on her own experiences.

These two features—intimacy of writing and the basing of Beecher's knowledge and authority to write on her personal experiences—are central for the transmission of the content of these particular works to the reader; however, if we employ the dominant Anglo-American model of the "philosophical"—what I am calling the "patrimonial" picture—to read Beecher, they are also the features we do not expect to find in standard philosophical works. The patrimonial picture of philosophy has distinct expectations about philosophical authorship. The philosophical author retains a certain level of impersonal detachment and writes for a "general" audience (which in the nineteenth century would have been a primarily male, educated audience), whereas Beecher, in these works at least, is metaphorically talking one-to-one with individuals in their homes. The knowledge imparted by the philosophical author is similarly abstract or universal, whereas Beecher's knowledge comes from her concrete experience or from the stories and experiences of others, and as such would appear to best be described as personal wisdom or advice. Historically and culturally, the public sphere and abstract knowledge have been associated with the masculine, while the domestic sphere and subjective or personal experience have been associated with the feminine. Because this is all many of us know, it is tempting to think that the patrimonial picture of philosophical authorship is objective, neutral, or ahistorical; we need to remember that this model of the philosophical author is not "fixed" but is rather an artificial construct.

It is important to recognize that this model of the philosophical author/ knower is at play in the two mainstream approaches to the history of philosophy. At first it may not seem so evident on the historical model, yet our search for historical accuracy—what a particular philosopher said on his or her own terms within his or her historical and cultural context—assumes something remarkably fixed about the notion of philosophical authorship. The search for a disinterested, historical rendering of a text is grounded on the text being written by a detached, impersonal author. The account of the text may be contextualized, but there is no conceptual room on the historical model to claim that the author him- or herself and the knowledge he or she is aiming to express are situated or contextualized. Yet we should not forget that human experience of particular cultural or historical contexts is different according to, among other things, gender. This is something that was made quite clear in Wheeler and Thompson's *Appeal*: they inhabited two almost separate worlds. Moreover, as Thompson makes clear in the *Appeal*, it is Wheeler's lived experiences as a woman that gives the work its epistemic authority.

This model of philosophical authorship is much more evident in the philosophical approach to the history of philosophy. In order for the philosophical approach to work—that is, for problems and questions to be timeless—authorship must be seen as objective, neutral, and ahistorical. The author must be able to talk to his or her readership in an acultural, ahistorical discourse in a timeless location. To answer the question "Is it true?" knowers—and therefore authors—must lay claim to universal knowledge of an objective reality.

Thus, on what I call the "patrimonial" picture of philosophy, some of Beecher's works cannot be counted as part of her philosophy, and accordingly, the knowledge she imparts in these works is of no particular use or interest on standard accounts of philosophy. Moreover, and more important, these works will also get left out if we try to read Beecher using either of the mainstream approaches to the history of philosophy. However, I hold that Beecher's nonphilosophical works are central to an understanding of her philosophy, and for why I wish to try to claim her works for our heritage in feminist philosophy. In order to see this, we need first to see why Beecher chose the particular forms of writing she did, what knowledge she is trying to convey, and to whom.

What Beecher Knew

Beecher's knowledge, unlike knowledge on the patrimonial picture, is concrete, situated, and practical. She draws on stories of the suffering of women and children and her reactions to this suffering. She uses her own experiences and those of her family as the foundation from which she develops the information she imparts in her works. The physical pain she has felt due to the poor health care typically received by women leads her to find out about alternative therapies and share this information. She is aware of her social status and uses its power to publish her thoughts and gain the attention of the educated middle classes, yet she also claims solidarity with servants by identifying with them as a friend and fellow American. The knowledge Beecher imparts in her letters also has an overarching goal; it is not knowledge of an objective reality or knowledge for its own sake, but rather is aimed at social and moral change.

Here lies our explanation for why Beecher chose the form of letters for certain of her works: her primary audience is women, for it is women who are to be moral leaders in humanity's move toward the divinely ordained greatest happiness. Obviously, Beecher could and did write using other forms, but letters were something that women would have been used to reading. Moreover, unlike philosophical treatises, letters were an acceptably feminine form for women to be allowed to read. The same point follows for Beecher's domestic advice manuals, and it is in discussing these works that this point can be brought out fully.

Sarah Leavitt has explored the specific structure of the genre of the domestic advice manual and its popularity. Leavitt shows that there was a new and growing audience for these manuals in nineteenth-century America, partly because most white women were literate and partly due to the fact that these white middle-class women were active consumers of reading matter, especially "women's fiction": romantic or sentimental novels with a moralistic tone, aimed at a female audience. Leavitt links the avid consumption of sentimental "moral" fiction with the popularity of advice manuals. Instead of characters teaching particular moral lessons, furniture and domestic activities became symbolically moral. Leavitt (2002, 12) argues that this "close connection with novels gave domestic-advice manuals a familiar literary form," and that this "format probably helped women readers to understand the emerging genre of advice manuals and to know what to expect. The dozens of domestic-advice manuals published in the decades after 1830 followed a clear pattern, established to guide women readers through the house. An extensive table of contents emulated the novel's list of chapter titles." Moreover, the style of writing in these manuals often followed the intimate writing of women's novels. In addition, many advice manuals were not simply about domestic affairs but were aimed at dispensing "moral" advice. Lydia Maria Child's *The Frugal Housewife* (1829), for example, is full of cautionary tales about profligacy and frivolity.

What is also interesting, although not discussed by Leavitt, is that the typical plotlines and characters of women's fiction of this era would have prepared

Beecher's readers for her moral and social philosophy. Nina Baym (1993, 19) has described women's fiction as having a basic plot that "exists in two parallel versions. In one, the heroine begins as a poor and friendless child. . . . In the second, the heroine is a pampered heiress" who becomes poor when her family dies or loses their money. Having engaged the reader by describing the sufferings of the heroine, the novel then proceeds to follow her as she learns to make her own way in the world. A perfect example of this type of novel is Maria S. Cummins's *The Lamplighter*, published in 1854, which tells the tale of the education and moral development of an abused orphan, who learns to respect others and to love God, and who then learns to make her own way in the world. As we shall see, Beecher's "ideal" women follow much the same course as they become educated, learn to follow the dictates of God, and achieve a certain level of independence.

Beecher's advice manuals follow some of these same genre conventions.[7] They contain tables of contents that list the information that will be given in each chapter, just as some novels "tell" the story through their table of contents. The style of writing is not particularly intimate in the sense that it does not engage the reader emotionally, especially when compared to some of Beecher's public addresses; in fact, it is often rather flat and turgid. However, Beecher's writing in her domestic advice manuals clearly shows that she is aware that she has a particular, concrete audience she needs to address and so—in this sense—her writing style could be described as intimate. For example, her introductory chapter to *Miss Beecher's Housekeeper and Healthkeeper* is addressed to "My dear friends" from "Your friend and well-wisher" (1873, 2–3). Moreover, women's novels of this era were rarely aesthetic masterpieces and their prose can be as stilted as Beecher's, so we should not have too high expectations of an intimate style of writing.

What is also fascinating is the way Beecher's "narrative" in the introductory letter to the *Housekeeper and Healthkeeper* mirrors that in women's fiction of the move from poverty to moral development. Beecher recounts that it was her "good fortune to be trained by poverty and good mothers and aunts" to do domestic labor, and how she ruined her own health and has now recovered by "strict obedience to the laws of health and happiness" (2). Beecher was taking some authorial license here, as she was by no means poor.

The social and moral philosophical concepts expressed in Beecher's domestic advice works and letters are no different from those explicated in her more traditionally philosophical works, nor are they "dumbed" down for her female audience. What we need to understand is that Beecher is using these genres, and especially that of a domestic advice manual, as the best way to reach her target audience: white middle-class women. Philosophical training is required to read philosophy, and this training was typically not available to nineteenth-century women; however, women had learned to absorb moral lessons from novels of a certain type and thus also from domestic advice manuals. Moreover, like letters, domestic advice manuals were socially appropriate forms for women to read. Beecher appears well aware of the need for the form of a work to be appropriate to the needs or skills of her target audience. In the case of *Letters on Health and Happiness*, which has content that is relevant for everyone, Beecher (1855, 11) states that she is writing in a simple enough manner that children can understand it and has made the work short enough that "even American *men of business* can be induced to read it." Again, however, the tone is one of intimacy; in her introduction Beecher asks if she can enter into people's "office or store, or study," and asks women if she may enter into their homes (7).

In Beecher's philosophical writings, there are some interesting differences in tone and structure from her letters and advice manuals. Perhaps the most significant is the fact that Beecher takes on a far more neutral, less intimate tone, even when she is speaking with an interlocutor (as in the case of *Letters on the Difficulties of Religion*), and instead takes up a position of critique and authority. The existence of these differences is perhaps no surprise. Philosophy has traditionally been written by men, with other men as the intended audience. Beecher's ability to "switch" modes demonstrates that there is no essential connection between gender and the form in which an author chooses to express his or her philosophical ideas.

When we read philosophy, we have learned to expect one of two things: a critique of an opponent, real or imagined, and an attempted demolition of his or her arguments, or a more general treatise. The first clearly requires some level of training in and knowledge of philosophy, but the second also rests on an assumption that the reader will have this training and knowledge. Historically, however, due to cultural restrictions on the education of women, female authors and readers have often been implicitly or explicitly excluded from participation in the philosophical enterprise. Moreover, as Janice Moulton (1983) has shown, "the adversary method"—often seen as the standard paradigm of philosophical technique in the West—is linked to aggression, a trait that has different social meaning and value for men and women. Linking aggression to philosophical technique serves to exclude women from philosophy, as it requires behavior that is not culturally constructed as feminine.

Thus the expected reader of philosophy will be the educated—presumably white and middle- or upper-class—man.

On the patrimonial picture of what philosophy "is," Beecher is not a philosopher, or she can be considered one only if we ignore a substantial amount of her published work and see it as *split* between philosophy and domestic economy. On the mainstream picture of how we are to do the history of philosophy, and, in fact, the patrimonial picture of philosophy more generally, we expect to find philosophical thought in the form of treatises, articles, monographs, essays, and the like. Autobiographies, letters, works of fiction, or poetry are less likely to be seen as primary source material for uncovering the thought of a philosopher, as they do not correspond to how we see philosophy. This is because these genres are more personal, more particular, more subjective, whereas the dominant picture of philosophy is as a universal, objective, and impartial search for knowledge. Like Beecher's positioning as author, her epistemic stance also pushes against the purity of the patrimonial picture of philosophy. Beecher does not frame herself as an autonomous, disinterested knower; rather, it is her experiences as a woman that leads to her philosophical insights and helps her form a bond with her audience so that she can communicate those insights. Beecher is not interested in the intellectual engagement of a male audience; she aims to raise the moral consciousness of women and thus to effect a more general social and moral change in the world.

On the patrimonial picture, philosophy is men writing for other men or, more precisely, for other intellectuals, who will typically be men. As I discussed in the introduction, the analogy of patrimony brings out the notion of male philosophical inheritance, and with this inheritance comes the notion of entitlement for the inheritors. Patrimony is also about the protection of this philosophical inheritance, especially from impurity, whether from the impurity of distortion by contemporary ideas or the threat to the autonomy of the discipline through impure subject matter or the form within which it is expressed.

Beecher, however, was reaching out to an audience who would have neither the leisure time nor the education to read "real" philosophy: women. In her domestic advice manuals and letters, Beecher is writing *philosophy for women*. This is not to say that women cannot understand, for example, the works of Kant, nor is to say that men cannot understand or respond to Beecher's work. It is to recognize that Beecher's advice manuals and letters were the best way to transmit her *particular* philosophy to women at a *particular juncture* in women's history of liberation and education. To argue that "it is just not philosophy" is to invoke a model of philosophical writing that has historically excluded women, a model that is itself an historical construct, one that is not independent of masculinist conceptions of what philosophy "is" and how it is to be "done." To exclude Beecher's "philosophy for women" is to reaffirm the historical male dominance of the world of philosophy.[8]

My analysis of Beecher appears to be similar to what Jorge Gracia calls "the literary" approach to the history of philosophy. Gracia sees this approach as part of what I am calling the philosophical approach in mainstream history of philosophy because its focus is on the philosophical value of texts and ideas. According to Gracia (1991, 259), the literary critic claims that that philosophers, "consciously or unconsciously, use literary form and style to convey the overall message they want to communicate." Gracia recognizes the validity of this approach, yet he claims that it can be problematic in that there is a tendency to treat the text in isolation from its historical setting and the author's intentions. Gracia does recognize, however, that this treatment of a text in isolation is by no means automatic and that the literary approach can be combined with other approaches. Gracia also critiques the literary approach as being somewhat peripheral, as most philosophical texts are written with the goal of clarity rather than using a particular literary form or forms to convey meaning.

Gracia's critique of the literary approach as contextually isolating may make sense in the context of the male canon, but it is clear that reading Beecher requires historical grounding in that we need to understand for whom she was writing. The question of authorial intention is—as always—more problematic and could be the subject of an entire work, but, as I have argued above, it is possible to identify Beecher's philosophical goals by her choice of genre, and one central goal was to write philosophy for women. Moreover, Gracia critiques the literary approach for being somewhat peripheral, yet it is clear that Beecher's choice of genre was vital for the substance of her philosophy. Thus, despite their initial similarities, there are some distinct differences in how I am approaching Beecher and what Gracia calls the literary approach, differences that point to the need to question again whether mainstream approaches to the history of philosophy are a good fit for early feminist philosophy.

It is not simply that we must place Beecher's supposedly nonphilosophical works into their historical and cultural context in order to see them as philosophical works, we must ask the broader question of what is to count as a

philosophical text and—indeed—what philosophy is. What I have been calling the patrimonial picture of philosophy underpins our contemporary
historical and philosophical approaches to the history of philosophy.
Whether—to use the oversimplified but convenient questions discussed in the
introduction to this book—we are asking what Beecher said or whether it is
true, we are working within a certain framework of what philosophy is and
how it is written or expressed. Moreover, we must recognize that the patrimonial picture of philosophy can allow only certain approaches to the study of
the history of philosophy as legitimate; indeed, its normalization of philosophy as adversarial sets up differing approaches being in opposition to each
other. We need to remember that this framework is itself a historical and
cultural construct, one that is potentially problematic and has historically
excluded women and the feminine.

If we maintain that the two mainstream approaches to the history of philosophy, or variants of those approaches, are the only ones available to us,
then we will lose sight of many of Beecher's works and therefore much of her
philosophical view. Instead, we should approach Beecher differently. Reading
Beecher's works together as a whole allows us to see what I am going to call
her "moral world," and throughout the rest of my account of Beecher I will
draw on the full range of her works to bring out her ideas. Once we have seen
this moral world we can understand Beecher's view of the moral role of
women; specifically, we can see how this moral role can lead to economic
independence for women and a surprisingly robust conception of moral
power.

We have already seen the importance of the question of the empowerment
of women for the analysis of historical works of feminist philosophy, and it
will be central for the rest of this chapter. It is only through taking an
approach to the history of philosophy that includes these three elements—
including Beecher's works that are not philosophical in standard terms; placing her work within its historical and cultural context; and bringing out how
her philosophy will empower women—that we can truly see the richness of
Beecher's philosophy and understand why we may wish to claim her as a
philosophical foremother. As I stated in the introductory chapter, the interpretive lens I want to develop is less about overturning standard or mainstream approaches and more about reflecting on the process of interpretation
itself and the political and ethical self-consciousness required for this reflection. The differences and similarities between the empowerment question I

wish to employ and the two mainstream approaches are something I obviously need to discuss. I will consider this issue briefly in the discussion of Beecher and return to it throughout the remainder of the book.

Beecher's Moral World

Beecher's moral world is strictly hierarchical, constructed by God to achieve utilitarian ends or goals. She explains in *The Moral Instructor* that God has constituted things so that we all have equals, superiors, and inferiors due to differences in intellectual abilities, age and experience, income and social station, or within the family or workplace (see 1838, 120–21; see also 1857, 175; 1860, 120; 1873, 264). This, Beecher holds, is the way providence has designed the world in order to bring about the greatest happiness overall. From the view of this divine system, every individual—no matter what social station they occupy or what mental powers they possess—is able to contribute to the greatest happiness of the whole, and is thus—in God's eyes—perfect as long as they act according to their appropriate place in the scheme of things. Humans recognize this grand design, for this is the "intuitive principle or belief in all rational minds" that *"happiness-making on the best and largest scale is the end or purpose for which all things are made"* (1873, 370).

According to Beecher, we call any action that best produces this end "right," but such actions are regulated by a system of laws: "the physical, social, and moral laws of God" (1860, 156). The laws regulating the mind are central to Beecher's moral system. She holds that the mind is motivated by the desire to gain enjoyment and avoid suffering, and is supplied both with the ability to judge the value of these potential enjoyments and the power to choose among them. The right choice is the one that actually produces pleasure unmixed with pain. It is here that we must understand that the law that regulates enjoyment is sacrifice: "always to sacrifice the lesser for the greater good" (1857, 36). When we are children we learn this in the context of our individual pleasures, and when we are adults we recognize that others suffer and enjoy due to this same rule, and thus we learn that *"the lesser good of the individual is always to be sacrificed to the greater good of the many."*

However, it is not simply that we are all isolated minds governed by the same rule. Beecher's moral world is constructed so that the enjoyments and pains that result from our actions extend to those connected with us: "Thus each mind is made dependent for happiness on the well-doing of those around them as much on its own obedience to law" (1857, 34). Given this dependency, the implications for the goal of the greater good are clear: "It appears that in this life *happiness* is the joint product of the obedience of each individual and the obedience of all connected with him to the laws of the vast system in which we are placed."

Within Beecher's moral system, then, the duties of self-sacrifice and obedience to the laws of the system are the way the divine plan for the greatest happiness will be achieved. Yet before we think that this is an overly repressive or austere system, let us not forget that the reason we choose to follow these laws is that they bring us enjoyment. She is clear that self-sacrifice is not to be identified with self-mortification (see 1841, 159). If we pursue the best overall happiness properly, God has designed these duties so that they are connected to some form of personal enjoyment for ourselves, thus—for example—"the principle of curiosity is gratified in pursuing useful knowledge" and "the palate is gratified by performing the duty of nourishing our bodies" (1873, 375). The problem is not with such pleasures themselves, but when these pleasures become disconnected from their attendant duties and are pursued for themselves. Moreover, even though the self-sacrifice of personal enjoyment is seen as the highest kind of right action in this system, we should recognize that Beecher believes that ultimately—as this sacrifice becomes a habit—it becomes a pleasure in itself (see 1841, 158).

Knowledge of these laws and their overarching purpose is not innate; it must be learned during the impressionable childhood years. The child learns from its experiences of seeing which behaviors are praised and rewarded as good and which are not. Gradually the child comes to understand that all human activities and plans are framed in this way, and thus that there is an overall design of things to produce good. Yet such learning is not automatic; it cannot be produced without what Beecher calls "the social influences of surrounding minds through the principles of *love, gratitude, sympathy,* and *example*" (1857, 217).

In what she sees as a parallel to the way God trained humans in the infancy of our race, Beecher holds that love for a morally superior mind combined with attractive teaching methods works best to produce obedience to these laws. This power of the morally superior mind is further enhanced when this person is a benefactor of the pupil. The latter will then desire to return the benevolence in some way, and the best way to do this is to bring pleasure to the benefactor through apt learning. This gratitude—and thus the learning of the pupil—is further increased if he or she sees education as based in the personal expense and self-sacrifice of the benefactor (see 1857, 41).

As we have already seen with Waithe's account (1991, 241), the role of the teacher is women's role, one that requires women "to educate and to provide moral example through acts of benevolent utility involving personal sacrifice and self-denial." What we can now also see is that this role will bring pleasure to women. Moreover, women's role as teacher goes far deeper than simply producing virtuous citizens. In order to be virtuous, children must learn the immutable laws of divine providence, and such is the constitution of the human mind that this can be learned only from a certain type of person and in a certain way: from a woman using her "feminine" skills to teach these laws and obedience to them. While we, as contemporary readers, may well be resistant to this stereotyping of women's "nature," we shall find that within the background of Beecher's moral world, the problematic notion of women as essentially domesticated, self-sacrificing moral educators is undercut. Within Beecher's moral world, women may have this role, but it becomes liberating and—to an extent—empowering.

Beecher's is clearly a utilitarian world. Despite its radical differences from classical utilitarianism—specifically, the grounding in Christianity and the emphasis on self-sacrifice—her theory has many of the structural hallmarks of the classical theory: the single principle; happiness as the end of humanity; and the idea that morality is learned, not innate. Even though Beecher sees the principle of the greatest happiness to be divinely designed, she is a classical utilitarian in the sense that her moral system is, at its core, a single principle theory with happiness as the end or goal of humanity. Finally, Beecher holds that even though it is natural for us to think as utilitarians, we must learn the behaviors, thoughts, and actions that will make us act for the greatest happiness overall.

Beecher's utilitarianism, however, is different in important ways from classical utilitarianism; it is what I call, for want of a better term, a form of "empowerment utilitarianism." Beecher has been able to make a theory that is very much in the masculinist ethical tradition available for feminist use, while at the same time avoiding the problems of the argument from expediency, a popular version of utilitarianism in the nineteenth century. As Molly Travis (1993, 394) explains, "The argument from expediency—a feminized version of utilitarianism—presumed men and women to be essentially different, and claimed, for example, if women were better educated they would make better wives, mothers, and homemakers and if women were allowed to vote, they would redeem politics with their moral sense and their insight into domestic concerns. The argument from expediency—claiming the benefits to society of women's difference from men—appeared less selfish and, thus, more feminine than the natural rights argument for justice and equality."

Beecher would agree that better education would make women better wives, mothers, and homemakers (although she did not agree with suffrage for women), and thus women's education is a societal good. However, and this is the crucial difference with both feminized utilitarianism and the utilitarianism of Wheeler and Thompson, Beecher also held that education was a good for women themselves, morally, socially, economically, and psychologically. In other words, as I shall show, women are to be empowered by education.

Beecher is not just interested in constructing a theory that shows how we can attain the greatest happiness of humanity, she wants actually to *produce* this greatest happiness: she wants her audience—specifically, her female audience—to become "happiness-makers." This is not to say, however, that Beecher's utilitarianism can be divided up into the theoretical and the practical—both elements are part of a whole for Beecher. Again, this shows that we must include Beecher's so-called nonphilosophical works in an analysis of her thought.

Throughout her nonphilosophical works aimed at women, and especially her domestic advice manuals, Beecher writes to persuade women to take up their moral role as happiness-maker in the home. She does not employ philosophical arguments, she appeals to women's pride in the role God has chosen for them, their nationalism, and their emotional reactions to the suffering of children; she speaks to them one-to-one as a friend and equal. Treatises may convince us of the cogency of a theory, but the persuasions of letters and advice from a friend will make us follow this theory. Beecher's utilitarianism is not just feminist in the sense that it has this practical component or that it utilizes feminine forms of writing for its expression, it is feminist because of the role women play in Beecher's moral world, a role that commentators have not yet truly recognized. This is something I shall return to after I have briefly discussed other commentators' interpretations of Beecher in the next section.

Beecher's Moral World and Calvinism

This next section is a little tangential, although it is required by philosophical thoroughness to recognize the alternative interpretations of other commentators. My reading of Beecher conflicts with Sklar's chronologically based account. Sklar (1973, 215) holds that even though *The Elements* is foundational for Beecher's work, by the 1850s Beecher had moved from a theologically grounded system to a secularized one. Sklar then reads the references to the laws of God in these later works as simply "a theological guise, their real import is social" (242). Any apparent vestiges of Calvinism are explained by Sklar as evidence of Beecher's struggle with her religious heritage; indeed, the developments within her social ethic—Sklar claims—are "shaped by her inability to abandon Calvinism in its entirety" (263).

Hall (2000, 74) claims that this is a misreading of Beecher due to a conflation of Beecher's rejection of some of the "'harsher' tenets of Calvinism" for a more wholesale rejection of the evangelical tradition. Instead, Hall redraws the distinction as one between religious doctrine and philosophical explanations of doctrinal truths: taking the primary tenets of Calvinism as the latter, Beecher rejects *these explanations* but not necessarily the fundamental doctrinal truths. Thus she rejects the Calvinist doctrine of irresistible grace, but still maintains that in order to choose salvation we require divine aid. Hall's explanation dovetails with Beecher's discussions of theology in her later works. In *Miss Beecher's Housekeeper* (1873, 423), for example, she clearly criticizes any theology whose theory of mind tends "to lessen hope and exertion in that training" through which we can escape most easily punishment in the afterlife. Yet she remains as adamant in her later works as in her earlier ones that our motivation to self-sacrifice is the fear of this punishment; her quarrel—she says—is with how this doctrine is to be interpreted, not with its fundamental truth (see 1872, 208–9).

While it is true that Beecher struggled with her Calvinist heritage in her personal life, I think that to see this as pointing to a dichotomy between the theological and the secular in her work is to misunderstand the nature of this struggle: it was a struggle *within* the framework of her religious belief. Moreover, framing Beecher as "trapped" by a male tradition and her own psychology may in fact serve to undermine Beecher's philosophical achievements. If we accept that Beecher kept a Calvinist worldview of divine order and human subordination to laws, but rejected its notions of sin and (as Hall also agrees) moral education, then the human role in the salvation of others—through education and example—now takes a prominent place. Beecher then sees women as the heaven-appointed candidates to fill this vacuum. In this way she turns on its head Calvin's notion that because God is our father, there is something of the divine in a human father. Instead, for Beecher, because God is our teacher, there is something of the divine in a mother. It is here we can see the first step in what will be a quite radical reenvisioning of women's role that will be both produced by and rooted in Christian tradition.

This dichotomy between the theological and the secular also plays out in the way Sklar seems to deal with those of Beecher's writings that are then consigned to the more "secular" category. Such works are seen as either adding little to her early arguments on domestic economy or female education, or—where there are notable differences—perhaps testifying to internal difficulties with Beecher's thought (Sklar 1973, 166–67, 246–57). Other more secular writings, such as Beecher's *Letters to the People on Health and Happiness* and *Letters to Persons Who Are Engaged in Domestic Service* are essentially ignored. Yet I believe that both works are important to an understanding of Beecher's account of the role of women.

Seeing Beecher's work as split between the theological and the secular reinforces the picture of the history of philosophy as a series of battles between opposing sects over timeless questions, a picture that has been critiqued by, among others, Rée (as I outlined in the introductory chapter). As I shall demonstrate with my examination of the work of Frances Wright in the next chapter, it is possible for there to be a synthesis between supposedly competing views that is not historically or philosophically problematic. Further, seeing Beecher's work as split in this way also serves to reinforce the notion, identified by Moulton and discussed in the introductory chapter, that philosophical practice is adversarial. As I argued in the introduction, the notion of philosophy as essentially combative is part of the patrimonial picture of philosophy I wish to question.

I hold that it is important to see Beecher's work as dedicated to explaining a divine system of laws. While her more philosophical works tend to focus on explaining intellectual and social laws, her works on home economics tend to emphasize explaining the physical laws and producing subordination to the system itself. Any analysis of her thought that tries to force too strict a separation between her more explicitly theological/philosophical work and her apparently practical work, courts the danger of not gleaning a true understanding of her moral system. Everything in Beecher's moral world is tied together: children's and women's health, the construction and organization of houses, and the social system. And she sees this harmony as tied to obedience to the laws: "The principle of subordination is the great bond of union and harmony through the universe" (1872, 188).

Indeed, we find that throughout Beecher's writings on home economics there is a clear sense of this organic whole, that every detail of the way we live our lives is fundamentally directed toward this happiness. For example, we find in *Miss Beecher's Housekeeper and Healthkeeper* that nature has fitted certain foods—such as milk and grains—with the proportions of elements that exactly match (and thus nourish) the elements of the body. The "good" or efficient housekeeper is then one who follows these physical laws in preparing food for her family, and is thus the "good" or moral housekeeper. The practical results of cooking—physically healthy children who are themselves ready and able to work for the ultimate goal of happiness—are obvious.

Beecher is clear that we must also follow these laws with the appropriate temper of mind: a benevolent and submissive one. The key to understanding this notion comes in *Letters to Persons Who Are Engaged in Domestic Service*. Here Beecher argues that it does not matter how lowly our task or activity may seem, it can be seen as an act of benevolence if it is done properly: "for the Glory of God" (1842, 196). In this way, then, she says that—for example—cooking properly with care and concern can show this benevolence. Beecher explicitly defines benevolence as something she says used to be called "charity." It is not about giving all you have or performing a few actions a year; rather, it is "in *every day life* that we can *all the time* be showing forth the temper of benevolence" (199).[9] Thus benevolence is far more than—as Sklar (1973, 248) defines it—a "willingness to act in sacrificial ways." For Beecher, it is closer to a way of life or a worldview that sees moral significance in the everyday.[10]

In this way, then, we can see not only how Beecher comes to value the domestic and educational role she allots to women, but also how her notions of subordination to happiness-making and self-sacrifice are nuanced. Humble domestic tasks are not mindless; they require knowledge and intellectual input. Done properly, they produce a sense of belonging or connection and purpose. This should not be underestimated, for we must consider the way Beecher's female contemporaries were each isolated in their own homes. Self-sacrifice is not to be understood as pure self-negation or self-denial. It is true that—for Beecher—the mark of moral character is the subordination of our other desires to this ruling purpose, but we must understand that this brings happiness to the individual and gives him or her social value.

We can see the importance of Beecher's discussions of the domestic—and thus her works on domestic economy—for her moral and social philosophy. These works are philosophy written for women, but they are also central to the way all the elements of Beecher's moral world become tied together. What we can also see is the way Beecher's version of utilitarianism that is expressed in her nonphilosophical works helps to glue together the different elements of her moral world: our lives—even down to the smallest detail—are designed to produce the greatest happiness both for others and for ourselves.

The Role of Women

I have tried to suggest that neither of the mainstream approaches to the history of philosophy is a good fit for understanding Beecher's work, in particular because of the apparently nonphilosophical subject matter and written form of some of her works. Neither of the approaches can allow for the more intimate model of philosophical authorship employed by Beecher in her domestic advice manuals, nor can either allow for an inclusion of these works in a discussion of Beecher's philosophy. Yet I have argued that we must include Beecher's nonphilosophical works if we are to truly understand her philosophical system, and I demonstrated the richness of this philosophical system once we use Beecher's apparently nonphilosophical works. Moreover, I have also argued that Beecher's chosen approach to authorship and the written form of her domestic advice works is vital for putting her philosophical theory into practice. She is writing a social and moral philosophy to improve the world for those who will actually carry out this world change: women.

What then would lead to a fruitful analysis of Beecher's work? In the previous chapter I identified the guiding question for a feminist perspective on the historical philosophies I am examining as "Does it [a particular philosophy/ theory/text] empower women?" This question requires us to examine the works of a philosopher within his or her particular historical and cultural context, not simply to understand what this philosopher said but to search for truths about the subordination of his or her female contemporaries and the knowledge that will end this subordination. Yet this question does not require us to remain locked in the past; it can also be used to ask whether the text can "speak" in some way to its readers in the present. This does not necessarily mean that we are to search for timeless truths in the text, for gender justice itself is not timeless in this way; rather, we are to look for intellectual and political connections in historical texts. Let us first see whether Beecher's philosophy could empower her contemporaries, and then ask whether it has the potential to "speak" to a modern "us."

What are women being asked to do specifically in Beecher's moral world? While a subordination to intellectual and physical laws may be unproblematic for the modern reader, the implications of obedience to the social laws of Beecher's era will no doubt be a cause for concern. For such laws establish not only a social hierarchy between the sexes, but one that consigns women to the home. The issue of Beecher's claims for the domestication of women seems an obstacle for any attempts to rehabilitate her as part of an early American feminist movement. The typical approach taken by commentators (no doubt based on Sklar's account) has been to emphasize the way Beecher allows for women's *moral* superiority over men: in homes and in schools, women will oversee the production of moral character, and ultimately— Beecher hoped—this will lead to a wholesale moral reform of the United States.

Sklar's account commits Beecher to a specific type of relational feminism: one that holds the traditional submissive role of women and aims to turn it "into a sign of superior moral sensibility" (1973, 136). Women's social and moral influence does not, then, come from human equality, but rather as a function of their difference from men (137). Essentially, Sklar sees Beecher's universe as "one bifurcated into masculine and feminine dichotomies," with Beecher building on traditional sex roles both to ensure cultural stability and to raise up women (154). Beecher focused on the domestic role of women because she believed that the way to "transcend social divisions" was to emphasize "the universality . . . of domestic values" (158). Sklar claims that Beecher's emphasis on submission and self-sacrifice was a conscious choice made because these characteristics were traditionally associated with women, thus making them pivotal in her social ethics, which "placed women closer to the source of moral authority and hence established their social centrality" (83).

Ultimately, this approach seems to produce more problems than it solves. Just as the theological/secular dichotomy employed by Sklar tends to keep Beecher confined within the "male" philosophical tradition, so does a location of her work within a relational/individualist feminism framework have the potential to narrow "our" feminist tradition. We cannot truly appreciate what I shall show is the radical nature of Beecher's work. Further, seeing domesticity as essentially about producing national unity through uniformity in practice reduces it to being simply a pragmatic tool that women are capable of wielding. It loses some of the significance that I have suggested, and will elaborate on further, that the domestic sphere had for both Beecher and the women she championed. Indeed, viewing it in this way inadvertently devalues the very thing that Beecher aimed to accord its proper value.

Finally, and most important, the notion of moral power that accompanies this view is—at best—a sop, for there is no doubt that it does not ameliorate the fact that women are consigned to the domestic sphere. Practically speaking, women will remain subordinate to individual men in the home. Politically speaking, they will remain powerless; Beecher held that arguing for suffrage for women is not going to give them the sort of power they can wield properly. Even more worrying is the fact that, while women's moral power is supposed to influence men to use their own power benevolently, Beecher often seems doubtful of men's potential for benevolence (Beecher and Stowe 1869, 468). It may then seem that no matter how much moral power women can lay claim to, they will never have the sort or level of influence hoped for by Beecher. Indeed, this is the fundamental problem with any of these claims for a "special" power for women that is supposed to function as a substitute for or an equal to the political power of men.

This problem is somewhat mitigated, however, if we do not see Beecher's work *just* through an oversimplistic binary of gendered separate spheres. Framed within the moral world I find throughout Beecher's work, we can form a more nuanced understanding of both the subordination of women and the moral power she believed they should possess. In order to resolve this issue of moral power, we must first understand that there is a notion of the subordination of women at play in Beecher's work that is distinct from what can be called the traditional model of women's domestic subordination to their husbands, brothers, and fathers. A typical mistake in interpreting Beecher is to assume that these are one and the same thing. In fact, we shall see that Beecher's account of the subordinate role of women can be seen both to work *within* her divinely ordered moral system and *against* the way American society is ordered. While Beecher's account did solidify certain elements of American society, it can also produce social change rather than simply confirming the status quo.

As we have seen, all humans are to contribute to the greater good of society in their own allotted way. Beecher believes that God's plan is for women to do this through their education and care of children, as well as through their moral influence over men. But we must be careful how we interpret this task. Beecher's clearest description of this *general* moral duty of women comes in an early work, *The Duty of American Women to Their Country*, in which Beecher (1845, 69) claims, "No woman is free from guilt, or free from the terrific responsibilities of the perils impending over her country, till she has done *all in her power* to secure a *proper* education to *all* the young minds within the reach of her influence." She states further that each woman will perform her duty differently: sisters can teach brothers, mothers can find nearby children to teach alongside their own, and others can go out West to set up schools (72–73).

We can see, as Beecher evidently did, that—once defined in this way—the moral task of women *does not require* them to be part of a traditional family, and thus they need not be subordinate within the domestic sphere.[11] Instead, Beecher argues that if women become economically self-sufficient, they can set up alternative households in which they can teach or adopt children:

> The distinctive duty of obedience to man does not rest on women who do not enter the relations of married life. A woman who inherits property, or who earns her own livelihood can institute the family state, adopt orphan children and employ suitable helpers in training them; and then to her will appertain the authority and rights that belong to man as the head of a family. And when every woman is trained to some self-supporting business, she will not be tempted to enter the family state as a subordinate, except by that love for which there is no need of law. (Beecher and Stowe 1869, 204; see also Beecher 1873, 266)[12]

Suitable occupations for women are the types of employment that "can be pursued in sunlight and the open air" (Beecher and Stowe 1869, 470). These include fruit growing, cultivation of cotton, manufacture of straw, or dairy farming (Beecher 1869, 10). This desire to give women financial independence is also part of her argument for proper female schooling and the establishment of teaching as "the true and noble profession of women" (1846b, 10). We are told, for example, in *Woman's Profession* (1872, 52) that if there were universities for women where they could learn women's work properly, they could establish their own homes and be independent.

Yet this recognition of the contingency of the traditional family must be understood to come out of Beecher's world of laws, not as conflicting with it. In this particular instance, Beecher considers how the divine plan that humans shall marry and have children—and thus learn and teach the virtues of self-sacrifice and love—can be accomplished in the face of the changing empirical conditions of nineteenth-century American society: fewer people were getting married due to factors such as the emigration out West of young bachelors. Beecher isolates what she calls "the distinctive feature of the family state"—in other words, the reason why the family state was created by God and its role in the overall divine plan—which, she states, is "*the training of a small number by self-sacrificing labor and love*" (1872, 43–44; see also Beecher and Stowe 1869, 18–19). Given this, it becomes clear that "those who are child-less may have as great a work to perform as the parental": they can obey at least the essence of the divine plan (1872, 44).[13]

In this way we can see that Beecher's *ideal woman* for accomplishing the God-given task of contributing to the social and moral progress of the United States (and thus the good of all) is the economically independent, socially valued teacher combating childhood illiteracy and the social and moral evils it produces. Moreover, even though this ideal was fully developed only in her later works, its roots are evident even in her earliest works. This, then, suggests that we can see Beecher's ideal as an integral part of her thought, rather than constituting any particularly radical change.

Clearly, men are not the center of Beecher's moral world; that place is reserved for children. Children are not sentimentalized; in fact, in *American Woman's Home*, she refers to the "useless, troublesome infant" (Beecher and Stowe 1869, 18). Yet because women's central task is to bring up children, their interests and importance become coupled with those of children (Beecher 1851, 97). This sort of self-sacrifice of women to children is not blinkered or instinctual; it requires intellectual thought and moral preparation. There is also a sense in which women freely choose it. While she holds that women are more equipped for it than men are, it is not "natural" per se; they must be trained for it both indirectly, through Beecher's writings, and directly through her schools. Indeed, she says that everyone is naturally averse to this notion of a duty of subordination (1872, 189). Least important, it would seem, are men, who—while they are obviously to parent children—seem to have as their central mission the support (financial and emotional) of these mothers (184). Thus, even though women are below men in the social world, in a *moral* hierarchy, women are higher.

We can now start to appreciate Beecher's account of the domesticity of women. It is not simply that she tries to revalue women's domestic role or to claim that there is a moral power that is supposed to accompany that role. Such projects seem doomed to failure anyway. She cannot directly challenge the power of men, but she can undercut the importance of men, and thus their power. Throughout her work, Beecher rarely discusses the role of men. At first this may seem to be because she is focused on raising women up, and men already have power; upon closer examination, however, we realize that in Beecher's system men are simply not as socially useful as women. In the world of domestic life and in the moral hierarchy, men are not very important, and once women are economically self-sufficient, men really do not seem to have much use at all.

Given the moral significance of usefulness, this is an important point for Beecher. If women were to achieve economic self-sufficiency, it would seem that men's main role is as biological fathers—not even necessarily as parents. If women's potential for moral power were to be fulfilled, then men would simply function as figureheads for nonconfrontational political negotiations and decision making, and even their outcomes would be influenced by women. Men's third and final role is as protectors of women, but this is problematic, as it is only from men—whom Beecher sees as having physical power over women—that women need protection in the first place.

Thus, while Beecher does keep women identified with the domestic sphere, she goes some way toward expanding the tasks that could be included within this sphere. What is clear, however, is that this need not entail the subordination of women to men in the individual home. Once this is recognized, the issue of whether Beecher's notion of moral power was simply an amelioration of the position of women also becomes clearer. First, Beecher's view differs greatly from the standard view of women's moral power as exemplified by Sklar, in that Beecher is offering a very robust form of moral power. It is one that will require both education and economic independence, and is supported by an ethico-religious system.

Second, while moral power is identified with women's sacrifice and subordination to the moral good, it should not be oversimplified as a personal moral superiority that comes from selfless behavior. It is not merely about individual character; instead, we must understand that Beecher frames sacrifice and subordination in terms of a general social usefulness. Women's moral power over children and those around them comes from the laws of the mind that govern the way the divine laws and their overarching purpose are learned. This moral power is to be understood as the control or regulation of the mind by a desire for good, whether it is control by the individual over herself or by a teacher over a pupil. It finds its basis as much in Beecher's philosophy of mind—perhaps more so—as in cultural archetypes of women. Understood thus, women's moral power is ultimately about their abilities to include others in a community of minds working together for the greatest happiness, an

inclusion that requires reciprocation and thus does not place the entire burden on the shoulders of women.

Thus Beecher's notion of moral power is not a bastardized copy of the civil
and economic power of men. Instead, it serves to undercut the economic and
domestic power of men and to raise women up—not in sentimentalized terms
of their nature, but in terms of their usefulness: a usefulness that is grounded
in an ethico-religious system. Moreover, even though women's moral power
is still framed within the domestic sphere, we must understand just how far
removed Beecher's concept of this sphere is from the confinement of isolated
and dependent women generated by the more orthodox nineteenth-century
ideals of domesticity.

Women's Rights and Women's Health

Yet this empowerment may *still* ring rather hollow in the ears of modern-day
feminist philosophers, for the type of power Beecher aims to give women
would have been available only to middle- and upper-class white women.
Moreover—despite Beecher's later criticisms of social distinctions based on
birth and a "caste" system that served to devalue labor—the inherent racism
and classism of her views cannot be ignored. These are implicit in the way
she ignores differences among women, and more explicit, for example, in the
fact that present in her call for these classes of American women to take up
their moral task and educate the millions of suffering and illiterate children
is the fear of the challenge to American democracy by a growing, uncontrolled
lower class. Perhaps most problematically, Beecher's view of the specific role
of women means that she is disposed to argue *against* women's rights per se
and *against* woman suffrage. Indeed, Beecher's elimination of the domestic
subordination of women simultaneously ensures that they are kept out of the
public sphere.

This is where we should understand that a crucial element in the way her
works on home economics were intended to empower women is the issue of
women's health. And again, this is why it is so necessary to include her works
on home economics as part of her philosophical oeuvre.

Commentators have tended not to attribute much importance to the fact
that throughout her works on home economics Beecher places a constant
emphasis on the health of both women and children. Indeed, in her *Letters to
the People on Health and Happiness*, she enters into a horrifying account of

the way fashionable clothes, eating habits, and the constant strain of child bearing all took their toll on middle- and upper-class women's health, while in the lower classes women were lured into dangerous factory work because of the pay. A further tragedy—if Beecher's information is accurate—is that women often avoided seeking medical treatment because sexual assault by physicians was quite common (see 1855, 137).[14]

If the picture Beecher paints of women's health and strength truly reflects the lives of women (of all classes), then we can see why her emphasis was not on arguing for the vote for women. In practical terms, what possible use would real political power have been? Instead, Beecher's instruction on domestic economy is aimed at dealing with the socioeconomic problems, and their attendant consequences, faced by her contemporaries. She aims to do this without recourse to arguing for political change either on behalf of women or for women to demand for themselves. This is because she held that women could not be involved in the political sphere due to the divine order of things. On a more pragmatic level, she was also concerned about the possibility of a backlash if women did try to claim political power. Indeed, she held that God had provided such social arrangements as a way of protecting the weakest members of society—women and children—from being oppressed and used by the strongest.

In discussing Beecher's criticism of women's suffrage, and her claim that moral power was the suitable substitute for women, we may mistakenly ignore the other ways that Beecher sought to empower women that were appropriate for their situation. These alternatives are part and parcel of her system, and could bring real changes for women. Beecher can be seen as arguing for empowering women in the sense that they are taking control over their own bodies, specifically through her home economics books, in which she aims to teach women basic medical skills. Indeed, these works are a lifeline for women's moral and physical health. Further, health and economic independence are interconnected for Beecher. Given the types of occupation she deemed suitable for women (e.g., dairy farming), we can see that physical health was necessary for such occupations and their likely consequences.

Thus, while the allotting to women the role of self-sacrificing servants will necessarily remain problematic, we can see that a wedge can be driven between service (in Beecher's sense of the word) and servitude. In order to be able to fulfill their allotted role, women in Beecher's world will require a surprising amount of independence in order to produce the power needed for that sacrifice. As we have already seen, the ideal of the self-sacrificing woman is not some perversion of the maternal role but is an economically independent, socially valued teacher setting up small orphanages to assuage the social evils caused by childhood illiteracy. Moreover, the sort of self-sacrifice Beecher has in mind is that of labor for the social good, a sacrifice that can best be performed by an independent and robust woman, physically healthy from manual labor and mentally healthy from intellectual stimulation—an image that stands in sharp contrast to the nineteenth-century ideal of the delicate, decorative, drawing-room flower.

Yet these surprisingly radical changes did not challenge traditional conceptions of women's roles; instead, they maintained both the social and the divine order. And it is here that placing Beecher's work within its historical and cultural context is vital to our understanding of her system and goals. While the desire to maintain this order is no doubt puzzling to the modern reader, it is in this latter point that we can see Beecher's true strength: we should not underestimate the power of religious belief, especially in the nineteenth century. From within our predominately secular society we may have forgotten that religious belief provided a worldview that framed all elements of a believer's life. To set up the moral rightness of a liberating social change, such as female suffrage, against religious belief is not to provide a moral dilemma, it is simply unlikely to make sense to the believer. Certainly, to expect the believer to discard religious belief as we do false information is to misunderstand the role belief plays in people's lives. Beecher was able to offer an argument for the moral rightness of a change in women's social, moral, and—eventually—economic station, one that was not merely divinely *sanctioned* but directly *entailed* by what she saw as God's plan for the happiness of humans.

As we saw with Wheeler and Thompson, the question to ask of Beecher is not whether her philosophy is true but whether, if it were put into practice, it would empower women. Placed within its historical and cultural context, it would seem that the answer is a clear "yes," that Beecher's notion of moral power will bring empowerment to women. She is both writing *about* empowerment for women and writing a philosophy *of* empowerment in that her philosophy is written for women; it is a philosophy of their own, written in forms that will be easily accessible. Moreover, both the structure of her philosophy and its expression are part of this goal in that she places her female contemporaries at the heart of her philosophical theory and aims to stir the appropriate emotions in her reader that will lead to their joining or supporting her cause.

Beecher and the Empowerment Question

In asking the "empowerment question," however, I do not want to remain locked in the past. I also want to ask whether it makes sense to say that Beecher can "speak" in some way to the modern reader: whether there is a political connection between Beecher and the modern reader that can be brought out by asking about empowerment of women. On the one hand, we do not want to treat Beecher as a museum piece, interesting but irrelevant; on the other, we do not want to try to extract her philosophy from its historical and cultural context, thus flattening it and losing its originality.

It can certainly be argued that Beecher's work has much in common with our modern feminist ethics. Traditionally, moral philosophy has ignored women's interests and the private sphere, denied women's moral agency, and devalued women's moral experience and the characteristics culturally associated with the feminine. In asking the empowerment question of Beecher's moral system, we can see that she does not simply challenge the devaluation of these elements, but rather makes them central to her system. Alison Jaggar (1991) has offered a set of minimum conditions for theoretical adequacy of any feminist ethics: an ethics that recognizes differences in the situations of men and women; an ethics that works toward an analysis of and resistance to subordination of women; an ethics that includes moral issues of the private realm as well as the public; and an ethics that acknowledges the moral experiences of women. On this set of minimum conditions Beecher could be claimed as a foremother of modern feminist ethics, albeit with some hesitation due to the political problems with her work.

It is important, however, to see that a connection of this kind does not commit us to talk of timeless issues. Modern feminist ethics *itself* is not conceptualized as a series of timeless problems. Beecher "speaks" to the modern feminist to the extent to which she has similar *political* commitments and goals as modern-day feminist philosophy, not just similar *philosophical* commitments or content. We are making connections between her philosophy and our modern philosophies that are more like Wittgensteinian family resemblances than the traceable trajectories of thinkers of the philosophical approach for the history of philosophy. (Obviously, transhistorical connections require the use of anachronistic concepts and are thus problematic for the historical approach.) In making these connections, we are part of a community of knowers, knowers who must be aware of the political and ethical dimensions of our interpretations of Beecher. Obviously, these historical–

modern connections we are making cannot be reciprocal on Beecher's part, but it can be claimed that she is part of this community of knowers, albeit a foremother, due to her consciousness of the political and ethical dimensions of both her theorizing and the way this theorizing played out in daily life.

As I said in the introductory chapter, traceable trajectories of thinkers are problematic in that they reflect what I call a "patrimonial" way of thinking about the history of philosophy. According to Rée, the picture of philosophy's past as a set of traceable trajectories of thinkers implicitly defines a philosopher as a successor to the canonical greats and the pursuit of philosophy as maintaining the intellectual practices of these greats. This "professionalized" picture of the history of our discipline functions to exclude women from the philosophical enterprise, since they typically lacked formal training; moreover, historically, women have been prevented from speaking publicly or publishing their ideas. Similarly, these trajectories function to exclude philosophical work that is on different subject matter or is in a different form or approach, such as that of Beecher.[15]

Seeing connections between thinkers, on the other hand, along the lines of a Wittgensteinian family resemblance allows us more flexibility as to who can enter into our canons and how. This notion of connectivity is something I shall explore more fully in the next chapter, on Frances Wright. What is crucial to see here is that a shift in how we think about philosophy is required. Looking for family resemblances means that we are looking to make creative connections between thinkers; moreover, we begin with a very flexible notion of what philosophy is and recognize that our disciplinary boundaries may be expanded as we add more philosophers to the canon. Traceable trajectories, on the other hand, are far more rigid. Moreover, while not necessarily adversarial in themselves, they are part and parcel of what Janice Moulton has identified as the dominant Anglo-American paradigm of philosophical practice itself as adversarial, and thus the framing of the history of philosophy as a series of battles between schools of thought. As Moulton argues, this linking of philosophical ability with aggression serves to exclude women from philosophy, as it requires behavior that is not culturally constructed as feminine. Thus, both the trajectories themselves and the philosophical skills required to identify and critique them have historically and culturally excluded women.

Modern feminist philosophers also have something to learn from Beecher about the use of nontraditional genres to transmit philosophical thought. This is not to say that modern female philosophers cannot read standard philosophical genres; rather, we can learn from Beecher that the act of reading in itself is empowering. We may not realize this until we remember that it is only recently that philosophy has been considered a suitable subject for women to study. Traditional genres of philosophical writing have reinforced a dominant picture of philosophy that is masculinist and has excluded women. Through reading Beecher *for her philosophy*, the modern reader is taking part in the feminist philosophical enterprise in that the reader is not accepting this picture of philosophy and the accompanying genres through which it is transmitted.

Thus Beecher's philosophy can "speak" to a modern "us," but it does not do so in quite the same way as the mainstream philosophical approach to the history of philosophy. Certainly, we can—if we wish—identify elements of her philosophy that reappear in our modern-day philosophy. However, focusing on the empowerment question means that Beecher's philosophy will *always* be placed within its historical and cultural context. To ask whether women would be empowered by her philosophy is to ask about practical results for an actual, historically and culturally located group of women. We do not expect that her philosophy will be of this kind of use for the modern reader. Indeed, as I claimed in the previous chapter, asking the empowerment question shifts our expectations away from trying to establish some sort of direct lineage in feminist philosophical thinking, as we are looking not just at what someone said but also outside it in the sense of the goals or potential results of his or her theory.

Asking the empowerment question of Beecher is not to use some kind of feminist version of the mainstream historical approach to her philosophy, because the modern reader is also included in the enterprise. In other words, the modern reader is not the disinterested, disengaged historical reader. Indeed, the importance of engaging the reader in such a way that he or she wants to end the oppression of women or bring about their liberation or empowerment is something we learn from Beecher *herself* through her explicit use of traditionally nonphilosophical genres that are aimed at speaking to her particular audience. Asking the empowerment question need not be simple or allow only a yes or no answer; there can be multiple and complex ways that a philosophy, text, or theory can be identified as empowering.

Beecher is not interested in the intellectual engagement of a male audience; she aims to raise the moral consciousness of women and thus to effect a more general social and moral change in the world. Moreover, asking the empowerment question is not to ask whether something is true or what was said, it asks how a philosopher's work can produce political and social change;

this is something that is seen across generations and is historically contextualized. More significant, the empowerment question leads us to see that feminist philosophy is a different enterprise from the picture of philosophy as a self-contained, autonomous endeavor that underpins the two mainstream approaches to the history of philosophy.

The empowerment question is more than an "interested" question that still could be part of the philosophical approach. The interpreters themselves are involved in the search (and its subsequent answers), as they must hold themselves accountable, and be held accountable, to the overall goals of the feminist philosophical enterprise. The mainstream philosophical and historical approaches themselves are not the difficulty; rather, the philosophical background against which these approaches are typically framed is the problem here. While there may be room for interested questions on the philosophical approach, on what I am calling the patrimonial picture of philosophy there is no room for the politically and ethically self-conscious interpreter, one who will be personally and politically involved with their chosen texts and theories.

Reading Beecher helps us see that any feminist perspective on how the history of philosophy is to be done will require a broadening or reconceptualization of both how we define philosophical texts and our notion of philosophical authorship. I am also claiming that Beecher can show us both that the act of reading can be empowering and how the reader can be part of her philosophical enterprise. It is in these ways that a feminist lens for the history of philosophy can allow for a different relationship with historical texts. If we are to read Beecher's philosophy properly, we must push against notions of the purity of the philosophy, the disinterested or autonomous knower, and how philosophical knowledge is "inherited" or passed on.

Even though I am claiming that the two mainstream approaches are not fruitful for reading Beecher, I am not arguing that they should be overturned or dismissed completely. Rather, I am more interested in reflecting on the process of interpretation itself and the political and ethical self-consciousness required for this reflection. Exploring the empowerment question will lead us to an alternative picture of philosophy from the patrimonial picture, one that I shall develop more fully in the next chapter, on Frances Wright.

Notes

1. Offen (2000, 90) sees two main strands in early feminism. A minor strand is "abstract individualism," where liberation is understood as "the ethical self-realization of

the individual beyond the constraints of sexual identity or 'spheres.'" However, most pre-1948 European thinkers—both for and against feminism—are seen by Offen to be "relational": "Most retained a holistic view of societies and agreed with their more conservative opponents that the sociopolitical relation of the sexes was the very glue that held the fabric of society together; they viewed women and men as embodied beings, marriage and sex/gender roles as inherently political and as essential for social cohesion, but they did want to alter the sexual balance of power in family structures by ending women's subordination. Some cautiously emphasized women's *instrumental* social roles and insisted on women's special nature as a positive social force, even as they appealed to principles of liberty and equality. But the dominant notion of equality remained moral and intellectual" (90–91).

2. Waithe does not include *Truth Stranger Than Fiction* (1850b) in this list; however, it continues Beecher's commentary from her *Address*. Presumably Waithe made this choice because the former was not published for general consumption but privately printed for Beecher to distribute to Protestant clergymen.

3. Waithe (1991, 242) states that these books must be "understood as an essential pragmatic consequence of her philosophical views."

4. Even though Hall quotes from Beecher's domestic economy books, he lists the same books as Waithe does as Beecher's "philosophical" works.

5. I have chosen to leave out Beecher's public addresses, as my focus is on her works that are in the nonphilosophical form, though both forms speak to her central concerns. Unsurprisingly, they do not usually take the form of a philosophical lecture and they are more typically aimed at rousing the emotions of women, especially to stir their moral consciousness and to promote what Beecher would have thought of as their womanly pride.

6. Beecher's *Industrial and Domestic Science* (186?) is not a work on domestic science but simply a circular for a proposed women's university.

7. It is certainly true that other writers of this era, for example, Helen Hunt Jackson in her *Bits of Talk About Home Matters* (1873), did use the domestic advice manual to transmit political messages, but none did as thoroughly and systematically as Beecher.

8. To recognize Beecher's domestic advice manuals and letters as part of her philosophical oeuvre is also to challenge the boundaries and concepts of traditional political thought, which has at its heart the division of social life into public/political and private/domestic spheres. Traditionally, the political life is identified with the life of men, the ideal being a life of autonomy and individualism. However, the domestic life, which is culturally associated with women, is one of connection with dependent others. Beecher does not question this cultural division, or the association of women with the domestic sphere; instead, she creates a political, social, and moral philosophy grounded in that sphere.

9. This account of benevolence conflicts with the interpretation of Sklar (1973, 247–48), who argues that by this period Beecher sees benevolence and rectitude as fundamentally at odds, with the social rules of rectitude being allowed to override religious benevolence when necessary. Again, this is grounded on the theology/secular dichotomy Sklar finds in Beecher's work.

10. While my account here diverges from Waithe's (1991), I do not think it necessarily conflicts with it.

11. Tonkovich (1997, 183), however, sees this notion as produced in great part by Beecher's own successful experiences of living in alternative familial arrangements with other women. Sklar (1973, 166–67) believes it was caused partly by the development of an urban industrial society, and partly by Beecher's inabilities to resolve the tensions she saw between the sexes and between the classes.

12. While there is no doubt that this view constitutes a change, it is not the radical change that Sklar sees from an initial framing of the family as a society in miniature to the

family as a female culture. This becomes clearer when we see how this possibility for women comes out of Beecher's worldview, and is in fact present even in her early works.

13. This also provides an additional response to Sklar's comments on the secularization of these laws (discussed above).

14. See also *Woman's Profession as Mother and Educator with Views in Opposition to Woman Suffrage* (1872), addresses that were originally given to all-female meetings on health.

15. These traceable trajectories of thinkers are part of the philosophical approach to the history of philosophy. The historical approach, in its more rigorous versions, cannot allow for this concept, as it would require the imposition of anachronistic concepts onto historical texts in order to construct these trajectories.

3 FRANCES WRIGHT

Interconnectivity and Synthesis

Ernestine Rose, speaking at the tenth National Woman's Rights Convention in 1859, said, "Frances Wright was the first woman in this country [the United States] who spoke on the equality of the sexes. She had indeed a hard task before her. . . . She had to break up the time-hardened soil of conservatism, and her reward was sure—the same reward that is always bestowed upon those who are in the vanguard of any great movement. She was subjected to public odium, slander, and persecution" (quoted in Kolmerton 1990, 111). Rose encapsulates the contributions of Wright to feminist thought and the feminist movement as well as her "rewards." Wright was groundbreaking in many ways, and she may have the dubious honor of being the most vilified of all the first-wave feminists. However, Rose could not have foreseen that despite her infamy in the early nineteenth century, Wright is now all but forgotten.

One reason why Wright has remained a minor figure in the history of American (or even British) feminist thought is that her work does not fit well into the standard categories of early nineteenth-century feminism as defined by Karen Offen (2000): relational and individualist feminism. This is partly because Wright is a socialist and partly because she is a philosopher. She is caught between two histories of feminism. Her socialism does not fit in well with the relational/individualist dichotomy of histories of feminism, and further, such histories of feminism leave little space for a feminist thinker who was primarily a philosopher. On the other hand, despite continued feminist work in revising the history of philosophy, Wright has been left out of the history of philosophy, even our new feminist revised canons.

Wright is similar to Catharine Beecher in that the interconnected structure of her theory is an actual part of the political and moral foundation of her theory. In Beecher's case, her theory has an ethico-religious foundation, and this connectedness comes out in her approach to writing. In Wright's case, this connectedness is produced through her version of utilitarianism and her "synthetic" approach to writing philosophy; Wright offers a revised version of utilitarianism and a philosophical system that combines both canonical theorizing as well as the mainstream and radical theorizing of her contemporaries. Like Beecher, Wright offers empowerment for women, but without the restraints of Beecher's religious moral world, Wright is able to offer a full and potent empowerment. However, just as the coauthorship of Wheeler and Thompson or the "nonphilosophical" works of Beecher do not "fit" well into mainstream approaches to the history of philosophy, so I shall find that these mainstream approaches cannot fully accommodate Wright's work or allow us to recognize its philosophical interest.

I am going to argue that one of the reasons for Wright's neglect by modern philosophers (feminist or otherwise) is that her work does not conform to the "patrimonial" model of philosophy that underlies mainstream approaches to the history of philosophy. Wright offers a philosophical system founded on a synthesis of several philosophies that are typically viewed as competing positions, and her system is aimed at producing concrete social and political change. Reading Wright on the patrimonial model of philosophy I identified in the introductory chapter will ultimately mean that we categorize Wright as not writing "true" philosophy, as her thought is not "autonomous" in the sense that its questions and topics are not distinctive to the discipline of philosophy; writing philosophy that is not "pure" in the sense that it is aimed at producing social change; or as a philosophical failure, in the sense that it lacks originality, theoretical purity, and simply does not correspond to our "story" of the history of philosophy as comprising opposing views and positions.

Yet we need not lose Wright as a potential foremother. We can see Wright as writing both within her historical and cultural context, *and* as having something to "say" to the modern feminist philosopher without falling into the discourse of timeless questions and problems. The individual components of Wright's philosophy probably have little use for us, but Wright leads us to a way of thinking about how feminist philosophy should look: a complete system. Most of us work in particular subfields or areas; few of us offer a fully worked out system. Through Wright we can learn how this system should look: it will need to be interconnected with the explicit dismantling of disciplinary silos—metaphysics, ethics, and so forth—that we have adopted from contemporary mainstream philosophy. More crucially, Wright's philosophy can function as an example of an alternative picture of philosophy to the patrimonial picture.

Wright offers us a theory focused on female empowerment, and indeed, one that will also bring about race and class empowerment. In the Wheeler and Thompson chapter I argued that the "Is it true?" question of the mainstream philosophical approach to the history of philosophy is not well suited for feminist philosophy; instead, I argued that we should ask "Does it [the theory/text/philosophy] empower women?" With Wright we can see what a genuinely empowering theory or philosophy would look like. We will then be in a position to examine critically, in the following chapter, the supposedly feminist work from the canon of John Stuart Mill, Jeremy Bentham, and James Mill.

Frances Wright's Life and Early Writings

Most of the secondary literature on Wright, thus far, has been in the form of either biographies or accounts of her role as the first female rhetorician in the United States; there has been little analysis of her feminist thought or of her thought more generally as philosophical thought. The major biographical works on Wright are Celia Morris Eckhardt's *Fanny Wright: Rebel in America* (1984); Paul S. Boyer's "Frances Wright" (1971), in *Notable American Women*; William Randall Waterman's *Frances Wright* (1967); and A. J. G. Perkins and Theresa Wolfson's *Frances Wright, Free Enquirer: The Study of a Temperament*.[1] None of them places Wright's activism or writings within the historical feminist movement and they rarely contain commentary on the philosophical foundations for her activism or written work. On the one hand, this lack of analysis is perhaps not surprising as Wright led an exciting life, in which she aimed to put her social and political ideals into practice through her Nashoba colony and promulgate these beliefs through her lecture tours. On the other, it is surprising as Wright self-identified as a philosopher as well as a reformer, and her lectures contain a systematic—if not particularly original— philosophy that grounds her feminism.

Frances Wright was born in 1795 in Scotland. Orphaned before she was three years old, Wright and her younger sister, Camilla, were brought up by their aunt. Wright found life with her aunt too restrictive, and both sisters went to live with their uncle, James Mylne, when Wright was eighteen. A professor of philosopher, Mylne was a liberal thinker who, among other things, was a utilitarian. It was during this time spent at her uncle's house that Wright took part in discussion groups on literature and philosophy and began writing herself. Wright wrote poetry, which is not particularly notable, and a play, *Altorf* (1819), that was later performed in the United States. More significant, Wright wrote a short treatise on Epicurean philosophy, which was later published as *A Few Days in Athens* and dedicated to Jeremy Bentham, the English utilitarian philosopher.[2]

In *A Few Days in Athens*, Wright discusses subjects that became part of the foundations of her later philosophy: namely, knowledge and the connection of virtue to pleasure. She argues for the Epicurean view that there is only one law or principle of action—pleasure—and claims that virtue is the highest pleasure, although other pleasures are also necessary to attain happiness. Wright explains through the figure of Epicurus that we should search for knowledge, and that the best knowledge is that which makes us more virtuous and happy, and which also makes us able to help others become virtuous and happy. This best knowledge is knowledge of ourselves. This knowledge is not the same as erudition, nor is it likely to be taught to us; indeed, Wright's Epicurus states that "the first and last thing I would say to man is, *think for yourself*" (1822, 12). What is particularly interesting about *A Few Days in Athens* for any analysis of Wright's later thought is her glowing portrayal of Epicurus's female disciple, Leontium, who outshines the other (male) disciples in both intellect and character, and Wright's claim that Epicureanism is open to everyone, not just philosophers. Both of these things point to her beliefs, fully expressed in her later work *Course of Popular Lectures*, that knowledge should be equally accessible to all and that women were as intellectually capable as men.

In 1818 the Wright sisters left for the United States, as Wright wanted to see what she later described in her autobiography as a new country of free individuals. During this period Wright wrote a series of letters describing her impressions of and travels in America. These letters, published in 1821 as *Views of Society and Manners in America*, are often a eulogy to the people, government, and social order of her adopted country. There are few instances of the more caustic writing style of her later works and little of the criticism that can be found in Wright's major work, her *Course of Popular Lectures*. It would seem that Wright is so excited by her new experiences and so disdainful of the "Old World" that she almost wills herself to see nothing but the best on her travels. The *Views* is certainly a fascinating travel document, but given Wright's biases, it does not serve well as a historical artifact. The *Views* does contain the four central topics—women's situation, slavery and race relations, education, and religion—that reappear in Wright's later work; however, there is little of the criticism that characterizes her lectures ten years later.

In the *Views* Wright clearly recognizes that women as a group are subordinated by men. She says that men naturally have multiple advantages; however, she criticizes men for reinforcing their sense of superiority through the maintenance of the weakness of women: "The vanity of the despot and the patrician is fed by the folly of their fellow-men, and so is that of their sex collectively soothed by the dependence of women: it pleases them better to find in their companion a fragile vine, clinging to their firm trunk for support; than a vigorous tree with whose branches they may mingle theirs" (1821, 427). Despite these comments, however, Wright is loath to criticize the situation of women in the United States. She claims that American women are treated in all social classes with gentleness and courtesy, and states that "much certainly is done to ameliorate the condition of women" (428). Wright praises the fact that, unlike Englishwomen—who are taught to see "the other sex a race of seducers rather than protectors, and of masters rather than companions"— American women are in charge of their own virtue (424). Although Wright's later notoriety stems in great part from her anti-marriage stance, she appears to have no concerns about the institution of marriage in the *Views*; indeed, apart from a footnote on the need for reasonable (i.e., nonrestrictive) divorce laws, she seems to romanticize American marriage. Even though Wright does suggest that Americans marry too early for them to have become knowledgeable enough to be good parents, she says that she cannot actually criticize early marriage as it seems to bring such happiness to both parties. Perhaps most surprisingly of all for the woman who was condemned later in life for her advocacy of sexual freedom for women, Wright admires the modesty in dress of American women.

Historical evidence shows that Wright was incorrect in her assessment of the situation of American women; while early nineteenth-century American women may have experienced different forms of patriarchal oppression from Englishwomen, their level of subordination ultimately differed little. The key to why Wright appears to be so willfully blinkered to the situation of American women is her belief in the correlation between the condition of women of a certain nation and the morality of that nation. Modesty in dress, according to Wright, is a reflection of the attitudes of a nation, not just an individual, whereas the fact that American women are in charge of their own morals reflects the fact that the country itself has high moral standards. In other words, as long as Wright continued to believe that the United States had more or less achieved its moral values of liberty, equality, and the pursuit of happiness, she was unlikely to hold up a critical lens to the situation of women.

The same resistance to critical analysis due to a romanticization of American life is present in Wright's account of American slavery. She places the blame for the existence of the institution on England, claiming that the early colonies even tried to pass laws that would prevent slavery but that England forced it on them. Further, Wright is prepared to believe the claim that Virginia slave owners are humane in their treatment of their slaves. Wright claims that in the North there is little of what is nowadays termed racial prejudice, and states that white Americans have been unfairly maligned for their treatment of black Americans. Indeed, she says that there is a "gentleness" of "feelings" toward freed slaves, and that black Americans in the North are neither treated like second-class citizens nor do they consider themselves to be so (1821, 71). While Wright recognizes that there is still segregation in the North, she argues that it is surely better to focus on the way that racial barriers are breaking down. Given the state of race relations even in the twenty-first century, it is hard to imagine that Wright's observations are even remotely accurate.

Although Wright, obviously, is disgusted by the system of slavery, she does not believe that simply freeing slaves is the solution. As we shall see, her later justifications for her plan to abolish slavery are grounded in her philosophical views. What is interesting in her early ideas expressed in the *Views* is how much she has accepted stereotypes about black Americans and how some of her beliefs about the capacity of black Americans to succeed as freedmen are little different from those of Southern slave owners. Wright holds that black Americans are a distinct race, a claim she based not so much on their physical characteristics but on "their greater laxity of morals" (76). Moreover, she holds that simply freeing slaves will not succeed, as they would not understand the (moral) value of liberty—"to give liberty to a slave before he understands its value, is, perhaps, rather to impose a penalty than to bestow a blessing"—and supports this by claiming that the ex-slaves of Maryland and Virginia are the most miserable and vice-ridden among black Americans

(518). Where Wright differs in her views from Southern slave owners is that she thinks that black Americans have the natural right to liberty and that their moral character can be improved with education.

Wright's interest in education is evident in the *Views*. She praises New England, in particular, for its system of public education, where "every child, male or female, black or white is entitled to a plain education" (417). Wright does recognize, however, that this education is not necessarily the same for girls and boys, and therefore she argues for educational equality. Wright's justification for the equality of education for women is that it will benefit the nation as a whole, in particular because properly educated women would be able to use their role as mothers to develop the national character. Here Wright appears to be relying on a "feminized utilitarianism" to make her argument: the goal of educating women is not so much for themselves but for the benefits to the entire community (Travis 1993, 394). In her closing comments on the status of women's education, Wright says that her correspondent may think she is about to propound "a Utopian plan of national education," but she says that she will leave this to the United States to do (see 1821, 430). Given that only a few years later Wright did herself produce just such a plan, one wonders whether the goal of producing this plan was already fermenting in her mind.

Considering that Wright was later condemned for her critique of religion and the church, her comments on religion in the *Views* are surprisingly mild. Her criticisms are reserved for the Church of England and certain sects that prey on the weak and ignorant, especially black Americans: "I suspect that the doctrines, or, more properly, absurdities of these wild fanatics, are what chiefly arrest the mental advance of the negro in these northern states, and form one of the minor causes which prevent that of the [Native American]" (216). Wright praises religious freedom in the United States and the fact that different sects flourish in a quiet and unassuming way: "Where religion never arms the hand of power, she is never obnoxious; where she is seated modestly at the domestic hearth, whispering peace and immortal hope to infancy and age, she is always respected, even by those who may not themselves feel the force of her arguments. This is truly the case here" (439–40). In her later years Wright did become far more critical of religious belief itself as well as the institution of the church. While part of this can be attributed to the influence of such people as Robert Owen, it would also seem that the increase in criticism is due to Wright's own, now fully worked out, philosophical system.

Upon its publication in England in 1821, Wright's *Views* were the target of the criticism of Tory reviewers; however, the book was well received by the Whig press. One reviewer wrote that the "moral sublime of the American democracy was never so deeply felt, and so eloquently described, as in these 'Letters of an Englishwoman'" (quoted in Eckhardt 1984, 48). Jeremy Bentham read the book and invited Wright, who had by then returned to Britain, to meet him, and it was through him that she met some of England's radical philosophers. Her biographers do not agree on the influence of Bentham on Wright. On the one hand, Eckhardt (52), for example, describes their relationship as one of "master and disciple." On the other, Waterman (1967), for example, claims that there is little trace of utilitarian philosophy in Wright's work, and that the influence of Bentham and his circle is confined to her later practical use of the utilitarian maxim to justify her proposed social and political reforms and her freethinking and anticlerical views. As we shall see, neither account is particularly accurate. Wright's philosophy is in fact utilitarian at its core, but it is synthesized with other contemporary philosophies to produce her arguments for social equality and reform.

Typically, biographers of Wright have spent more time focusing on the influence of the Marquis de Lafayette, the French hero of the American Revolution, than on Wright's philosophical influences. Eckhardt, in particular, offers a detailed and empathetic account of Wright's relationship with Lafayette. Certainly, this relationship with the sophisticated, older aristocrat is one of the most fascinating in Wright's life; however, my concern is that too much emphasis on their relationship—which appears to have been a romantic/sexual one—can play into the criticisms made by Wright's contemporaries of her sexual immorality, and thus to see Wright's radicalism as lived only through her personal life rather than as also founded on a carefully formulated philosophical system.

It was as companions to Lafayette, however, that Wright and her sister, Camilla, returned to the United States in 1824. It was on this trip that Wright saw the miseries of slavery firsthand, when she saw a slave ship and realized the reality of the slave system: "My heart is sick. . . . I have seen [my fellow creatures] manacled when sold on board a vessel bound for New Orleans. . . . I cannot write on this subject and yet it preys so continually on my mind that I find it difficult to write on any other" (quoted in Bederman 2005, 445). It was during her tour of the United States with Lafayette that Wright encountered the Scottish reformer Robert Owen; in 1825, after her second visit to the

Owenite community of New Harmony, Wright decided to create a community for slaves to work out their freedom and be educated. Later on, Wright would claim that she was not influenced by Owen, but her letters at this time show that her ideas for the community were strongly indebted to him (Kolmerton 1990, 115). It was Wright, however, who saw the possibility of the application of Owenite principles for the abolition of slavery. Owen himself had little interest in the issues of slavery and race relations; indeed, people of color were excluded from the community of New Harmony (Perkins and Wolfson 1939, 127).

In October 1825, Wright published her "Plan for the Gradual Abolition of Slavery" in the abolitionist journal *The Genius of Universal Emancipation*. Wright's plan was to buy slaves and a farm, and use the surplus profits of the farm generated by the work of the slaves as a way for them to buy their own freedom. While working to earn their freedom the slaves would also be given an education that would prepare them for their liberty. This element clearly reflects Wright's perspective on ex-slaves expressed in the *Views*. Wright's calculation was that it would take the average slave about five years to pay off the original purchase price and overhead. The initial idea was to recolonize the slaves to, for example, Liberia or Haiti. Wright believed that as the idea spread, and thus more and more slaves left the United States, slavery itself would vanish. It would therefore seem that Gail Bederman (2005) is correct in claiming that Nashoba itself was never envisioned as a utopian colony; it was rather a means to the end of making the United States a utopia. However, by the time Wright wrote justifying the founding principles of Nashoba in 1828—in her "Explanatory Notes on Nashoba," published in the *New Harmony Gazette*—she appears to have changed position and now argues that the goal of Nashoba is to produce true racial equality through education and intermarriage. It is hard to explain this shift. Perhaps Wright did want this all along but had accepted recolonization as the only way to find supporters.

Owen's influence on Wright and the founding principles of this community of slaves will be discussed later in this chapter. For the present it need only be noted that Nashoba was a failure from the moment of its inception. Wright herself recognized that Nashoba had failed, not simply because it was in dire financial straits and had not succeeded in attracting the necessary interest, participants, and slave laborers, but also because of its failed ideals. Writing in 1844, Wright says that she had begun reform in the wrong way, for reform could not be effected by a few individuals but only by humanity as a collective. She now sees her role as educator, teaching about the advancement of human knowledge and human happiness. What is interesting about her realization is that it is the wellspring for her decision to begin a career as a public lecturer and reflects the foundational thought of the philosophy propounded in her lectures.

In 1828 Wright visited New Harmony again and began to coedit the *New Harmony Gazette*, which was renamed the *Free Enquirer* when it was moved to New York. She also began a series of public lectures, which were published as the *Course of Popular Lectures* (1829). Wright was certainly a stirring public speaker, and these early lectures were well attended; indeed, this period was the apex of Wright's intellectual and public career, when halls were filled to capacity and she would receive thunderous applause at the conclusion of her lectures (Eckhardt 1984, 185). Yet she was also excoriated for daring to step outside a "woman's sphere" and taking on the "masculine" role of public speaker: "She has leaped over the boundary of a feminine modesty, and laid hold on the avocations of man, claiming a participation in them for herself and her sex. . . . She stands condemned of a violation of the unalterable laws of nature, which have erected a barrier between man and woman" (quoted in Kolmerton 1990, 129).

After Wright finally recognized that the Nashoba experiment was a failure, she left the United States in October 1829 to take the slaves to Haiti, where they would be able to live as free men and women. She was accompanied on the journey by William Phiquepal (D'Arusmont), whom she had originally met at New Harmony. Wright became pregnant by Phiquepal and married him. According to Eckhardt's biography, Wright realized that despite her antimarriage sentiments, having an illegitimate baby would be social death for both her and the child. The D'Arusmonts lived in France until 1835, when they decided to return to the United States and Wright began to lecture again; this time, however, Wright's lecture tours were unsuccessful.

According to Eckhardt, what Wright had miscalculated was that in the years she had been in France, there had been a strengthening in hostility toward women who stepped out of their "natural" place and that Wright had come to symbolize such women; indeed, the accusation of "Fanny Wrightism" functioned as a way of discrediting liberal causes (Eckhardt 1984, 244). Whereas in Wright's earlier lecturing years she had been part of a network of speakers and organizations, she now isolated herself from these people and groups both through this political choice and through personal disputes. In short, Wright could still provoke attention, but she was no longer influential.

Wright left the United States in 1839 and lived in semiretirement until her death in January 1852. Wright's marriage, which never appears to have been particularly successful, ended in divorce in 1850. Wright's relationship with her daughter, Sylvia, also foundered after the divorce and they remained estranged. While Wright did continue her work, her lectures and publications were largely ignored. She wrote an account of her life in 1844, which offers little insight or information for a commentator seeking to understand Wright's life and thought; at its worst, the volume is what Eckhardt (1984, 275) has described as a "revisionist history." Wright spoke in public again in 1847 in London, but the content of her lectures seems to have been above the heads of her audience and the talks were not well attended.

The fact that the later years of Wright's life were intellectually fallow should not detract from the achievements of her early years, in particular the thought of her *Course of Popular Lectures*. We have two standard competing narratives of the development of an individual's philosophy. On the one hand, we have the prodigy narrative (e.g., A. J. Ayer's *Language, Truth, and Logic*) or the masterpiece narrative (e.g., Thomas Hobbes's *Leviathan*). On the other hand, we have the slow maturing to greatness (e.g., Plato). Against the background of a picture of philosophy as a trajectory of great men, such narratives make perfect sense and may not appear to be just that: narratives. Unfortunately, women have not been so easily included in either of these narratives. Prodigies and masterpieces require public recognition (and are usually associated with being a man), while maturation requires both recognition of your life's work as well as a life within which you can actually do such work. Moreover, the dramas of Wright's earlier life should also not be allowed to overshadow an examination of her philosophy, specifically the *Course of Popular Lectures*. As I discussed regarding Wheeler, there is a tendency to consider the private lives of women philosophers in ways that we do not for male philosophers—yet discussions of private lives are rarely of *philosophical* importance for *either* gender.

Course of Popular Lectures

In the preface to the *Course of Popular Lectures*, Wright outlines the reasons for her change in attitude from the *Views* toward certain aspects of American society and culture. She says that her eyes have been opened to the situation of (white) women and black Americans and that she now sees "the political anomaly and moral injustice presented by the condition of the coloured population in the slave-holding states, as well as by the feeling exhibited, and practices legally countenanced, towards that race, generally throughout the union" (1829, vi). In other words, she is talking not just about slavery in the South, but also about what we would nowadays call racism—both racial prejudice and institutional racism—in the North. For Wright, slavery is not a distinct wrong; it is, she believes, caused by ignorance and thus shares the same foundation as all other social evils, such as poverty. Given the cause of social evils, it is no surprise to find Wright claiming that "the melioration of the human condition can be reached only by the just informing of the human mind," and she sees herself as laying out the groundwork for this education of the mind in her following course of lectures (vii).

The situation of women is described as one of the two main "strongholds" in the "citadel of human error," the other being the control of the public press by people who are too ignorant or too scared to publish the truth (vii). Women's mental development and education, according to Wright, are neglected. Wright says that this leads to two things: their dependence (presumably on men), and their vulnerability to control by religion and religious leaders. Indeed, her decision to write this series of lectures was prompted by a series of religious revivals in Cincinnati, because it was "invariably women" who were "victims of this odious experiment on human credulity and nervous weakness" (viii).

This is a central point in understanding Wright's attack on religion and her promotion of true knowledge throughout her lectures. Even if Wright does not always spell out the implications for women of her philosophy, it is feminist at its core as it leads to the amelioration of the condition of women. Moreover, it is interesting that Wright sees women as the most influential half of the nation, presumably because of their influence on their children. Removing women from ignorance will also allow them to exert this influence properly; thus Wright is also offering women a form of power.

Moreover, it is clear that the change in Wright's attitude in the *Lectures* toward the situation of women and black Americans is not simply one of recognition of their situation. It is not merely that she now realizes that the public education women receive is unsatisfactory or that what we would call racism exists; rather, the change rests on a development of philosophical thought, which saw an early expression in *A Few Days in Athens*, now prompted by her personal experiences at Nashoba.

Wright's Philosophy

As I mentioned above, little has been written on Wright as a philosopher; indeed, the vast majority of the academic secondary literature on Wright is on her role as an early female rhetorician or her Nashoba experiment. It is not clear why this should be so. Her intellect was respected by Jeremy Bentham, among others; indeed, Henry Rogers, an American lecturer in natural philosophy, wrote after hearing Wright speak that she was a "prodigy in learning, in intellect and in courage, she awes into deference the most refractory of bigots" (quoted in Eckhardt 1984, 183).

The *Lectures* presents a philosophical framework within which Wright has a—somewhat rudimentary—epistemology, metaphysics, ethics, and politics. Before we are tempted to dismiss her work for not offering a fully fleshed out philosophy, we must remember that she is not writing philosophy for its own sake but for the practical goal of social change. Her ultimate goal was "*practical equality, or, the universal and equal improvement of the condition of all, until, by the gradual change in the views and habits of men, and the change consequent upon the same, in the whole social arrangements of the body politic, the American people shall present in another generation, but one class, and, as it were, but one family—each independent in his or her own thoughts, and all co-operating, according to their individual taste and ability, to the promotion of the common weal*" (1829, 216). Here it would seem that Wright is arguing for a people undivided by race, class, or gender. For Wright, there was one way and one way only that such equality could be achieved, and this was through education. However, Wright was not talking about equal access to schools and colleges; in fact, her epistemological commitments required a radical reconceptualization of what education was and how it was delivered.

The first three lectures are essential for an understanding of Wright's philosophy; the other lectures are either expansions on the topics raised in these three, or discussions of practical political and social changes that come out of her basic philosophy. In the first lecture, "On the Nature of Knowledge," Wright explains that knowledge is not what is taught in schools; rather it is "acquaintance with ourselves" and "with all things to which we stand in relation" (7). We obtain this knowledge through observation, specifically, our senses and "our faculties, as awakened and improved in and by the exercise of our senses." For Wright, the truth or falsity of our opinions rest on the truth or falsity of the evidence they are based on; in other words, "just opinions are the result of just knowledge" (5). If we later discover that our opinions were incorrect, then it is because we did not do a proper initial investigation or there is a problem with our recollection of our sensory perceptions.

Despite the fact that knowledge is discovered through the senses of individual knowers, what we discover will agree with that of others: "As we can only *know* a thing by its immediate contact with our senses, so is *all knowledge compounded of the accurately observed, accumulated, and agreeing sensations of mankind*" (13). Moreover, the goal of knowledge is not just to improve ourselves but to ameliorate the human condition, and thus knowledge should be shared. We can benefit from the knowledge of others, although—for us—this will not be knowledge. For Wright, the distinction between what she calls true knowledge and what she calls belief is that in the latter case we are basing our opinion on the observations of others. This belief will be stronger or weaker depending on such factors as the known veracity of these other observers or whether they are reporting their own immediate experiences of those of a third party.

The immediate consequence of Wright's view is its effect on the content and delivery of education. If knowledge is acquired through the senses, then students will learn through practical demonstrations in which they can hear, touch, and see. If they are taught through lectures then they will only believe, not know. This also means that the different disciplines will be divided into two groupings—those of knowledge and those of belief—with the study of chemistry, for example, classified under knowledge and that of history under belief. It is interesting to note that Wright is mistrustful of those who are currently educators because she believes that they are unlikely to question the material they teach, as they do not want to lose their jobs.

Wright's introduction of the issue of education for women and her own authority to lecture publicly is subtle. The third category of mental content—aside from true knowledge and grounded belief—is prejudice: unquestioned or badly grounded beliefs. She says, however, that we are reluctant to question our prejudices. She then claims that those who are outraged by her speaking in public are prejudiced, presumably because they cannot accept that a woman can have knowledge or should be able to teach or lecture. Truth, Wright counters, does not have a sex. What is interesting is that she also implies that women have a great deal of influence over the destiny of the human race. Truth itself may be sex-neutral, but it would appear that Wright is hinting at something more than equality of access to education for women. She states that the growth and equality of access of knowledge is the only means to ameliorate the condition of humanity and says that she believes that "my sex and my situation tend rather to qualify than to incapacitate me for the undertaking" (16).

Rather unhelpfully, Wright does not elaborate on this comment. What does she mean by her situation actually being a qualification for the task of social change? It is unclear. Given that this claim is immediately followed by a criticism of the current education system and other methods of disseminating information, such as learned journals, she may be claiming that the fact she has *not* had the "proper" education is a point in her favor, as she has fewer layers of prejudice or misinformation to peel off and is more likely to cast aside her own prejudices, since they do not come from supposedly reputable sources, such as college professors. Wright's claim that her biological sex is also a qualification would seem to reiterate her belief that women have an important role to play in the task of enlightening humanity; this belief is made more explicit in the second lecture.

Even though Wright claims that her discussion of women is incidental to her discussion of knowledge and education, she returns to the subject of women again at the end of the first lecture, saying how happy she is that there are so many women in the audience. This prompts a lengthy discussion of gender relations. Wright criticizes the way that women are encouraged to remain ignorant. She claims that women's lack of knowledge keeps men in control, and thus men deliberately keep their wives and daughters in ignorance in order to "make the better servants and easier playthings" (21). Given the content of Wright's discussions about women and the time she spends on this issue in the first lecture, it would seem that her inclusion of a discussion about women is anything but incidental. Rather, it would appear that the ways she includes her comments on women are more likely to be rhetorical strategies aimed at not immediately alienating her audience.

The second lecture, "Of Free Enquiry Considered as a Means for Obtaining Just Knowledge," expands on Wright's claim that just knowledge comes from "a judicious education and a free spirit of enquiry" (21). Wright soon returns to the issue of educating women, and now she is less cautious in her claims than in her previous lecture. This time she states clearly that the improvement of the human race depends on the improvement of the situation of women: "Let women stand where they may in the scale of improvement, their position decides that of the race. Are they cultivated?—so is society polished and enlightened. Are they ignorant?—so it is gross and insipid. Are they wise?—so is the human condition prosperous. Are they foolish?—so is it unstable and unpromising. Are they free?—so is the human character elevated. Are they enslaved?—so is the whole race degraded" (24). For Wright, women influence the human race, not only through their children but also through their lovers and husbands.

Clearly, then, Wright believes greatly in the influence of women, but as we shall see, this influence is a far cry from the "feminine" moral influence of Catharine Beecher's women. Moreover, while Wright may appear to be agreeing with a popular view among nineteenth-century reformers, such as James Mill or Charles Fourier, that social progress could be measured by the level of women's emancipation, there is more going on here. According to Wright, there is something about men that allows them to be easily controlled by women: "Men will ever rise or fall to the level of the other sex; and from some causes in their conformation, we find them, however armed with power or enlightened with knowledge, still held in leading strings even by the least cultivated female" (31). It is not clear whether men are controlled through their sexuality by their wives and mistresses or whether they are just generally weak willed in the presence of women. Either way, Wright comes to the radical conclusion that if only one sex is to be enlightened, then it should be women, not men; indeed, she even makes a claim for the superiority of women, as they are "by far the most important and influential" half of the human race (24). These views would seem to answer Wright's claim in the previous lecture that her sex was a qualification for lecturing her audience on the truth.

Wright is not simply offering a utilitarian argument that educating women will benefit the human race, nor is she arguing that women should replace men in the social hierarchy. The betterment of the human race will come about only through collective engagement with the work of inquiry, and Wright states emphatically that this can come about only when humans work collaboratively as equals. Here Wright is not just talking about sexual equality, she is also talking about racial (and class) equality. For Wright, equality of education is foundational to equality and equal rights: "Equality! where is it, if not in education? Equal rights! they cannot exist without equality of instruction" (25). Here Wright means that we cannot exercise our equality of rights without this equality of instruction; moreover, Wright argues, without equality there can be no liberty.

For Wright, it is freedom of inquiry that will lead us to understand and respect these rights of liberty and equality, and the rest of the second lecture is devoted to the praise of free inquiry and an examination of its benefits. It is here that Wright shows her debt to Enlightenment thinking; indeed, there are even echoes of Kant's essay on Enlightenment in her connection of knowledge and freedom and her call for fearless inquiry.

The third lecture, "Of the More Important Divisions and Essential Parts of Knowledge," is deceptively titled. Wright has shown us "the nature and object of just knowledge" and the means for obtaining that knowledge—free inquiry—and she states that she will now turn to a discussion of "those parts or divisions" of knowledge with which we should be most concerned (38). What follows, however, is far more than a discussion of the different branches of knowledge, such as physics, as Wright establishes her account of morality within her metaphysics and epistemology and initiates her criticism of organized religion.

Knowledge, for Wright, falls into two categories: knowledge of ourselves and knowledge of the world around us. In the first category she places anatomy, physiology, and the natural history of humans. The second category she calls "physics," and this includes astronomy and animal biology as well as what may properly be called physics. Once we have knowledge of these things, then we may study, for example, history, since we are now in a position to judge what we are told about history in relation to what we know about the nature of man and the world and thus to judge whether we should believe what we are told. Her basic account of knowledge and its acquisition is now complete, and Wright is free to pursue the implications of this account, specifically, how religious "knowledge" and moral knowledge fit into it.

Wright on Religion and Moral Philosophy

Wright's critique of religion begins in the third lecture and is then a frequent central theme in her other lectures. For Wright, what the clergy teach is not truly knowledge, as it is "knowledge" of things we cannot see. Unlike physics, or even history, there are no facts we can observe about heaven or angels. Even those supposed historical facts from the Bible are about miraculous events that contradict our experience of how the world works. Wright's criticism of religion, however, is not simply grounded on her epistemology; she sees religion as the enemy of the free inquiry she believes is central to the acquisition of knowledge, and she urges her audience to substitute priests and preachers with "experimental philosophers" as teachers (46). Interesting enough, Wright's criticism of religion is also practical. She points out that $20 million is spent each year in the United States on the existing religious system, a lot of money that gives little knowledge and produces hysterical fanaticism instead of reasoned inquiry. Wright recognizes that her opponents will argue that we need religion to give us a rule "to regulate our actions, frame our opinions, chasten our feelings, and render the term of our existence one of utility and delight," but she argues that this rule can be found under the "the science of human actions or of human life": morals (71).

Wright's moral philosophy is introduced in the third lecture when she imagines an interlocutor claiming that moral knowledge falls outside the scope of her account of knowledge, as moral truths appear to our feelings, not our senses. Wright responds that we have a sensibility toward the pains and pleasures of others; we first learn to distinguish pain from pleasure in ourselves, and this sensibility then allows us to estimate the feelings of others. Here Wright is offering a form of moral sense theory. Further, Wright claims, it is the "beneficial or injurious consequences of actions [that] make us pronounce them virtuous or vicious." In other words, actions that produce pleasurable sensations are deemed good and those that produce painful sensations are deemed bad; the "man of cultivated sensibility then refers his sensations and applies his experience to others, and sympathises in the pain or the pleasure he conceives them to feel" (49–50). Wright is clearly writing here as a utilitarian. In this way, Wright can claim that moral truths are based on fact: they are grounded on human physiology and psychology.

This somewhat simplistic utilitarianism and moral sense theorizing is made more interesting by the way Wright bases it in her metaphysics and epistemology. For Wright, we are part of a whole; the elements of our bodies may change but they will always be part of the matter of the universe: "We stand, in our very nature, allied and associated with the air we breathe, the dust, the stone, the flower we tread; the worm that crawls, the insect that hums around us its tiny song, the bird that wheels its flight through the blue ether, and all the varied multitude of animal existences, from the playful squirrel to the lordly elephant." Once we see ourselves as part of the world in this way, "how calculated to awaken our intellectual faculties and excite our moral feelings! Our sympathy is attracted to every creature, our attention to every thing. We see ourselves in the midst of a family endlessly diversified in powers, in faculties, in wants, in desires; in the midst of a world whose existence is one with our own, and in whose history each mode of being is an episode" (39).

Wright's account of morality, or what she calls the "science of human actions or of human life," is further developed in the fifth lecture (71). Continuing with her notion of the interconnectedness of humans, she states that the standard notion of dividing actions into those that affect only ourselves and those that affect others is nearly impossible to make. Wright argues that nearly any action we consider cannot be seen independently of its effects on others and the effects of these effects rebounding back on ourselves. She claims that the only actions that truly just affect ourselves are those that involve "the gratification of the appetites appertaining to our nature" (78). A careful calculation of the costs to ourselves of the gratification of these appetites will show us that there is a middle path of temperance between overindulgence and unhealthy self-denial; here Wright takes a stance that is clearly influenced by Enlightenment thinking when she claims that our passions need to be governed, not denied, and that reason has the power to keep our passions in check.

Wright continues to maintain in the fifth lecture that we have a natural principle of sympathy for others, and she now wants to show that this view is in accordance with what she sees as the view of many philosophers—presumably she is thinking especially of Bentham here—that individual self-interest lies at the foundation of morality. Wright is able to synthesize these two views by arguing that "self-love and self-interest, rightly understood . . . always lead to justice, beneficence, gentleness, truth, candor, and indulgent toleration" (79). She says that if we calculate the consequences of our actions we can see that selfish enjoyments are brief, whereas pleasures we share with others or that we give to others remain in our memory and give pleasure whenever we are reminded of them, even if these pleasures also contain a loss of pleasure or inconvenience to ourselves. Thus rational calculation of our self-interest means we will promote the happiness of others. For Wright, there is something more to morality that is "better than any process of reasoning" and "which prompts us to spring forward to the relief of suffering" (79–80). We also have an emotion, "variously called by philosophers the moral principle, emotion, faculty, or sympathy," which leads us to actively seek the pleasures of others, even at times in preference to our own (80). Despite the power of this emotion, Wright still maintains that it should not be the sole guide to moral action; instead, moral action should be directed by our intellect.

This moral faculty is to be developed through education, and thus we can again see how education is the cornerstone of Wright's philosophy. Properly educated, the human race will develop morally, eschew the superstitions of religion, and respect the equal rights and liberties of others. Wright is clear about the interconnections of equal rights, the development of the moral faculty, and education: "Equal rights must originate in equal condition . . . equal condition must originate in equal knowledge, and that sound knowledge . . . in similar habits, and those good habits . . . in brotherly sympathies" (217). According to Wright, the foundation for these sympathies and habits will be a system of national education, one that will be for rich and poor, male and female, black and white.

In this way, we can see that Wright's moral philosophy has utilitarianism as its core, which she then synthesizes with moral sense theory and Enlightenment notions of the relation between reason and passion. Viewed through the lens of mainstream history of philosophy, this synthesis is potentially problematic. As we saw in the introductory chapter, the history of philosophy has become framed as one of competing positions or sects—even if these are not in reality as much in tension as our historical narratives tell us they are—and thus there is little space for a philosophy that combines competing "isms." As I shall show, it is not really whether supposedly competing views can be combined or synthesized that is the difficulty; rather, it is the underlying picture of philosophy, specifically its "purity" and its ideals of originality, that is at stake here.

I would argue that the fact that Wright's philosophy is primarily one of synthesis should not be seen as a weakness. What we shall see is that Wright's can be interpreted as a feminist philosophical approach, one that aims for interconnections among different perspectives and theories, rather than the critique of opposing views in order to maintain one's own as the "winner." Moreover, we can also draw on Wright's philosophy to develop what I am offering as a feminist interpretive lens or perspective for the history of philosophy.

Before we can understand Wright's feminist philosophy, however, we need first to understand her feminism. Most commentators have either seen Wright as merely arguing for equal education for women, which does not make her particularly original, or have focused solely on the problematic issue of Wright's rejection of the institution of marriage and her championing of "free love." Neither approach does justice to the complexity of Wright's feminist thought, a complexity that comes out of her thought's philosophical foundation.

Wright's Feminism

Wright's feminism does not fit neatly into either of the categories typically associated with nineteenth-century feminism. At first it may seem that Wright is an Enlightenment feminist in the tradition of such figures as Mary Wollstonecraft. While Wright, like Wollstonecraft, holds that the two sexes are physically different, she believes the mind is gender-neutral—and that this trumps mere physical differences—and any apparent differences in the psychology of the two sexes is due to training, environment or education. For example, Wright holds that "the mind has no sex but what habit and education give it" (quoted in Waterman 1967, 74). Moreover, she claims that it is the duty of parents to treat their daughters in the same way as their sons "as *human beings*," for they share the same basic nature (quoted in Waterman 1967, 53).

Offen (2000, 90) has characterized this type of feminism as one where women's liberation is understood as "the ethical self-realization of the individual beyond the constraints of sexual identity or 'spheres.'" Indeed, it would appear that Wright is so entrenched in this view that she does not offer much to women beyond an education that will produce this ethical self-realization. She appears to accept that even though education will make women knowledgeable and moral beings, they will not enter into the public sphere. What is remarkable here is that Wright—despite her own public career as a journalist, lecturer, and newspaper editor—does not offer any kind of proposal to change the opportunities offered to women, once educated.

Yet Wright also appears—at least initially—to hold views similar to what Offen calls relational feminism. As we have seen, Wright contends that women—as women—have a moral/social power to influence the progress of humanity. Yet, even though Wright appears to maintain this fundamental difference between the sexes, she does not subscribe to the typical conclusions of relational feminism: namely, that motherhood is the way that women exert this influence, and women have a gentle "nature" that is complementary to men's stronger one. Instead, it would appear that Wright believes that men have the weaker nature and women the stronger; men's nature means that they are susceptible to the control of women, not just as mothers or wives but as—Wright even goes so far to say—lovers. Moreover, Wright rarely mentions motherhood, and when she does, it is not to sentimentalize the role but rather to ask whether parents (both mother and father) are fit for the moral responsibility of raising a child properly.

Wright does not seem to be either a purely relational or an individualistic feminist; thus it is perhaps not surprising that she has not figured prominently in histories of European or American feminism, as she is outside the mainstream of the movement. Discussions of Wright's feminism are more likely to be found in works focused on Owenism or the socialist movement more generally.

There is little doubt that Robert Owen was strongly influential on Wright's feminism. Barbara Taylor in *Eve and the New Jerusalem* (1984), an analysis of Owenite feminism, sees Wright's visit to Owen's New Harmony community in 1824 as a turning point for her feminism. Even though she was heavily influenced by his ideas, Wright was not simply repeating Owen's views on marriage and sexuality. Owen himself was not particularly feminist in that his criticisms of marriage were not aimed at alleviating the particular oppressions experienced by married women; instead, he believed that marriage caused unhappiness for both sexes and he argued for the sexual liberation of both.[3] As we shall see, much of the impetus for Wright's criticism of marriage was—unlike Owen's—a recognition of the restrictions and servitude of married women.[4]

Wright followed Owen in arguing that women should be as free as men to experience sexual pleasure; however, Owen grounded his arguments on a variety of sexual theories, including the view that children conceived in unhappy marriages would be physically inferior, whereas Wright focused on a rejection of patriarchal codes of morality that prevented women from experiencing this pleasure or—once broken—led to prostitution or promiscuity: "Ignorant laws, ignorant prejudices, ignorant codes of morals . . . condemn one portion of the female sex to vicious excess, another to as vicious restraint" (quoted in Eckhardt 1984, 156).[5] Further, for Wright, the enjoyment of sexual relations (controlled and rational, obviously) for both men and women brings happiness and therefore is good, since whatever promotes human happiness is virtuous. Thus Wright's views of women's sexuality and her rejection of patriarchal marriage come naturally out of her utilitarian philosophy.

The Community at Nashoba

What then were Wright's views on family life, communal living, and the relations between the sexes? The publication of selections from the Nashoba journal in *The Genius of Universal Emancipation* was a defining moment in both the fortunes of Nashoba and Wright's reputation as a free love advocate. It occurred during a period when Wright had left the community to recover her health and had left her sister, Camilla, and James Richardson in charge. The inflammatory passages published from the journal were those that dealt with the sexual relations between members of the community. One of the male slaves had attempted to sexually assault one of the female slaves, Isabel. Camilla refused the request of the female slaves, Nelly and Isabel, to have a lock put on the door to protect them from future attempts at assault. Her justification was that a lock was inconsistent with the doctrine of Nashoba, which held that "the proper basis of the sexual intercourse to be the uncon-strained and unrestrained choice of *both* parties," and that this doctrine, once enforced, would give "to every woman a much greater security, than any lock can possible do" (quoted in Waterman 1967, 116). A few days later Richardson announced that he was going to live with Mamselle Josephine, a daughter of Mamselle Lolotte, a free African American woman brought in to manage the school at Nashoba.

Upon questioning by Charles Wilkes, an old friend and erstwhile supporter of Wright's, Camilla responded that she disapproved of marriage itself, "which I regard a not only in the utmost degree irrational, in requiring of two individuals to love each other during life, when they have not the control of their affections for one hour, but in the highest degree pernicious in com-pelling these individuals to continue united, when the feelings that brought them together may not only have changed, but, as I have know in several instances, have turned to utter aversion" (quoted in Waterman 1967, 118). Camilla attributed these views to Wright and states that Wright was prevented from publishing them only because of her current illness.

Wright herself wrote to Richardson stating her concern that he saw fit to publish the journal. If they were to change and improve the world, she said, it would have to be done slowly, without deliberately provoking those who would oppose them. Part of Wright's concern is that the founding principles of Nashoba deserved "a statement temperate in its language and complete in its reasoning," and she asks whether it is really advisable to launch them "naked and defenseless in the midst of the enemy leaving to that enemy itself the task of developing them." She points out that "all principles are liable to misinterpretation but one so much as ours. If good taste and good feeling do not dictate their expression and guide their practice they will fall into . . . contempt" (quoted in Waterman 1967, 121). These comments are key to understanding Wright's feminism. Yes, she certainly held radical views on marriage and sexuality, but what made these views distinct from those held by Richardson or other radicals, or even Owen himself, was that Wright held that her principles must be explicitly grounded in reason and justifiable through argument. In essence, then, Wright's views were those of a philosopher as well as a social reformer.

For the modern reader, Camilla's (and Wright's?) complete lack of comprehension of the sexual vulnerability of the slave women is unconscionable. Moreover, even though Richardson may have genuinely believed he was breaking down racial barriers in his relationship with Mamselle Josephine, his actual actions—living with but not marrying a woman of color—continued the race/gender/class privileges long exercised by white men in the South; no doubt Mamselle Josephine herself would have far preferred the economic security and social status provided by marriage, and one wonders just how much the relationship with Richardson was freely entered into on her part.

For Wright's contemporaries, however, it was not just Wright's actual and supposed views on marriage that were shocking, but that Nashoba was grounded on principles of *both* sexual and racial equality. Moreover, in her "Explanatory Notes on Nashoba" (1828, Feb. 6, 133), Wright went so far as to suggest that the racial problem in the United States could be solved through the amalgamation of the races: "the olive peace of brotherhood be embraced by the white man and the black, and their children, approached in feeling and education gradually blend into one, their blood and their hue."

What were Wright's philosophical principles that underpinned the Nashoba colony? Was Camilla Wright's understanding of her sister's views accurate? After her return to the Nashoba colony Wright published her "Explanatory Notes, respecting the Nature and Object of the Institution at Nashoba, and of the Principles upon Which It Is Founded: Addressed to the Friends of Human Improvement, in All Countries and All Nations." This was written on board her return ship from Europe and is dated December 4, 1827, and it was published in the *New Harmony Gazette* in 1828.[6] In these "Explanatory Notes" (1828, Feb. 6, 132) Wright sets out her reasons why the institution of marriage and the marriage law had no role to play at Nashoba.

> No woman can forfeit her individual rights or independent existence, and no man assert over her any rights or power whatsoever beyond what he may exercise over her free and voluntary affection; nor on the other hand, may any woman assert claims to the society or peculiar

protection of any individual of the other sex, beyond what mutual incli-
nation dictates and sanctions, while to every individual member of
either sex is secured the protection and friendly aid of all.

The tyranny usurped by the matrimonial law over the most sacred
of the human affections, can perhaps only be equalled by that of the
unjust public opinion, which so frequently stamps with infamy, or condemns to martyrdom the best grounded and most generous attach-
ments which ever did honor to the human heart, simply because
unlegalized by human ceremonies, equally idle and offensive in the
form and mischevious in the tendency . . .

Let us correct our views of right and wrong, correct our moral lessons, and so correct the practice of rising generations! Let us not teach
that virtue consists in the crucifying of the affections and the appetites,
but in their judicious government! Let us not attach ideas of monastic
chastity, impossible to man or woman without consequence frought
with evil, nor ideas of vice to connexions formed under the auspices of
kind feelings. Let us enquire, not if a mother be a wife, or a father a
husband, but if parents can supply to the creatures they have brought
into being, all things requisite to make existence a blessing!

Wright is saying that marriage law—as it stands—takes away freedom from
women and puts men in power over them. The community will protect and
look after all its members, and thus women do not need marriage as a means
of protection. It would appear that women's need of protection is the way
that women have some kind of power or control over their male partners.
But Wright is not just talking about personal liberty; she also wants to talk
about freedom from societal or popular prejudice: so-called morality. She
claims that popular opinion condemns relationships grounded on affection
that are not sanctioned by the marriage law. For Wright, sexual relations—
and the enjoyment of these relations—between men and women outside marriage are not in themselves wrong; it is uncontrolled and irrational sexual
relationships that are morally problematic. For Wright, morality is simply
what promotes human happiness, and she stated in "Explanatory Notes" (as
well as in her later *Course of Popular Lectures*) that whatever promoted happiness is virtuous and whatever prevented or countered it was vicious. In other
words, Wright's utilitarianism is a core principle in her critique of marriage
and her defense of freedom of sexual relations.

Wright's views on marriage are directly connected to her more general discussion in "Explanatory Notes" on liberty and happiness, and again Wright's utilitarianism is at the heart of this more general discussion.[7] Wright claims that *"men are virtuous, in proportion as they are happy, and happy in proportion as they are free"* (Wright 1828, Jan. 30, 124). According to Wright, however, people are currently restricted by societal conventions and conditions that prevent them attaining happiness and virtue: society is divided artificially into classes, with some people living a life of luxury and ease and others a life of physical hardship and labor. The economic success of a country is not measured by how many individuals are wealthy, but rather the mass of wealth in commercial circulation; public opinion prevents the cultivation of individuals and the development of classes. Finally, talented and independent women remain childless (and thus do not benefit the development of the race), as they do not want to enter into an oppressive marriage and public opinion forbids them to have children outside marriage: "In what class do we find the largest proportion of childless females, and devoted victims to unnatural restraints? Certainly among the cultivated, talented and independent women, who . . . shrink equally from the servitude of matrimony, and from the opprobrium stamped upon unlegalized connexions" (1828, Feb. 6, 133).

In the United States, political liberty has been obtained, but true freedom—"universal in all the objects it embraces and equal for all classes of men"—will come only with moral liberty: "the *free exercise of the liberty of speech and of action*, without incurring the intolerance of popular prejudice and ignorant public opinion" (1828, Jan. 30, 124). With this moral freedom, people can then rationally inquire into their institutions and remove the prejudices, institutions, conventions, and structures that stand in the way of happiness and virtue: "The means shall be sought, and found, and employed to develope [*sic*] all the intellectual and physical powers of all human beings, without regard to sex or condition, class, race, nation or color." Ultimately, people will learn "to view each other as members of one great family, with equal claims to enjoyment and equal capacities for labor and instruction, admitting always the sole differences arising out of the varieties exhibited in the individual organization."

Thus it would appear that Richardson and Camilla Wright had grasped the basics of Wright's views of sexual relations and race relations; however, their understanding appears to be limited in that they did not understand—or chose not to repeat—the grounding principles of equality and liberty that are so central for Wright herself. Moreover, they also appear to have missed the fact that Wright's views on marriage and race relations are part of a larger utopian vision for a country of free equals connected by fellowship. I would argue that underpinning this vision is Wright's own version of utilitarianism. The moral goal of this utopian vision is human happiness, which is measured in proportion to human freedom. Following the classical utilitarianism of Bentham, all humans are to count as equal in the attainment of this goal; the happiness of one group of individuals is not to be allowed to count as more than that of another. Where Wright differs from more standard utilitarian thought is that this happiness cannot be achieved without a recognition not just of human equality but of our interconnectedness with one another. We do not act or live in a metaphysical, epistemological, or moral vacuum; our actions, lives, and searches for knowledge all have consequences for the happiness of others.

It is fascinating that Wright's critics and even some of her more sympathetic commentators fail to see the philosophical grounding of her rejection of marriage. It is certainly true that Benthamite utilitarianism has been critiqued for its foundation in human pleasure, but these critiques did not bring out the implications of his utilitarianism for human sexual relations. In Wright's case, however, her critics were unable to see beyond her views on human sexual relations, namely, her reputation as an advocate for free love and the blending of the races. For example, consider William Leete Stone's reaction in the *New York Commercial Advertiser*: "She recommends the encouragement of early prostitution . . . condemns and discards altogether the marriage contract and in effect recommends transforming this glorious world . . . into one immeasurable brothel" (quoted in Eckhardt 1984, 187). Yet it is hard to see how Wright earned this reputation when she said relatively little on the subject and she herself married. Her views certainly remain implied in the *Course of Popular Letters*, but there is little doubt that these are lectures on philosophy. It was only as a reaction to the problems of Nashoba that Wright explicitly expressed her free love views.

In short, it would seem that it is because of Wright's gender that criticism of her was focused on sexuality. The unfortunate consequence of this for commentaries on Wright is that her opponents have been allowed to dictate the discourse. Consequently, Wright's feminism is discussed mainly by modern (pro-Wright) commentators for her views of free love, while little is said about its philosophical underpinnings or her feminist thought more generally; yet the *Course of Popular Lectures* and the circles she moved within show her to be a philosopher first and foremost.

What then of Wright's philosophy? I think a case can be made that she is offering not simply a philosophy that leads to feminist conclusions, but a feminist philosophy. In order to make this claim, however, I need to be able to explain what I mean by this in a historical context—specifically, a nineteenth-century American context.

Wright's Philosophy, Feminism, and Feminist Philosophy

There is little doubt that Wright's philosophy draws from many sources; one commentator summarizes her philosophy in the following way: "Wright's philosophy was primarily synthetic. . . . The ideas behind Nashoba and her first lecture tour were compounded of Owenite anti-marriage and anti-religion themes, the utilitarianism of Bentham, the rationalist empiricism of Adam Smith, the common-sense philosophy of Thomas Reid, the feminism of Mary Wollstonecraft, and the antislavery feelings of British Whiggery" (Connors 1999, 39). Added to this, Wright herself said that Nashoba's foundational principles of moral liberty and equality were those of William Godwin (Eckhardt 1984, 151).

Wright uses her utilitarianism to bring together these disparate strands. At its core Wright's utilitarianism, as we have seen, is Benthamite: vice and virtue are understood in terms of pleasure or pain, and good or virtuous actions are those that produce pleasure. However, Wright adds to Benthamite utilitarianism in two main—but interconnected—ways. A standard criticism often made of utilitarianism (or any form of consequentialist philosophy) is that it can lead to some kind of moral paralysis in our attempt to consider or calculate all the possible consequences of an action, or in our recognition that a seemingly harmless act can have distant problematic consequences. What is interesting about Wright is that recognition of this interconnectedness of our actions is a cause not for paralysis, but rather for moral education and maturity. This is then linked to her second addition to Benthamite utilitarianism: her view that we have a natural principle of sympathy for others. Recognition of our interconnectedness will further this principle, and—in its turn—this principle allows an understanding of our interconnectedness. Wright herself recognizes the divergence of this principle from Benthamite utilitarianism and—as we have seen—aims to show that this principle of sympathy is compatible with Benthamite individual self-interest.

I would like to claim that these two divergences from Benthamite utilitarianism—and Wright's attempt to bring them together—constitute something more than a mere synthesis of Benthamite utilitarianism with other philosophies; rather, Wright can be seen to be developing a perhaps rudimentary form of *feminist philosophy*: not a philosophical system that merely leads to feminist conclusions or reforms, but one that is feminist in its actual structure. Wright's attempt to interconnect the different philosophical elements she draws on is itself feminist—or at the very least, non-patrimonial—in that she is eschewing an "adversarial" picture of the history of philosophy: one where there are "winners" and "losers." Moreover, in offering a synthesized philosophy, Wright is implicitly rejecting the patrimonial picture of philosophy as a series of competing isms, which demands that we must take a position on one ism or another.

Instead, and in keeping with her view of truth, Wright wants to make connections between the different elements of philosophical thought that appear true to her—or more specifically, that will bring about social change. Here, her philosophy is not a completely autonomous enterprise. In other words, it does not fit the dominant Anglo-American model of how philosophy "is." Moreover, and again in contrast to the patrimonial picture, her philosophy is not autonomous in that she draws on both philosophical theory and empirical data about the situation of women and African Americans. Indeed, given her concept of knowledge, she cannot do otherwise than build her theory on empirical data. I am hesitant to say that her philosophy of connection comes out of a "woman's perspective"; rather, it would appear to come out of Wright's own version of utilitarianism: hers is a philosophy of interconnections, both among human individuals and in terms of its philosophical structure.

So what do I mean when I claim that Wright is offering an early form of feminist philosophy? As I argued in the chapter on Catharine Beecher, reading for empowerment in historical feminist works requires a level of ethical and political involvement on the part of the interpreter. We can—if we want—take an approach similar to the mainstream philosophical approach and read Wright for content similar to modern feminist philosophy, albeit content placed within its historical and cultural context, but we can also read Wright for a "conversation" based on similar political and social goals. Obviously, this latter conversation between the modern reader and Wright is asymmetrical as it takes place across the centuries, but it is an important trope as it brings out both our relationship with these texts and figures as one in which we are part of a community of knowers with ethical and political responsibilities toward these texts and figures, as well as the need for self-consciousness about our own goals of the equality and empowerment of women.

The core difference, on my working definition, between feminist philosophy and mainstream philosophy is that the former does not claim to search for knowledge for its own sake, but rather for the sake of a political goal: resistance to, and elimination of, the subordination of women. Using this definition, Wright's thought can be identified as an early form of feminist philosophy; it is fundamentally a social philosophy designed to bring about social change, not just for women but also for the other oppressed groups of working-class and black Americans. Wright is demanding the inclusion of the interests of these groups, and part of her ultimate goal is to give them moral agency and political empowerment.

In addition to her social philosophy, an early form of feminist philosophizing can be found in her metaphysics and epistemology. Modern feminist epistemologists have pointed to the way that women have been excluded from access to knowledge or have been labeled as incapable of knowledge in some way. Wright was an early precursor of this view; moreover, she takes it further, stating that denying women access to knowledge prevents the progress of the human race. Wright is not here arguing for some kind of "feminine" epistemology: she is not saying that there is some special "women's knowledge" or "woman's way of knowing" that will be added to the sum of human knowledge.

Wright's epistemology is at its heart part of the traditional "masculinist" enterprise criticized by feminist philosophers. The ideal knower on this tradition is a solitary individual who obtains knowledge independently of other knowers; again, as with moral philosophy, this knower reflects the experiences and ideals—not of humans in general, but of middle-class, white Western males. However, Wright shares with some (but not all) modern feminist epistemological projects two elements: that knowledge has a political goal and that knowledge itself is ultimately accumulated agreement among the community of knowers. Like some modern feminist epistemologists, Wright does not hold to the rigid dichotomy that is traditionally drawn between pure knowledge and the political values of the knower. For Wright, knowledge for its own sake is not the ultimate goal; rather, knowledge must be shared, and the ultimate goal of knowledge is the amelioration of social injustice. Even though Wright's knower is not the situated knower of modern feminist epistemology, her knower does not generate a universal account of knowledge in the traditional manner.[8] Traditionally, it is only through being free of one's particular concrete situation that we can generate a universal account of knowledge. For Wright, not only are we accumulating knowledge for the sake of others as well as ourselves, but we must not conceive of ourselves as separate from the world around us. It is through agreement with others that we can generate a universal account of knowledge, and it must be remembered that—for Wright—this agreement is a collaborative enterprise conducted among equals.

There is also implicit in Wright's metaphysics a rejection of the traditional masculinist, value-neutral, objective ideal from which we must understand reality. This ideal of intellectual detachment is something that has been critiqued by modern feminist philosophers. Wright merely shows that we are part of the reality we observe; she does not move toward the modern feminist claim that we are particular materially and socially situated selves.

Once we see Wright's work in this way, it brings to the fore elements of her feminist view that would otherwise be overshadowed by an emphasis on her views of free love and marriage; both her critics and her supporters have tended to focus too strongly on Wright's sexual morality. In fact, there is proportionately little said about marriage in the *Lectures*. Instead, Wright's argumentative goal is equal education—the accessing of true knowledge—for women. Further, while she specifically identifies women more than other groups, Wright holds that social inequalities will be dismantled only through collective inquiry into knowledge, which—in its turn—will require a system of national education that will produce the foundation of a sense of interconnectedness with our fellow creatures.

Where Wright differs from other early feminists in her belief that education will bring about social justice is that she is not simply arguing for education for white women of the upper or middle classes (as does, for example, Mary Wollstonecraft). Where she also differs from most other early feminists is that she grounds her views on education on a philosophical structure, which leads to Wright's radical conclusions about the equality of the races and classes, not just the genders. Indeed, Wright's ethics, epistemology, and metaphysics could not lead to any other conclusion. Thus Wright's work is a fascinating amalgam of nineteenth-century feminist thought, with its emphasis on education as the solution for women's subordination, and a harbinger of modern feminist thought with her recognition that all oppressed groups—not just women—need to work together to bring about social justice. Indeed, it would not be implausible to call Wright the first feminist philosopher.

Ultimately, Wright's own version of utilitarianism lies at the core of her philosophy. As we have seen, Wright's utilitarianism is one of interconnectivity among humans. What is often seen as a problem for classical utilitarianism—moral totalitarianism, if you like—is something that Wright sees as a strength for her view of morality. On her account, "there is a wrong and a right way of doing every things; a wrong and a right way of feeling everything; a wrong and right way of saying everything. We are therefore moral or immoral at every moment of our conscious existence" (Wright 1829, 76–77). This notion of interconnectivity among humans plays out in her ethics, epistemology, and metaphysics. Moreover, I want to argue that this notion also plays out in the structure of her philosophical system, specifically in the way she synthesizes different philosophical views together. Her epistemological and moral goal is to find truths that will lead to the development and thus happiness of the human race. We are to work together to find these political, social, moral, and practical truths.

Given my criticisms of mainstream approaches to the history of philosophy, can I legitimately claim that Wright was an early feminist philosopher? Although I do not argue that Wright preempted the work of modern feminist philosophers, my claiming of her as an early feminist philosopher is grounded on the possibility of a conversation between Wright and us moderns. Obviously, as I mentioned above, I do not literally mean a conversation; rather, I am using the notion of conversation metaphorically or as a trope. For if we cannot allow this conversation to take place, it would seem that we lose our potential foremothers. In other words, it seems that I am assuming that there are certain similar elements between her philosophy and our modern philosophy that allows for this conversation to take place, so it may seem that I am utilizing some form of the philosophical approach, albeit a more "interested" one than is typical.

What exactly allows this conversation to take place? Is it truly "timeless" questions or problems about gender equality or social justice? Is it an agreed-on set of disciplinary standards or criteria? Surely, the ability for us to have a conversation with Wright is not generated by our reading her work through the lens of these questions or standards; rather, Wright's work *itself* produces the conversation. We do not so much read Wright historically from our current vantage point—Wright allows us to read *forward*. Wright shows us that knowledge—specifically, knowledge that will bring about social and political change—is an interconnected, collaborative enterprise, in this case, interconnected and collaborative across time. As Wright states, this interconnected, collaborative enterprise requires self-consciousness about the ethical and political dimensions of all our actions. I would argue that this claim can be applied to our feminist theorizing, whether it is our own modern theorizing about feminist philosophy, Wright's own historical theorizing, or our modern interpretations of her historical theorizing and texts. Thus what I am calling our conversation with Wright (or other historical figures) takes places within this interconnected, collaborative enterprise.

Wright offers a synthesis of competing philosophies, and in so doing she is offering us a different view of philosophy from the patrimonial picture. For Wright, we are to work together to discover philosophical "truths"; however, one central element of the dominant Anglo-American picture of philosophy is the philosopher as lone thinker, a paradigm that is distinctly masculinist. In some ways similar to the solitary (male) artistic genius, the "true" philosopher is one who demonstrates the mistakes of previous theorizing and produces "his" own distinct system that furthers philosophical knowledge. Janice Moulton has called this way of constructing philosophy adversarial because it requires the identification of other philosophers and their views as opponents, which lies in sharp contrast to Wright's synthetic, cooperative view.

We also saw the patrimonial picture in the Wheeler and Thompson chapter as one tied into mainstream epistemology with the knower as a solitary individual, whether in the rationalist or the empiricist tradition; an individual free in ways that women culturally and materially have not been—free of the hindrances of the emotions, the body, or other historical particulars. On the patrimonial picture, this is how the solution to philosophical problems is, or is supposed to be, achieved. In Wright's case, however, solutions to philosophical problems, which are also social and moral problems, are resolved through cooperation and require a political and ethical awareness of both one's motivations and the consequences of one's actions.

It is the fact that Wright's philosophy is a synthesis of other, supposedly competing, schools of thought that should make us question the paradigms used in mainstream histories of philosophy. We can certainly identify what Wright said, but at a meta-level her philosophy does not fit into our mainstream pictures of the history of philosophy, either philosophical or historical. Whether we take philosophers to be answering permanent problems, whether we see the history of philosophy as a series of sectarian battles, whether we take the history of philosophy to be about choosing a position or about grouping philosophers into classifications, there is little room for a synthesizer.

It is here that we may find part of our answer to why Wright has been ignored as a philosopher. Certainly, the focus on Wright's radical views on sexuality has drawn attention away from the examination of Wright as a philosopher, but her neglect by philosophers, including feminist philosophers, may also stem from our picture of the history of philosophy. Wright may not seem worthy of examination because it appears there is nothing "original" about her philosophy, nor is it theoretically "pure." It comprises—among others—moral sense theory, utilitarianism, Owenite socialism, and Enlightenment rationalism. Yet I would argue that this expectation of originality and theoretical purity is part of the patrimonial picture of the history of philosophy. Further, synthesis of potentially competing theories may be seen as muddled thinking; as we have seen on the adversarial model, one theory must emerge as the "winner." Another part of our answer as to why Wright has been ignored as a philosophy would seem to stem from the fact that she does not treat philosophy as an autonomous discipline; rather, she draws on empirical data to create an argument for social and political change, and her work is wrapped up in, and generated by, the social issues of her time. Moreover, the knower is not an autonomous individual, but one among a collaborative group of knowers who hold themselves responsible to the subjects of their theorizing and the way this theorizing is done. Here again, the issue of the purity of philosophy is played out, albeit in a different way.

In the previous chapters I argued that the question that should be asked of historical works is "Does it empower women?" In Wright's case, the answer would appear to be a resounding "yes" if we mean "Would it empower her contemporaries?" Leaving aside some of her more extreme claims about the power of women, empowerment will come about through education. This is not the weak empowerment of most nineteenth-century feminism in that it is not simply an individual empowerment. Wright saw, unlike many of her contemporaries, that offering women equal education is not particularly empowering if nothing else changes; equal education may lead to individual development, but not much else.

Yet it may still be hard to remove ourselves from the binary thinking common to mainstream history of philosophy. Does the fact that Wright's philosophy would empower her contemporaries mean that it cannot empower "us"? Given the differences in our social and political situations, the answer would appear to be that it cannot. Perhaps we need to broaden our notion of empowerment, however, and not make it so strictly a replacement for the "Is it true?" question. I do not want what I am offering as a feminist perspective for doing the history of philosophy to be simply modeled on mainstream approaches with women or gender just somehow thrown in; there needs to be a political component that reflects the fundamental political goal of feminist philosophy. The "Is it true?" question asks for content and arguments we can use for our modern philosophizing. The "Does it empower women?" question need not just be about argumentative content. It can also be about whether it stirs passion, pride, anger, or other politicized emotions in the reader that leads to a change in their way of thinking. Surely, then, there is something empowering about Wright's philosophy, namely, her way of writing and the interconnective and collaborative nature of Wright's enterprise as a whole. More significantly, Wright makes us recognize our epistemological, ethical, and political responsibility as members of a community of knowers, a sense of responsibility that is a necessary accompaniment to empowerment.

Beecher, Wheeler, and Thompson can give us some of the building blocks for the feminist interpretive lens for the history of philosophy I am aiming to offer, but it is Wright who can offer us the core foundation. Specifically, we can learn from Wright's interconnective and collaborative epistemology. We search for our feminist foremothers as part of a collaborative enterprise they and we share to empower women and to bring about social justice. We look for connections between their work and between their work and ours. Our goal is to search for Wittgensteinian family resemblances, not traceable trajectories of great thinkers. Yet this is neither anachronistic nor committed to the claim that gender justice is a timeless problem. Approaching texts and philosophies looking for connections means that we are abandoning the patrimonial view of the history of philosophy as a series of competing views, and thus that philosophy must be done (or is best done) in an adversarial manner. We no longer read texts *just* for what they contain, or for what they add to our discussion of timeless problems, but for what we can learn politically and personally from these texts. With the empowerment question we are placing a political and practical goal at the heart of the enterprise of the history of philosophy, not historical accuracy or timeless truths. Ultimately, as we saw with Catharine Beecher, we are broadening our notions of what philosophy is and how it is to be done.

Even more crucially, Wright's philosophy *itself* can offer an idea of how an alternative—feminist—picture of philosophy to the patrimonial picture might look, although I am *not* suggesting that this is the only possible alternative. Wright's picture is one of the (constantly) ethically and politically self-aware knower who collaborates with a community of like-minded others to produce political change. This knower is linked to others by shared political goals and a shared sense of responsibility to one another, those goals, and those whose lives he or she wishes to change. On this picture, commitment and responsibility are inherited as much as ideas, positions, or texts.

We can then extrapolate from this alternative picture of philosophy an alternative way of approaching the history of philosophy for us moderns. I have argued for the fruitfulness of using an empowerment question for early feminist philosophical texts. The sort of picture of philosophy we can draw from Wright can provide the theoretical foundations for this question. In brief, we both read for political and social change in a work and bring a political and ethical self-consciousness of our role as interpreters and intellectual grandchildren of these early feminists.

To ask whether I am offering a distinct methodology or a truly new question is perhaps to miss the point, although this question is something I am careful to discuss further in the final chapter. As I said in the introduction, I am not interested in arguing that mainstream approaches to the history of philosophy should be overturned or dismissed completely—that is to remain within the patrimonial picture of philosophy. Indeed, if my "new" lens or perspective—the empowerment question—seems to share elements with mainstream approaches, I am not overly concerned; after all, the sort of alternative background I am proposing is open to synthesis and collaboration. I shall return to this discussion in the final chapter, but first I want to use the empowerment question in a different way. Instead of using it to argue for the feminist philosophical elements of someone's thought and to recapture forgotten or neglected philosophers, I want to show that it can be used to critique the supposed feminism of canonical figures.

Notes

1. Thanks to Lori Ginzberg for identifying these sources. See Ginzberg 1994.

2. In reviewing Wright's biography here, I have drawn on the work of Eckhardt, Waterman, Perkins and Wolfson, and Kolmerton. Without their exhaustive research on the life of Wright, I would not have been able to write this section.

3. According to Taylor (1984, 297), Owen argued in several instances that women needed the help of those whose moral qualities and intellectual capacities were more fully developed (presumably middle-class men) in order to organize for their own liberation.

4. It would appear that Owen himself thought that Wright had gone too far in her views of relations between the sexes. According to James Mylne, Wright's uncle, Owen said to him that she had gone "to much more extravagant lengths than he himself who as I have long known has very little limit to his extravagances" (quoted in Eckhardt 1984, 146).

5. See Taylor 1984 for a discussion of Owen's views of sexuality that ground his rejection of marriage.

6. Information found in Waterman 1967.

7. The following is based on Waterman 1967, 125–27.

8. The concept of the situated knower means that the historical particulars of the knowers, such as their embodiment, relationships with others, and social status, affect both their access to knowledge and the way their knowledge claims are expressed, justified, and accepted as authoritative.

4 TEA AND SYMPATHY WITH JOHN STUART MILL

I now want to use the interpretive lens of the empowerment question, which is admittedly still in its embryonic stage, to examine the works of Western *canonical* philosophers who have been claimed as feminist rather than neglected, forgotten, or misinterpreted. I believe that this type of application will allow me to develop the feminist perspective for doing the history of philosophy I want to offer. In this chapter I turn to canonical nineteenth-century (male) philosophers who have written on the subject of women. I briefly discuss claims that James Mill and Jeremy Bentham held feminist views, and I show that these claims are questionable. My central reason for discussing the elder Mill and Bentham is to demonstrate the way that modern commentators' use of the mainstream approaches to the history of philosophy, and the underlying "patrimonial" picture of philosophy of these approaches, have defined the discussion of the feminism of both James Mill and Bentham.

I focus primarily on John Stuart Mill, specifically his work *The Subjection of Women*. Mill has been praised for his feminism, and *The Subjection* has been seen as a—perhaps *the*—major work of nineteenth-century philosophical feminism. I argue that modern commentators have misunderstood Mill's work, in part because it has been interpreted employing the philosophical approach to the history of philosophy. Using the admittedly still skeletal feminist or empowerment question to the history of philosophy I have sketched out, I am able to resolve the tensions modern-day feminist commentators have seen in *The Subjection*. More specifically, I demonstrate that the work is not about the empowerment of women. Somewhat more controversially, I argue that, ultimately, *The Subjection of Women* is as much a work about the moral requirements for the English in their role as "civilizing" colonialists as it is a work about the liberation of women; indeed, *The Subjection* may have been mistakenly placed in what could be called the feminist "canon."[1]

The Standard View of Bentham's Feminism

Until recently, the feminism of the canonical utilitarian philosopher Jeremy Bentham was not in dispute. The standard account of Bentham's feminism is best exemplified by Mary Mack in *Jeremy Bentham: An Odyssey of Ideas, 1748–1792* (1962). Mack states that "Bentham was a covert feminist, eager to put the untapped brains and energy of women to use but wary of deep prejudices" (112). She claims that "few social facts angered him more" than the situation of women, and states that "throughout his entire life he deplored their inequality. The waste of so enormous a reservoir of potential intelligence was profoundly non-Utilitarian" (323).

Mack assesses Bentham's actual support of women in the following way:

> In the area of women's rights, eighteenth-century England was still bar-barian. Everything remained to be done. At the same time, Bentham was well aware how little could be done. Few social issues were more boring to the public or more deeply submerged in prejudice, as he con-tinually observed, from the early *Principles of the Penal Code* to the *Con-stitutional Code*. Open ardent feminism was an ideological luxury that Bentham could not afford. All the same, he did what he could to further the equality for women. As early as the 1770s he offered a "Proposal for the restraining of the male sex from the exercise of certain trades: in favour of purity of manners, and of the employment of the female: Staymakers, Hairdressers." (323)

In sum, Mack's claim is that Bentham was a feminist who, at least in part, was critical of the situation of women because it was a waste of potential resources for the greatest happiness; however, he did not actively work for the right of women to vote or for other measures of equality, as he held that "violent and universal" prejudice against women's equality or suffrage would have doomed any attempt from the start (416).

While it will not determine the question of Bentham's actual feminism, these sorts of arguments in support of a claim for his feminism need to be eyed critically. First, Mack is attributing a form of "feminized utilitarianism" to Bentham. Even though Mack is focusing on the contribution to society women could make due to their intelligence, a gender-neutral attribute (rather than through a typically "feminine" capacity, such as nurturing), she is still mounting an argument based on women's usefulness to the community instead of one based on the injustice of keeping equally intelligent beings in a position of subordination.

This approach is vulnerable to standard criticisms made of classical utilitarianism, the most obvious being that there is nothing about Mack's interpretation of Bentham's views that would prevent women remaining subordinated if it could be shown that this promoted the greatest happiness overall. Once we look more closely at Bentham's writings on women, however, we shall see that Mack has oversimplified his view, and thus pursuing this line of criticism may not be particularly productive.

What are we to make of Mack's approach itself to interpreting Bentham's feminism? While it will become clear that evidence of Bentham's feminism can in fact be drawn from his philosophical works, Mack is employing a "psychological" approach to the history of philosophy to explain why Bentham did *not* follow through on his beliefs. According to this strategy, the investigator focuses on the psychological factors that led an individual to hold they ideas he or she did. As we saw with Anna Doyle Wheeler, while we are certainly interested in these factors, they are not particularly germane to any philosophical interpretation or evaluation we intend to accomplish. Psychological factors can potentially explain the causes that led to a philosopher's ideas, but they cannot explain the *philosophical* reasons, nor does knowledge of these causes aid us in any attempt to make a judgment about those ideas.[2]

At first, it may also seem that Mack is taking a historical approach in that she places Bentham's work within its historical–cultural context; however, she does so in order to explain why Bentham was never an active proponent of women's rights. Yet, even if we allow that Mack is describing but not evaluating at this point, she is incorrect about the social context. Judging by the amount of literature published on the situation of women, the relations between the sexes, and women's "nature" during the centuries before Bentham was writing, the topic of "women" was one of extreme fascination not just for popular writers but for philosophers, too. In fact, it is more likely than not that Bentham's philosophical forefathers (and foremothers) wrote on women.

Thus Mack's arguments for Bentham's feminism seem rather outdated and lacking in evidence compared with the level of work done on analyzing the feminism of canonical figures in the last couple of decades. Indeed, much has changed in the discussions of Bentham's feminism since Mack was writing. I think Mack's arguments are worth including, however, so that we can see the variations in the ways that the history of philosophy is being done and how narratives about historical figures become written and developed in ways that reflect social, political, and philosophical changes.

Ball, Boralevi, and Bentham

Bentham's reputation as a feminist was first questioned in the 1980s by Terence Ball. Ball's work is in many ways typical of historical interpretive scholarship from the later twentieth century; this interpretive work often aimed at critiquing the misogyny of canonical figures or identifying them as potential feminists. Ball (1993b, 230) identifies the two main reasons for Bentham's categorization as a feminist: "his defense of women's suffrage and his dissent from the anti-feminist stance of his foremost disciple, James Mill." As we saw in the chapter on Wheeler and Thompson, Mill had argued in his 1820 essay "Government" that women could be excluded from political rights, since their interests were involved with that of their fathers or husbands. According to Ball, Bentham argued that Mill has not offered any actual reasons for the exclusion of women, and—on the contrary—the utilitarian principle requires that the interests and happiness of women be considered equally to that of men. Moreover, Ball claims that Bentham appears to move beyond this claim of formal equality between the sexes to argue that—because women are more subject to physical pains and weaknesses than men—women should be given more political power than men. Ball quotes Bentham as stating that in relation to this deficiency on the part of women, "the principle of equality affords another reason, not merely for admitting the female sex to an equal share in the constitutive, but even to a greater share than in the case of the male" (231). Further, Ball claims that Bentham holds that not only is the enfranchisement of women required by moral—that is to say, utilitarian—principle, it also will produce a practical good: the amelioration of the present social situation of women.

Thus far Ball agrees that Bentham's reputation as a feminist appears to be justified. However, Ball then argues that—ultimately—Bentham arrives at the conclusion that women should not be given the vote: the same conclusion as

James Mill. The first reason Bentham gives, according to Ball, is one of expediency. Bentham states that "the prepossession against their admission is at present too general, and too intense, to afford any chance in favour of a proposal for their admission" (quoted in Ball 1993b, 232). Ball claims that Bentham's argument here falls foul of his own "fallacies of delay": the procrastinator's argument—"Wait a little, this is not the time"—and the snail's pace argument—"One thing at a time! Not too fast! Slow and sure!" (quoted in Ball 1993b, 233).

The second reason Ball finds in Bentham for denying the vote to women is a question of principle. Ball takes this principle, quite naturally, to be that of utility and he turns to Bentham's *Introduction to the Principles of Morals and Legislation* (1780) for an explanation. Ball (1993b, 233) claims that, essentially, Bentham holds in this work that there are *innate* differences in women's nature that make "her less able than men to make rational political judgments—that is, decisions based upon the principle of Utility." Ball quotes Bentham as saying that women are more inclined to superstition than men are—"that is, to observances not dictated by the principle of utility"—and that women have a tendency to have sympathies only for their immediate families rather than a more abstract sympathy for humankind, and thus that women are less able to think in the moral terms required by the principle of utility (quoted in Ball 1993b, 233–34). In order to make this argument, Ball requires that there be slippage between Bentham's views on women's (utilitarian) moral judgment and the capacity required to vote, and that Bentham hold certain aspects of women's intellectual and moral nature to be fixed. We shall return to these points with Lea Campos Boralevi's response to Ball.

According to Ball (1993b, 234), Bentham is not simply prepared to deny women the vote, he is also prepared to prevent them from "serving on juries, holding public office, and even from attending parliamentary debates." The central reason Bentham gives for these added restrictions is that women will prove a sexual distraction for men. Bentham also deals with women's situation in the home. According to Ball, Bentham reinforces the status quo of men in that he sees them as holding a parental power in relation to their wives, except that men can also demand sexual services from a wife that a father cannot demand from a child; Bentham certainly is not calling for male tyranny, but he does not believe in sexual equality in the home. Thus Ball concludes, drawing on a wide variety of sources, that "Bentham's reputation as a feminist is almost entirely without foundation" (237).

Lea Campos Boralevi has been the main critic of Ball's argument that Bentham's feminism is a myth. Boralevi's central point is that Ball has not dealt with Bentham's comments on women or women's suffrage in chronological order. She claims that what may appear to be conflicting views when seen piecemeal become evidence of an intellectual evolution when seen relative to the time and order in which they were written.

Boralevi's main point of contention with Ball is whether Bentham justified the exclusion of women from political rights on principle as well. She finds Ball's use of *An Introduction to the Principles of Morals and Legislation* to be arbitrary as this work was written in 1780, many years before Bentham became interested in women's rights. Moreover, she claims that Ball has misinterpreted Bentham in claiming that Bentham held in this work that women were unable to make political judgments. Boralevi argues that Bentham was talking about religion, not politics. She does not directly tackle Ball's claim that women's type of partialist moral thinking makes them unsuitable candidates for utilitarian moral agency; however, she makes a strong case that Bentham thought women's moral biases toward chastity and modesty were socially constructed. From there we can extrapolate, on Boralevi's behalf, that partialist moral thinking could also be the result of the social environment in which women found themselves.

For the moment I will follow the interpretive approaches of both Boralevi and Ball and ask "What exactly *does* Bentham say?" In the passage under dispute (1780, 35.25), Bentham is discussing differences in the quantity of sensibility in women. He does claim that women are more inclined to religious superstition; however, contrary to Ball's interpretation, religious superstition is not connected to political judgment. The crucial point in this passage is why Bentham thinks women are more prone to superstition. He says this is because of women's physical and moral differences from men:

> The health of the female is more delicate than that of the male: in point of strength and hardiness of body, in point of quantity and quality of knowledge, in point of strength of intellectual powers, and firmness of mind, she is commonly inferior: moral, religious, sympathetic and antipathetic sensibility are commonly stronger in her than the male. The quality of her knowledge, and the bent of her inclinations, are commonly in many respects different. Her moral biases are also, in certain respects, remarkably different: chastity, modesty, and delicacy, for

instance, are prized more than courage in a woman: courage, more than any of those qualities, in a man. (1780, lvi)

Looking carefully at this passage, Boralevi appears correct that Bentham is not making claims about women's innate nature. Bentham's final comment about gender differences at the end of this passage reinforces this point, as he states in the case of "pecuniary circumstances" that women are "in general less independent" (lvii). It would be hard to imagine Bentham thought that women's economic situation came out of an innate nature. However, even though Bentham does not appear to see these differences as unchangeable, he is clear that they affect women's ability to follow the principle of utility: "In general, her antipathetic, as well as sympathetic biases are apt to be less conformable to the principle of utility than those of the male, owing chiefly to some deficiency in point of knowledge, discernment, and comprehension." Certainly it is possible to see this as an implicit call for the amelioration of the situation of women: depriving women of intellectual growth deprives them of their ability to follow the principle of utility and thus moral agency and the possibilities of contributing to the betterment of society. Unfortunately, Bentham does not actually make this claim here or anywhere else.

Boralevi does agree that Ball makes good points in his discussion of Bentham's claim that women should be excluded from attending parliamentary debates, from serving jury duty, and from holding political office, and she acknowledges that this exclusion limits Bentham's feminism. Finally, Boralevi interprets Bentham's comments on family life differently from Ball. She holds that Bentham was not a revolutionary, but points out that we should not expect him to be so. He was a reformer, however, and "many of his proposals can be reduced to a list of clauses, to be inserted in the laws which were directly concerned with the condition of women, in order to protect them from the abuse of masculine power, which for the moment appeared impossible to overthrow" (Boralevi 1993, 251).

Boralevi's conclusion, therefore, is that despite certain limitations, Bentham can be claimed as a feminist because he recognized that women's nature was not fixed and could be altered by changing society, and because he produced strong arguments for women's enfranchisement. Based on the strength of her argument and her attention to the detail of Bentham's writings, Boralevi would appear to have the upper hand in the debate. Indeed, Jim Jose in "Contesting Patrilineal Descent in Political Theory" (2000, 160) states that Boralevi has "definitively refuted" Ball.

Now that we have clarified whether Bentham is worth considering as part of the feminist philosophical canon, we need to ask how this conclusion was—and should be—reached. Both Ball and Boralevi appear—at least initially—to be taking a version of the historical approach.[3] As we have seen, the historical approach focuses on the identification of philosophical ideas and reasons, but "that aim is secondary and pursued only insofar as it serves an overriding historical aim. There is a fundamental emphasis on historical accuracy, faithfulness to sources, and the construction of an accurate account of the philosophical past. Philosophical enlightenment is only secondary and, when present, is considered to be precisely a consequence of the correct understanding of the past" (Gracia 1991, 235).

Both Ball and Boralevi aim for what Rorty, Schneewind, and Skinner (1984, 49) have called "historical reconstructionism." Their philosophical task is given a succinct definition by Jorge Gracia (1991, 241) as "one of description, purely objective description, purged from any element of interpretation and particularity of evaluation." This approach need not be confined to questions of historical accuracy; it can also uncover philosophical questions that have been forgotten or neglected. However, the question of the philosophical truths of purported answers to these questions is beyond the scope of the historical reconstructionists' approach. In essence, their task is conceptual translation, rearrangement of texts, and identification of influences (Gracia 1991, 243).

Thus, in the case of Bentham, it would appear that a version of the historical approach to the history of philosophy has allowed him to be categorized as a feminist or proto-feminist, albeit a conservative one. As we have seen, Boralevi builds her case through detailed reading of the texts, careful chronological tracing of Bentham's arguments, and an interpretation of Bentham's view of the nature of women that fits far better than Ball's with the views of Bentham's intellectual contemporaries, such as Mary Wollstonecraft, or recent predecessors, such as David Hume.

Yet this does not close the matter. What is interesting are the reasons why Ball and Boralevi are offering an account of Bentham's feminism. Ball wants to build James Mill into a canonical trajectory of philosophers with feminist sympathies, whereas Boralevi wants to argue that Bentham is the forefather of feminism. While the identification of influences is a worthy historical enterprise, both Ball and Boralevi ultimately leave behind the cool eye of the historical approach and move into versions of what I call the philosophical

approach when they discuss the broader justifications for their interpretations
of Bentham.

Ball, Jose, Bentham, and Mill

In "Utilitarianism, Feminism, and the Franchise" (1980), Ball raises the two
connected questions of the origins of the view that Bentham was a feminist
and how this view has been perpetuated. Ball locates the origin of this view
in the, apparently mistaken, belief that Bentham disagreed with two of his
disciples, James Mill and Étienne Dumont, who have the reputations of being
antifeminist. Bentham's contemporaries are seen as the source of this supposedly mistaken belief; both William Thompson (Ball appears to neglect the
existence of Anna Doyle Wheeler, Thompson's coauthor) writing in *Appeal
of One Half of the Human Race*, and John Stuart Mill, writing in his autobiography, state that Bentham believed in the equal political rights for women.
Ball, however, dismisses Thompson as having misunderstood Bentham's position and the younger Mill as having a "faulty" memory. Unfortunately, Ball
does not offer any support for this dismissal.

Ball then claims that Bentham's reputation as a feminist has been maintained by the belief that he was influential on John Stuart Mill's feminist
views, including Mill's work *The Subjection of Women*. As we shall see, Ball is
correct that there are major differences between the purportedly feminist
views of Bentham and those of the younger Mill. As it stands, however, the
mere existence of these differences between the views of Mill and Bentham
do not lead us to any firm conclusion about Bentham's feminism or lack
thereof.

Ball's arguments about Bentham's feminism do not take place in a vacuum;
they are part of a larger argument to demonstrate that James Mill, who is
usually seen as an antifeminist, can be—at least partially—rehabilitated as a
feminist and thus can be awarded a place in the history of feminist thought.
Ball's basic contention is that, even though Mill argued for coverture in "Government," Mill's *History of British India* has feminist implications, primarily
due to Mill's criticism of established traditions of oppressive treatment of
Indian women. Ball argues that the essay on government was simply a sketch
of political ideas, whereas the *History* was a more properly worked out
account, which offered an analysis of India judged on utilitarian principles.
Mill critiques Hindu society for the degradation of Indian women and their

dependence and infantilization, and Ball (1980, 93) claims that he finds "in Mill's criticism and condemnation of Hindu practices an implicit, and even impassioned, defence of the rights of women."

What Ball appears to be missing here, however, is that Mill's focus is to show a continued need for English supervision of India. Mill argues that the arrival of the English and their technology has undercut any economic justification for the subordination of women; their continued mistreatment is a reflection on the Indian character and culture. The question is then whether James Mill is pro-feminist or merely pro-colonialist. Jim Jose makes a similar point in "No More Like Pallas Athena" (2004). Jose argues that Mill's arguments for women's progress were for women to be raised up to be men's helpmates. While this would certainly result in improved social status for women and a lessening of social restrictions on them, Mill's intention, according to Jose, was to show "the lack inherent in Indian society, a lack that justified, even necessitated, the extension and consolidation of British rule and its concomitant social values" (7).[4]

If we ask the empowerment question of James Mill's *History*, the answer is a clear "no" to James Mill being a feminist of any kind. The only level of power he offers women is that which will benefit the ruling British power. The empowerment question allows us to examine Mill's claims in his *History* as culturally and historically embedded and thus allows us to see that Mill's focus is on British rule. Moreover, as we have seen, reading for empowerment also encourages us to consider Mill's audience. Unlike the other philosophers I have considered in previous chapters, Mill was clearly writing for an audience of male legislators and not the actual women in need of liberation. If we were to look only for an ahistorical and acultural discussion of, for example, women's rights, then it would be far easier to agree with Ball and consider welcoming James Mill to the feminist canon, or at least to consider him an ally.

What is interesting about Ball's claims about Bentham's and Mill's feminism is that it points to Ball's acceptance (conscious or unconscious) of the patrimonial picture of philosophy or intellectual thought. As I argued earlier in relation to Wheeler and Thompson, part of this patrimonial picture is the passing down of influence from male master to male pupil in a chain of inheritance. On the surface this chain of inheritance is simply an intellectual inheritance; however, there is also an accompanying, hidden inheritance of male privilege. Male philosophers can claim a privilege to write for other (male) philosophers. Even if these philosophers are criticized or placed in the opposing camp, their right to philosophy itself and their right to be called philosophers is not questioned. Thus, in James Mill's case, an intellectually threadbare set of politically contentious concerns is welcomed as a coherent, progressive philosophical perspective on women's rights.

Even though Ball does not believe that Bentham influenced John Stuart Mill, the fact that there was not this passing down of influence from (male) master to (male) pupil is seen by Ball as counting against claims that Bentham was a feminist. Indeed, Ball accepts the patrimonial picture in that he sees William Thompson and James Mill as the major influences on the younger Mill. In other words, the patrimonial picture itself is in place for Ball; other commentators merely have the wrong figures as participants in it. Ball's neglect of the existence of Thompson's collaborator, Anna Doyle Wheeler, only serves to confirm Ball's acceptance of this picture. Indeed, Ball's only references to Wheeler are as an inspiration both for Thompson's feminist views and for Mill's personal life, in that Thompson's "chaste and cerebral" relationship with her may have provided a model for John Stuart Mill's relationship with Harriet Taylor Mill (1980, 111). Yet, as we have seen, Wheeler was far more than an intellectual muse.[5]

In closing, I would like to suggest that Ball's acceptance of the patrimonial picture may have made him more open to developing arguments for the feminism of James Mill. Ball may appear to be interested in creating a new narrative of feminists, proto-feminists, or allies within the history of philosophy, but he is focusing solely on the male canon framed within the meta-narrative of the history of philosophy as a trajectory of great thinkers and their inheritors. Ultimately, Ball's arguments are simply about identifying "correctly" successors and inheritors: he questions Bentham's right to be called a feminist and bestows the title on James Mill. What we can also see, and I will develop this further in the next section, is that the patrimonial picture may lead to a history of feminist philosophy as male dominated or could even be distorted by the supposed contributions of canonical male philosophers, for certainly, James Mill was no feminist.

Bentham and the History of Feminist Thought

Returning to Bentham, even if we allow that Boralevi has shown Ball's contention that Bentham was no feminist to be unsubstantiated, this does not mean that we must automatically accept that Bentham *was* a feminist. My concern here is less to do with whether Bentham was a feminist and more to do with Boralevi's approach to reading Bentham's work that leads her to claim that he was a feminist.

Both in her response to Ball and in her later monograph on Bentham and social justice, *Bentham and the Oppressed*, Boralevi makes the sweeping claim that Bentham is the "father of feminism" (Boralevi 1984, 18; 1993, 252). In her monograph, Boralevi (1984, 18) tempers this claim a little by stating that it is to be understood in the sense "that he provided it [feminism] with its ideological weapons." However, she also adds the following claim about the feminist debt to Bentham: "The evolution of Bentham's attitude towards abortion . . . provides us with further evidence in support of the claim that some of the most important issues of contemporary feminism can be traced back to Bentham's utilitarianism." Despite their differences, both Boralevi and Ball accept the patrimonial picture of feminist thought; they simply differ as to who are the major figures on that picture.

Boralevi (1984, 23) makes her case on the "feministic implications of his utilitarian philosophy" and "historical evidence which points to his originality." The historical evidence of his influence is weak. Boralevi argues that Bentham's *Introduction*, which she relies on heavily for her discussion of his "feministic implications," influenced later feminist thinking. She holds that he influenced both John Stuart Mill's and William Thompson's feminist thinking. This claim relies for its plausibility on a simplistic understanding of the feminist views of Mill and Thompson. As should already be clear from my account of Wheeler and Thompson's *Appeal*, it is Bentham's *moral philosophy* that was the central influence on Thompson; there are few similarities between their views and conclusions on the situation of women. Moreover, Boralevi—like Ball—neglects the fact that Anna Doyle Wheeler was Thompson's coauthor.

Similarly, we shall see that there are few similarities between John Stuart Mill and Bentham. Without evidence of connections in thinking, it is hard to make the claim of the influence of one thinker on another. Boralevi's final claim is that even though Bentham did not have a direct influence on Mary Wollstonecraft, who is often acknowledged as the first feminist philosophical thinker, he contributed to an intellectual milieu in which her *Vindication of the Rights of Woman* was made possible. Here Boralevi demonstrates a lack of knowledge of the history of feminist thought. Wollstonecraft had direct, explicitly acknowledged influences like Catherine Macaulay, and feminist thought in England can be traced to such figures as Mary Astell, who wrote on equal education and the oppression of marriage in the late seventeenth century. Thus, even if we accept Boralevi's claims of Bentham's influence, we are in danger of leaving out female figures from our canon. Here I would claim that despite her aim to produce a history of feminist thought, Boralevi's tacit acceptance of the picture of the history of philosophy as one of male thinkers and inheritors produces a distorted narrative of the history of feminist philosophy.

What then are the feministic implications of Bentham's utilitarian philosophy? Essentially, Boralevi repeats in *Bentham and the Oppressed* the claims she makes in her response to Ball: Bentham was in favor of female suffrage and education; he demanded equality for women, but he recognized that women's unequal condition in society may require different treatment and he made proposals for their protection accordingly.

This is still not enough to demonstrate that Bentham is the father of feminism. At best, we can see that utilitarianism is compatible with feminism; but that only tells us something about utilitarianism, nothing about feminism. It may be tempting to say that utilitarianism requires or leads to feminism. This, as we shall see, certainly seems to be the view of Wheeler and Thompson; however, this leaves the problematic case of James Mill and his outright declaration in his essay "Government" that women should be excluded from the vote. In Mill's case, utilitarianism clearly does not require or lead to feminism.

Boralevi explores the general relationship between utilitarianism and feminism in her article "Utilitarianism and Feminism" (1987). Here she endeavors to show that historical feminism is in fact "produced by classical utilitarianism" (159). Boralevi claims that there are three dimensions of this relationship. The first is "that utilitarianism was a positivist and empirical philosophy that ignored a question which has inflamed argument for centuries: do women have souls? In doing so it excluded an important intellectual justification for the subjection of women." Equality of interests is the second dimension of the relationship between utilitarianism and feminism identified by Boralevi: "The principle of utility assumed a fundamental equality in the structure of human psychology. Women as well as men, according to this theory, have interests which should be taken into consideration." Boralevi's final dimension is her claim that "the psychological axioms of utilitarianism provided the intellectual and ideological background of feminism and offered a general view of human nature and social life compatible with the political goals of historical feminism." Boralevi supports this by pointing to the reactions of Bentham, John Stuart Mill, and William Thompson to James Mill's exclusion of women from the franchise in his essay on government. Boralevi takes their condemnation of Mill as evidence of their belief that feminism and utilitarianism were connected.

However, this historical evidence shows something only about the beliefs of early utilitarians; it does not show the level of theoretical connection that Boralevi needs to support her claim that classical utilitarianism actually *produced* historical feminism. She attempts to demonstrate this causal relation by showing that the structure of historical feminism reflects the structure of classical utilitarianism rather than the other political theories of the time. As we have seen, classical utilitarianism focused on societal reform (the vote and laws related to marriage), and this was to be carried out through legislation and education. Classical utilitarians, on the whole, did not discuss the economic aspects of the liberation of women. Boralevi (1987, 175) claims that this is mirrored in historical feminism: "Historical feminism . . . restricted itself to women's right to vote and to equal education, without touching the economic structure of Victorian society. It might be argued that this was done only for strategic reasons—so as not to appear *too* revolutionary. Nevertheless, the limits (or merits) of historical feminism were not 'strategic' but the direct ideological consequence of the limits (or merits) of classical utilitarianism."

Boralevi, therefore, is now interpreting Bentham's feminism according to a more mainstream philosophical approach. I have already questioned this approach in general as problematic for examining the work of historical feminist philosophers, so I would now like to examine how Boralevi's specific approach affects the feminist project, specifically, the field of feminist history of philosophy. The immediate problem is that Boralevi ignores other strains of early feminist thought, such as relational and socialist feminist thought, and focuses only on the dominant "liberal" strand, which does indeed connect well with utilitarianism. Thus women such as Wright and Wheeler become excluded from Boralevi's account of historical feminist thought. The deeper problem is that feminism thought itself has become subordinated to utilitarianism. Even though I have been arguing that utilitarianism need not be a male-dominated school of philosophy and that some striking female feminist philosophers were utilitarians, utilitarianism is typically identified with its leading male proponents. Not only has Boralevi done nothing to change the maleness of the historical trajectory of utilitarian thinkers, she has ensured that women can play little role in that trajectory.

Again, the patrimonial picture is at work, whether in terms of ideas or individuals. As usual, we stand to lose figures from our historical canon, such as Anna Doyle Wheeler, since making Bentham the "father" of feminism means that only those who follow his example can be "true" historical feminists. However, and more important, there is something else going on here in that we have lost ownership of a theoretical idea and a movement. This is not to say that *only* women can be feminist philosophers, but we do not want to lose our only toehold in the male-dominated canon. In what other philosophical field have women been the leaders and originators? Implicit in the empowerment question I have been asking throughout is this notion of ownership, one that stands in contrast to an unearned inheritance. Wheeler and Thompson, Beecher, and Wright all call in their different ways for empowerment for women; the relative strengths and weaknesses of these different calls are grounded on how much women are to claim this empowerment for themselves.

The disputes surrounding Bentham's feminism, or lack thereof, as well as those concerning James Mill and John Stuart Mill, also point to a troubling part of the development of a history of feminist philosophy. While we continue to dispute whether canonical philosophical figures were feminists, we miss the opportunity to include noncanonical figures into our histories and may even run the risk of making the history of *feminist* philosophy—of all things—male dominated. My concern is that while we are happy to give over the history of feminist *activism* to women like Stanton, Anthony, and Pankhurst, there is still a struggle to let women dominate feminist or proto-feminist *philosophy* of the nineteenth century. Why is this the case? It seems to be that proofs of Bentham's or James Mill's feminism contain an implicit understanding that these proofs of the feminism of a canonical male philosopher will add to the intellectual solidity of feminist thought—vestiges of the patrimonial picture all over again.

Indeed, even in the case of John Stuart Mill, I believe that the desire to read a defense of women by a major philosopher has blinkered some commentators to the weaknesses and problematic nature of the younger Mill's views. Moreover, I hold that these weaknesses will be clearly exposed if we analyze Mill's work through the lens of women's empowerment, and not through either of the mainstream approaches to the history of philosophy.

John Stuart Mill

I now want to turn to the feminist thought of John Stuart Mill, specifically his 1869 work, *The Subjection of Women*.[6] Mill's *Subjection* is clearly an important piece of the history of feminism. As Susan Moller Okin points out, it is significant for four reasons: it is the only major work of feminist theory written by a well-known Western philosopher; it was politically influential; it is a good piece of argument, which intertwines many of the major elements from his other works; and it raise questions about sexual difference and sexual equality that are still pertinent to feminist discussion today (see Okin 1988).

While there is plenty of disagreement over Mill's type of feminism and its level of progressiveness, the amount of literature on Mill's feminism attests to the level of importance his work has been given.[7] The recent edited collection by Maria Morales (2004) is a good showcase for this wide range of work. Further support for Mill's importance, for example, can be found in Okin's introduction to a 1988 edition of *The Subjection of Women*. Okin sees Mill's work as significant for both historical and contemporary feminism:

> It is the only major work of feminist theory written by a man who is generally considered a great theorist within the western political tradition. . . . Both the essay and Mill himself played central roles in the important advances in women's rights that were made in England in the late nineteenth century. . . . [It] is one of John Stuart Mill's finest pieces of arguments. . . . In this work Mill employs and expands on a number of the most pervasive themes of his political philosophy. Here we find, either reiterated or applied and sometimes both, his arguments for individual liberties and justice, his concerns for the protection of interests and the improvement of human beings through political participation, his deep interest in psychology and the development of human character, and his fundamental belief in human progress. . . . [It] has continuing significance for feminist argument. Though many of the explicit grievances with which it is concerned have now been redressed, the broader issues it addresses remain pertinent. (vi)

Much of the work on Mill—even if critical—still rests on the assumption that Mill deserves a place in our feminist canon. Yet this is the very issue I wish to address: does Mill actually deserve a place in our feminist "canon"? I intend to argue that he does not deserve the beatified role he has been given. In so doing, I will also be able to resolve the problems and tensions that some feminist commentators have found with Mill's work. I intend to show that a central feature of *The Subjection*—its problematic nationalism—has been missed by feminist commentators. While nonfeminist commentators have noted Mill's interest in British colonialism and the "science" of the national character, feminist commentators have remained focused primarily on discussing what form his feminism takes, his use of utilitarianism to argue for the raising up of women, and his views on marriage.

In other words, the majority of feminist commentary on *The Subjection* has followed the mainstream philosophical approach. Even if not explicitly stated as such, commentators have looked for Mill's answers to supposedly timeless questions about "women": arguments and discussions on the vote, educational equality, marriage and sexuality, work, and so forth. As Okin said, Mill's *Subjection* raises questions about sexual difference and sexual equality that are still relevant for today. In the Morales collection, for example, the majority of the essays are on liberal feminism, Mill's use of utilitarian arguments, radical feminism, and his views on marriage.

Throughout this book I have questioned whether the notion of timeless questions is a good fit for feminist philosophy, and I have tried to show the complexity of nineteenth-century feminism. I now want to press on this issue and ask whether the philosophical approach restricts our analyses of Mill to the point that it skews our understanding of his feminism. I intend to show that once we stop seeing Mill as arguing against the subjection of women, understood as some kind of general, ahistorical group, and recognize that he is arguing against the subjection of a particular, contextualized group—nineteenth-century, middle-class Englishwomen—we begin to see the arguments of *The Subjection* in a new, more controversial light. Indeed, from the perspective of this new—and more problematic—account of his feminism I uncover, I even go so far as to suggest that we may wish to reconsider our views of his utilitarianism itself.

While I do hold that it is important to place Mill's *Subjection* within its historical and cultural context in order to understand its arguments, the sort of historical interpretive perspective I am recommending differs from the mainstream historical approach. First, I am placing Mill's work within its historical and cultural context in order to discover whether it has anything to offer philosophically or politically for the feminist philosophical project. It is not that I struggle to take the philosophically disinterested stance necessary for the mainstream historical approach; rather, I believe that the feminist project requires an overt political/philosophical stance.

Second, the sorts of social and cultural elements and entities I wish to examine in *The Subjection* are—from the perspective of the mainstream historical approach—anachronistic. I hold that rather than look at what Mill—or

any other philosopher for that matter—says about "women," we must understand that "women" are also classed, raced, and—in Mill's case—of a specific
nationality. The "women" Mill wishes to liberate are a particular historical
and cultural construct, and we must draw on current feminist philosophical
work to understand this. In contrast, for the mainstream historical approach,
the knowledge we gain from the examination of texts is value-free in the sense
that we aim not to distort this knowledge by interpreting it through our own
historically situated position or by using our contemporary philosophical
concepts.

Thus the "philosophical entities" I am examining in *The Subjection* are in
tension with the notion of philosophy as "pure" or autonomous, in that I am
taking an overtly politicized and anachronistic stance to examine the philosophical subject matter of Mill's work. As I claimed in my introduction, this
notion of purity does not simply function as an ideal, it also functions both
literally and metaphorically to maintain philosophical inheritance. My
"impure" interpretation of Mill's *Subjection* and my questioning of his utilitarianism theory serves to disrupt his inheritance as a feminist philosopher
and perhaps even as a "good" utilitarian.

Let us now examine Mill's *Subjection* in the light of the question of whether
it offers empowerment for women, and if so, what kind. Let us also ask the
attendant questions of who was the audience and epistemic authority for
Mill's work. We have seen in the previous chapters that one of the hallmarks
of a text that aims to empower women is that it gives women some form of
epistemic authority. In the case of Thompson, he says that as a man he cannot
feel women's oppression, but thanks to Wheeler he is able to understand how
oppression affects women's lives and it is this knowledge that supports the
argument of the *Appeal*. Beecher uses her knowledge of women's lives drawn
from her own experiences and that of others, whereas Wright makes the more
radical claim that her gender makes her better qualified to argue for social
equality. Beecher's target audience is primarily women, unless she is fund-
raising for schools for them, whereas the target audience for Wright and
Wheeler and Thompson comprises both genders.

The Subjection of Women

Mill did in fact consider the situation of women in an earlier work, the essay
on marriage written for Harriet Taylor Mill in 1832 or 1833, but *The Subjection*

is his systematic examination of the "woman question." The central argument in this earlier work is on divorce and the form that marriage should take. Even though he states that these issues cannot be considered without the woman question, his aim is not to provide any thoroughgoing critique of women's situation; it is *The Subjection of Women* that is a systematic account of the status and situation of women.

In the first chapter of *The Subjection* Mill begins with his central claim. He says that the principle that regulates the current social relations between the sexes is one of "legal subordination" of women to men. He argues it is wrong in itself and is "now one of the chief hindrances to human improvement"; he wants to replace it with a "principle of perfect equality" (Mill 1869, 1). He says that the subordination of women was never chosen because it produced the most happiness for all concerned, but rather it began from the early relations between the sexes (which were based on physical strength) and then was simply converted into laws. For, as he says, "laws and systems of polity always begin by recognising the relations they find already existing between individuals" (8). He argues that the legal subordination of women is not a new institution, but a version of the original form of female "slavery" to men.

Mill's analogy of the subordination of women to slavery runs throughout *The Subjection*, and—at first glance—it may be easy to see it as a rhetorical device aimed at his opponents; after all, as he says, they base their views on prejudice and feeling, not reason. Upon closer examination, this would not seem to be the case. He sees slavery as a regularized institution that began (like the subordination of women) from a "mere affair of force between the master and the slave" (9). However, he says that with the progress of civilization and the improvement of the moral sentiments of humankind, we now recognize that what he calls "the law of the strongest" is an unacceptable basis for laws and institutions (11). Thus this same "law" cannot support the inequality of rights between the sexes. It is crucial to notice here that while Mill apparently uses universal talk of "we" and "mankind," he is in fact specifically referring only to one or two nations.

This is the first indication of the way Mill is placing his argument for civil equalities for women within a specific nationalist context. In his continued discussion of the history (and gradual demise) of the law of force, Mill compares England with other countries. Thus we are told that the English put an end to the tyranny of the nobility faster than did the French, that—unlike other countries—they have recognized that military despotism is merely another example of this law, and that—in contrast to the United States—there was a far greater strength of antislavery feeling there. In part this latter senti-ment was due to the fact that few English people stood to profit from Ameri-can slavery, but Mill also points to the feeling of "abhorrence" of the English to slavery (17). On their own such comments do not seem to amount to much, but we shall see that they comprise Mill's overall contextualizing of his argument for the civil equalities of women: the subordination of women is not "English," for it is against their national character and it will hinder the progress of England. Moreover, this contextualization can be used to explain why Mill does not offer a full-blown argument for the equality of women.

Mill considers various "standard" arguments against the equality of women: it is in their best interest, they actually want inequality, and so forth. The crucial argument is the one that will reappear throughout: the issue of the nature of the two sexes. Mill argues against those who hold a sex-complementary view of the roles and capabilities of the two sexes by claiming that at this juncture we quite simply cannot know the nature of each: "What is now called the nature of women is an eminently artificial thing—the result of forced repression in some directions, unnatural stimulation in others" (38–39). Indeed, he says that of all oppressed groups their character has been the most distorted.

Mill begins here what I will show to be an important discussion of the way environment forms character, and the mistake he believes people make in not understanding this phenomenon. Significantly, he uses examples of how peo-ple are mistaken about national character to prove his point about women here. This analogy will prove relevant for our own understanding of Mill's later ambiguities on the issue of the natural and the artificial. At this point it is important to see that if he is basing his argument on national character in this way, it would seem that this latter notion would have been comprehensi-ble to his audience, whereas the modern reader is far more comfortable deal-ing with notions of social construction in relation to gender than with the concept of national character. For this reason, we must be careful not to dismiss or under-evaluate Mill's comments on national character.

In chapter 2, Mill discusses the oppressive state of marriage for women generated by the laws of England. However, he does not wish to dissolve the institution as such; in fact, he posits his ideal of marriage: a voluntary companionate relationship between two equals. For Mill the legal equality of married people is not simply about promoting the happiness of two individu-als, but "it is the only means of rendering the daily life of mankind, in any high sense, a school of moral cultivation. . . . The only school of genuine moral sentiment is society between equals" (78–79).

Even though Mill argues for the legal equality of women, such as ownership of their own property, he does not promote the desirability of women actually making money; instead, he sees the customary division of sexual labor as the best way in a society that is in other ways just. Indeed, he claims that in the same way men choose a profession, it is understood that (with some exceptions) women choose a domestic role when they marry. He thinks that the power of earning money offers dignity and protection to women, but for them to earn money as well as to fulfill their customary caretaking role would be exploitative. As I shall show, these arguments become more intelligible when placed within the context of national character.

Having dealt with the issue of the legal inequalities faced by women, Mill turns in chapter 3 to "the other point which is involved in the just equality of women, their admissibility to all the functions and occupations hitherto retained as the monopoly of the stronger sex" (91). It is in this chapter that Mill tackles arguments based on sexual stereotyping against women being given the vote or holding political office. Recalling his arguments from chapter 1, Mill again reaffirms his claim that because women have been artificially socialized, we are unable to make claims about their true nature. Mill further claims that if women were left as free as men in the development of their nature, and "no artificial bent were attempted to be given to it except that required by the conditions of human society," it may well be that there would be little or no difference in the character and capacities of the two sexes (105).

Yet immediately after making this statement, Mill allows himself to make some "empirical" generalizations about women's intellectual tendencies: their tendency toward the practical and their capacity of intuitive perception. In his favor, Mill does not go so far as to say that these tendencies could never change, and he also argues that intuitive thinking, as opposed to (masculine) speculative thinking, is equally important for human knowledge as it does not lose itself in abstractions.

Here Mill appears to accept certain sexual stereotypes and even to use them to hold a sex-complementary view of the search for knowledge. While he certainly indicates that these two characteristics he sees in women may change, he does not explain how it is that he can distinguish between these somehow more acceptable "fixed" characteristics and those he rejects as corrupted, which are the more artificial products of socialization.

Things become more complicated when Mill discusses the claim that the nervous susceptibility of women means that they are unfit for public life. Mill responds by stating that this tendency is not restricted to one sex, but is a combination of environment and inheritance. He then qualifies this claim, however, by stating that a greater number of women inherit this temperament. He then adds a further qualifier that attempts to make this tendency a "good" one: sensibility and enthusiasm are often qualities associated with leadership.

In an attempt to develop his point, Mill points to the way excitability can be found in the natures of different nationalities and how it has not hindered the successful development of their nations. Mill here invokes nationalistic stereotypes; thus he reminds us of the "fact" that the French and Italians are more emotional than the English. The analogy is simple: in the same way that the different "races" do the same things differently, but with equal success, so can women and men on average. Moreover, with a proper education, women would achieve equally with men. Here again Mill is reinforcing his tendencies towards a sex-complementary view.

It is important at this point to see that the few characteristics Mill ascribes as "feminine" are those that would connect well to women's domestic role. Intuition, practicality, and a nervous energy would be important characteristics for women not simply as household managers and family caretakers, but also for their central role as moral educations of their families.

Returning to his earlier claim that we cannot make arguments based on women's nature because we are not in a position to know what it is, Mill adds further weight to this claim by pointing to the different views of women's nature from different countries. These views come from the social circumstances of the countries, affecting women's development—mere empirical generalizations—rather than from proper philosophical analysis. Thus Englishmen think women are frigid whereas the French think they are fickle, and these two divergent views stem directly from cultural valuations of sexual fidelity.

Yet it is interesting to note that even though Mill wants to argue that sexual character is an unknown, he is clear enough about *national* character. We are told that we should not depend on Englishmen's views of women, as they are not in a position to judge human nature of any kind. This is because "both in a good sense and a bad sense, the English are farther from a state of nature than any other modern people. They are, more than any other people, a product of civilization and discipline" (124). The French, on the other hand, are not so much ignorant of human nature but prejudiced.

In the fourth and final chapter Mill asks whether the liberation of women will bring about an overall benefit to society. He says that legal equality in marriage will clearly benefit women, but he is now asking whether a more general advantage can be gained from the civic and legal equality of women. He argues that the advantage of having the relation of marriage regulated by justice is far-reaching: "The moral regeneration of mankind will only really commence, when the most fundamental of the social relations is placed under the rule of equal justice, and when human beings learn to cultivate their strongest sympathy with an equal in rights and in cultivation" (177). Here sympathy is understood as a sense of commonality and common interest. He claims that many of the moral flaws in men come from their upbringing. For how, he asks, can a boy not remain uncorrupted by the present state of affairs? He can never truly follow the laws of justice and the claims of respect based on conduct alone, if his character has been formed from the law of force and the unearned superiority of maleness.

The second benefit to be expected from the freeing of women from their subordination is more practical: more people available for the higher service of humankind. This in its turn would give women a more beneficial influence over other people's beliefs and (moral) feelings. This moral influence is something he says has always been in one form or another women's greatest contribution to society. Mill makes it clear that women—once given social and political emancipation—would have a major role to play in influencing public opinion. Yet he also emphasizes that the most significant moral improvement they would bring about would be through their influence in their individual families.

Mill finishes the chapter by arguing that that women want—and need—freedom equally with men, and that such freedom will bring individual happiness. At this point Mill seems to double back somewhat on his earlier comments on women's domestic role, for he says that once women have raised a family they should be allowed to enter into the public sphere in some way. Having done their duties as a mother, they should not be thrown on the scrap heap, as it were. Not only will they have suitable skills, but to deny them this is to deny their self-fulfillment as individuals and thus their happiness. Here it would seem that Mill is not claiming that women's domestic role is particularly "natural," but rather pragmatic. I shall show that this ambiguity, along with the importance of women's moral influence, becomes clearer with its contextualization within Mill's concept of national character.

Analysis of *The Subjection*

Thus there are four main problems that I (and other commentators) find in *The Subjection*. First, despite Mill's progressive views on the legal equality of women, he is often criticized for not challenging the traditional sexual division of labor (Shanley 1988, 387). Second, even though the mere fact that Mill supported women's equality was pretty radical for his time, overall his work is conservative. Third, his discussion of the "nature" of women seems to be ambiguous at best. Finally, Mill's arguments in chapter 4 sometimes run dangerously close to a form of "feminized utilitarianism": the justification for sexual equality is that it will be good for society as a whole.

So far, these problems have not been resolved to the satisfaction of modern commentators. Yet I would argue that using either or both of the mainstream approaches to the history of philosophy will not help us resolve these problems. We will not find the solution if we approach Mill's work as a response to an ahistorical question about social inequality. On the other hand, just placing *The Subjection* within its specific historical and cultural context will also not lead us to resolve its four main problems, because the historical approach, by its very nature, is not focused on dealing with philosophical problems.

When we read Mill, we are not reading about *women*, we are reading about nineteenth-century *Englishwomen* and their particular set of material and social conditions. It is certainly tempting to read historical philosophers to see what they say about women, as this would seem to be the obvious way to construct some kind of canon for feminist philosophy or to produce a history of our own, albeit a minimal one. However, women are also classed, raced, or in Mill's case, of a particular nationality. Thus for women reading runs the danger of becoming a specifically feminist form of reading texts for univocal questions. What starts as a non-problematic "interested" question ends up becoming a restricting question.

This is linked to the more general problem of timeless questions or problems. Certainly, Mill deals with issues that are still current in feminist discussions: economic equality, women's nature versus their socialization, and the sexual division of labor. As I shall show, however, treating these issues separately from the context within which Mill placed them is the difference between finding "Mill the major early feminist" and finding "Mill the problematic nationalist and the—at best—questionable feminist." In other words, it is the difference between reaffirming without questioning the male line in feminist thought and the genuine production of a feminist "canon." Our search needs to be for whether a particular philosopher offered—within their theoretical, cultural, and historical confines—empowerment for women. The search for timeless questions, problems, and issues may or may not be the way to do "standard" history of philosophy, but it offers little that is ultimately fruitful for feminist history of philosophy.

Conversely, I am not simply arguing that we analyze Mill using the mainstream historical approach. While I have placed *The Subjection* within its historical and cultural context and within the context of Mill's other works, the interpretation of Mill that I have given requires the "importing" of modern—anachronistic—categories of analysis that conflict with the self-restrictions of the historical view.

I would argue that the way to resolve—or perhaps to dissolve—these problems will be by examining *The Subjection* using the perspective for the history of philosophy I have begun constructing: to ask whether *The Subjection* will empower women. What I wish to promote is a historicized lens that is also politicized and can allow for connections to modern-day thinking.

It would seem clear based on the four problems listed above that Mill is not offering empowerment for women. He simply wishes to offer women legal and economic protections and to defend them against the typical criticisms that were made of their abilities and nature. While Mill does hold that women should be given the freedom to achieve fulfillment and happiness as individuals, and he also argues that women should have a role of some kind in policy making, it is clear that, for whatever reason, Mill sees women's primary role as domestic caretaker. It is possible to argue that there is some level of empowerment for women, along the lines discussed by Catherine Beecher, in the way that Mill holds that women—once equal—will have a significant role to play in influencing public opinion, albeit primarily through their influence in the domestic sphere. Like Beecher, Mill sees this influence as contributing to a greater social good; however, I intend to argue that Mill's greater social good is not a general Beecheresque moral good but a pragmatic nationalist good. In other words, what little power is offered to women is offered for a specific purpose, one not necessarily for the good of women themselves.

As we have seen from previous chapters, the notions of audience and epistemic authority are connected to the question of empowerment of women. Unlike in the works of Wheeler and Thompson, Beecher, and Wright, epistemic authority is not given to women in *The Subjection*, by which I mean that women are not given a voice either through the author him- or herself or through the author's expression of what he or she takes to be women's thoughts on their own oppression. Indeed, given Mill's ambiguous comments about women's nature, it is not entirely clear how Mill would allow epistemic authority for women. Similarly, Mill's audience does not appear to be women (as in the case of Beecher) or both genders (as in the case of Wright or Wheeler and Thompson); indeed, Mill does not seem to be speaking to women at all. Moreover, while Mill is clearly arguing against the oppression of women, there does not seem to be the passion that Wright, Beecher, and Wheeler and Thompson all express in their own distinct ways. Perhaps this is simply Mill's style of writing; more likely, however, the reason is that he has a different audience. He is writing primarily for an audience of *Englishmen*. Mill's appeals to nationalist pride or to the development of the nation are not simply rhetorical strategies to get this audience to accept the equality of women; rather, the equality of women and the development of the English national character are intimately connected.

It is here that we can start to see clues as to what underlies *The Subjection*. Mill does offer some level of equality and liberation for his female contemporaries, but not much; however, it is clear that he genuinely thinks he is offering them something significant. If we look for gender equality or justice understood as some kind of timeless question or problem, we will not be able to pinpoint what it is that Mill thinks he is offering. Moreover, and obviously, if we just place *The Subjection* within its historical and cultural context and nothing more, we will not be able to explain and understand its problems. If we press on the arguments of *The Subjection* using the empowerment question, however, then we can see it from a new and fascinating perspective. What we will find is that Mill does offer a minimal level of empowerment to women, specifically Englishwomen, of an unusual kind. As Englishwomen, they will be given an important role in the moral development of the nation itself. It is because of this role that we can see how Mill sometimes produces strong arguments for gender equality, but it is also because of this role that he struggles to move beyond the traditional domestic roles for women.

National Character

The key to understanding Mill's arguments for the empowerment of women—both those he made and those he did not (but perhaps should have)—can be found in his conception of national character. It is important to recognize that talk of national character was common in political thought in the nineteenth century. It is even more important to recognize that national character was a significant notion for Mill; after he had finished *A System of Logic*, he apparently wanted to write a work on the science of ethology: "the science which corresponds to the art of education; in the widest sense of the term, including the formation of national or collective character as well as the individual" (Mill 1973, 869). Moreover, his discussions of national character occur in a wide variety of his writings. By the 1860s, however, Mill no longer aimed to write an actual study of national character and instead discussed it in relation to the types of government that would be appropriate for certain nations (Varouxakis 1998, 387). This shift in ambition does not undercut the arguments in this chapter, but rather strengthens them because of the diversification of Mill's interests.

Mill does not really offer an actual definition of national character; the clearest statement of this concept is probably in *Logic* (1973, 905): "the character, that is, the opinions, feelings, and habits of the people" of a particular country. For a fuller account it is best to turn to the work of Georgios Varouxakis, who has written the most widely on this topic. Varouxakis has demonstrated that Mill's views on national character are important and have been mistakenly neglected.

Even though Varouxakis stresses the ambiguities of Mill's account of national character, he identifies its fundamental elements. For many of Mill's contemporaries, race was part of national character and Mill initially shared this view; however, Varouxakis claims that by the 1840s Mill did not often discuss the relation of race to the formation of national character. Mill was not always clear about how to identify groups that had a "character"; for example, he sometimes saw the Scottish as having the English national character and sometimes as having one of their own. Mill held that national character was subject to development, although by the 1860s he was less confident about how easy these changes would be.

Varouxakis (1998, 376) argues that Mill understands national character in two connected ways. The first was as the end of legislation and social reform: "Institutions could not be considered advisable if they did not conduce to the improvement of the collective character of the people who were to live under them." The second was as a fact: "the need for legislators or social reformers to take them into account in the calculation of the means they were to employ in order to achieve their goals (attaining to a better collective or 'national' character being one of the main goals)." Varouxakis takes the second way as the one that eventually became central to Mill's thought on the issue.

Mill's analysis of Bentham's philosophy provides the clearest demonstration of Mill's views, and on the whole, Mill understands national character primarily in the second way in this work. Mill critiques Bentham for his lack of understanding of human life; for Bentham, all human behavior is dictated by self-interest and partly by our like and dislike of others. Mill claims that Bentham does not recognize that humans are also motivated by the desire to be morally excellent for its own sake, not because of external sanctions. In other words, Bentham fails to recognize the existence of a conscience as well as the human desire for higher things, such as the love of beauty.

For Mill (1969a, 98), Bentham's theory of human life fails because it does not recognize the role of self-culture in the individual and the fact that the "regulation of . . . [a human being's] outward actions" will be slow and incomplete without the former. Moreover, Bentham's theory fails society in that it does nothing for the "spiritual" interests of the larger community: the desire to develop as a society. Instead it is national character that performs this function: "That which alone causes any material interests to exist, which alone enables any body of human beings to exist as a society, is national character: that it is, which causes one nation to succeed in what it attempts, another to fail; one nation to understand and aspire to elevated things, another to grovel in mean ones; which makes the greatness of one nation lasting, and dooms another to early and rapid decay" (99). Mill offers a succinct and harsh criticism of this failure of Bentham's theory; he states that a social philosophy not grounded on an account of national character is "an absurdity." For Mill, a true social philosophy for England (or France, the United States, etc.) is one that theorizes about the development of national character.

The English National Character

Despite Mill's statements that France and England had achieved the same level of civilization, it is clear from Mill's praise of England, and his critique

of France, that he believed that England's civilization was the most significant.[8] In *The Subjection*, Mill states that the English were far more advanced
than other nations in their rejection of the law of force (indeed, Mill holds
that the English have a natural feeling of abhorrence to slavery), military despotism, and absolute monarchy; the motivation for this rejection, he states,
comes from a feeling of disgust for this type of law. A central reason for
England's advancement was that the English had achieved the understanding
that "the pursuit of personal liberty was of intrinsic worth to the individual"
(Smart 1992, 528). Indeed, for Mill, "autonomous self-development was the
central dynamic of social progress."

For Mill (1977, 409), it is the "striving go-ahead character" of the English
that meant they were "the foundation of the best hopes for the general
improvement of mankind" and thus could rule for others. He discussed this
notion in his work "England and Ireland," for example. Those countries who
were backward—in other words, those that lacked capacity for self-
improvement—should even be grateful for the chance to be subjects of the
Empire (Smart 1992, 530). And Mill sometimes even resorted to problematic
stereotypes in order to demonstrate the backward nature of these countries.

It is in virtue of the English character and its level of development that the
Empire was a model for other countries. This reflects a common understanding of the role of the Empire at this time. The general understanding of the
relation between England and her Empire had moved from a simple case of
economic greed to a belief in her duty to "civilize" its subjects through such
things as education and religion. Mill's nationalism was not simplistic; rather,
he held that social progress was primary. However, if the march of progress
was stalled by another country, then Mill held that "colonialism, annexation,
and even benevolent despotism were legitimate" (Smart 1992, 533).

Despite their superiority, Mill did not believe that the English had reached
their full potential; he was critical of the English national character, in particular, for its lack of sympathy.[9] In one of Mill's earliest writings, the 1840 essay
on Coleridge (see Mill 1969b), he held that the English were too cautious and
lacked a desire to think critically. Mill's view of the problem of these flaws
can be seen to underpin his later—and harshest—criticism of the English.
This comes in *The Subjection* when Mill complains that the English have
learned to follow what he calls the rule—here he means the social rule—to
the point that they actually *feel* according to the rule. Thus, in a sense, the
rule has become human nature. For this reason the English cannot pass judgment on human nature, which—inevitably—means that they cannot see

beyond the artificial "nature" of women. For Mill, the English are the product of the highest civilization yet their distance from human nature is both an advantage and a disadvantage.

Englishwomen and the National Character

Given Mill's view of the English national character, it is possible to offer an account of the nature and the role of women in *The Subjection* that answers the questions and concerns about these issues. It is clear throughout the text that Mill is focusing on the situation of Englishwomen specifically. *The Subjection* is primarily a discussion of the social injustices faced by this subset of women; it is only the first part of chapter 1 that contains any substantial general discussion of the subjection of women in general.

Mill's claim in *The Subjection* is that women are to have a moral influence in public affairs primarily through their moral influence at home in the household, an influence that best described as the development of sympathy: a feeling of commonality and shared interest with others. It is this character trait that Mill feels is underdeveloped in the English. Given that Mill seems to hold that women are typically more sensitive and sympathetic, it would appear that it is men who are the most in need of character development. This is supported by the fact that in Mill's discussion of women's moral influence, he often discusses this as occurring through their roles of wife and mother, specifically as mother of male children.

Placing the discussion of women's role from chapter 4 within the context of national character gives Mill's "solution" for the liberation of women a greater depth and thus a greater interest. Rather than see women's role solely as helping individual men in their home, men who will then make better policies, it is plausible to see it as one of the development of the English national character. Thus women are given significant social and political power, but it is power only for a certain class of Englishwomen; moreover, it is secondhand or indirect power.

What then is the moral, social, and political role of the Englishman? Why does he need to be developed in this way? First, so that policy makers will choose the type of government and social system within their own country, which Mill holds will benefit the country and help individuals with their self-development. But, more problematically, also so that the role of the Englishman in government and social policy outside his own nation is one that will help other nation and their subjects move toward civilization. In a nutshell, the maintenance of the British Empire.

Placed within this context, the issue of Mill's version of the sexual division of labor (women in the home, men in the public sphere) undergoes a shift. In the same way that women are restricted, so were Englishmen of certain classes and positions to fulfill their moral task: benevolent rule and civilization of other nations. The division of labor is truly about labor. On Mill's account, neither sex would have had rewards at the expense of the other: men benefited from women's domestic role, but only in order for them to fulfill their own roles. Mill's account reflects the common colonialist sentiments of his era best expressed in Rudyard Kipling's famous 1899 poem "The White Man's Burden," in which Kipling holds that white men from civilized countries have an (onerous) duty to raise up and serve the peoples of their colonies. To expect Mill to challenge or even recognize the problematic sexual division of labor in *The Subjection* (as we modern commentators may do) is to fail to see the bigger picture of what Mill hoped to achieve with this arrangement.

Moreover, within a nationalistic interpretation, Mill's account of the nature of women, and its problematic ambiguities, become less central for his arguments in *The Subjection*. Although this is not to say that they become any more clear! Similarly, Mill's conservative account of women's economic independence becomes a lesser element in his argument for the equality of women. Mill's discussion of property in relation to national character may also add to understanding why Mill claims that women should own property but at the same time wishes to deny them the opportunity to earn money for themselves. Ownership of property may not be simply Mill's way of giving women some level of independence from their husbands or making them less vulnerable to the caprices of those husbands. There may be some connections here with his solution for the "Irish question": the possession of property. Mill held that property would make the Irish a better or more civilized people in that they would become more forward thinking, prudent, moderate, self-respecting, and so forth. Thus it is possible that Mill's primary motivation for supporting the possession of property for women has less to do with economic justice and more to do with the improvement of women's characters.

In these ways, the main problems that feminist commentators have found with *The Subjection* begin to change: the sexual division of labor has an explanation, as does the conservative nature of the work, while Mill's discussions of the nature of women become less problematic; indeed, the latter two issues drop out of the picture as central concerns. Moreover, even though it may be repugnant to the modern reader, women have an important and interesting role to play in Mill's schema. The role of women makes Mill's imperialism a softer, gentler version of the Empire-as-moral-duty arguments prevalent at that time. Further, his moral, political, and social idealism is not a Rousseauian parasitism on women. Moreover, there is a sense in which Englishness cuts across gender lines: despite gender differences, both sexes are privileged and mentally developed by being English. Thus, using the empowerment question allows us to see the complexities of Mill's *Subjection* and—to an extent—resolve the main problems that modern commentators have found with the work.

What of the empowerment of Mill's female contemporaries? What does using the empowerment question offer us here? Certainly, Mill provides a form of moral power to women, in many ways similar to that of Catharine Beecher, but unlike Beecher, he offers little toward *tangible* empowerment for women as individuals or as an oppressed group. It would appear that even though Mill wishes for justice for women, this is connected with the usefulness of women for the English nation and its rule over the colonies. It would then seem that asking the empowerment question raises the ultimate question of whether Mill should remain in the feminist "canon" at all. I would argue that if Mill's arguments for women are connected to the development of the British Empire (as I have claimed), then he is offering a feminized utilitarianism of such a problematic sort that he should not be given a place in the feminist canon.

Utilitarianism

Although this next section is not part of my main argument, I think it is a worthwhile tangent. The account of Mill's philosophy that comes out of a women–national character context does not end here. Of further interest is how easily this account slips into Mill's utilitarian theory.[10]

There is a gap of roughly thirty years between Mill's remarks on Bentham and the publication of *Utilitarianism*. Yet just as Mill responds to specific critiques that had been made of Bentham's theory, so he can also be interpreted as letting his own critiques of Bentham direct some of his positive theorizing. More important, an examination of the hallmarks of Mill's "civilized" character finds that they are exactly those required for a utilitarian moral agent. Moreover, just such a character would value a society grounded on utilitarianism.

In the crucial part of his arguments in chapter 2 of *Utilitarianism*, Mill argues—perhaps deliberately, perhaps not—for two elements that are central to his critique of Bentham: the need for a theory of human life and the understanding that we are not motivated purely by self-interest. Regardless of whether this replaying of these elements is deliberate, their function is the same: to enhance his own account of utilitarianism and to separate his account from that of Bentham.

Mill (1863, 9–10) states explicitly that he is offering a theory of human life that provides the "grounding" for the "Greatest Happiness Principle": "Actions are right in proportion as they tend to promote happiness, wrong as they tend to produce the reverse of happiness." Mill states that pleasure, and freedom from pain, are the only things desirable as ends; and that all desirable things (which are as numerous in the utilitarian as in any other scheme) are desirable either for the pleasure inherent in themselves, or as a means to the promotion of pleasure and the prevention of pain (10).

The crucial difference between Bentham and Mill here is that the latter gives different values to pleasures: some are more desirable as ends than others. If you value the lower it is because you do not know better. Moreover, following the utilitarian rule is not meant to produce the individual's happiness, but the greatest amount of happiness altogether. We shall be impartial between our happiness and that of others: we do not perform moral actions based on our own self-interest.

The connections—perhaps sometimes just echoes—to his earlier work on Bentham come out when Mill adds further background elements and assumptions to fill in the "gaps." Our choosing a life aimed at the fulfillment of our capacities for the higher pleasures comes from a natural tendency toward moral and personal development. We are unwilling to behave like beasts because we have a sense of dignity (albeit at different levels). Mill explains the phenomenon of those who recognize the superiority of the higher pleasures but sink into the lower, as the result of a lack caused by the fact that their occupations and the society in which they live do not support the necessary exercising of their higher faculties.

In response to the potential criticism that happiness is not an achievable goal for many (and thus cannot be the end of morality), Mill argues that "the present wretched education, and wretched social arrangements" are the only things that truly prevent happiness from being attained by most people (19).

Mill argues further that a central cause that makes life unsatisfactory is the lack of a cultivated mind: one that is open to knowledge of the world around it. Significantly, Mill argues that there is no reason why this type of intelligent interest "should not be the inheritance of every one born in a civilised country" (20).

Thus the utilitarian moral character—one who has the goal of self-improvement and who values a refined life for themselves and others—appears most likely to come from living and being educated in a certain type of society. It is this character who will understand the goals of utilitarianism and will desire to further them.

Is it then such a great leap to identify this utilitarian moral character with the English national character? For Mill, as I have shown, the English national character is characterized by a high level of self-development, a characteristic that was central for social progress. Further, the character of the English, because it was so civilized, formed a moral model for others. Regardless of whether Mill recognized this similarity, the English national character is the sort of character needed not only theoretically for his utilitarian theory, but also in actuality to drive it as a social policy.

According to Mill, as we have seen, the English character is not perfect, though it could be. It requires the development of sympathy, a feeling of commonality and shared interest with our fellow beings that comes about through the moral education given by women. Similarly, the development of a properly utilitarian character requires a certain type of society, one grounded on the moral influence of women depicted in *The Subjection*. Whether this was Mill's intention or is simply something that was an unanalyzed part of his thinking, the role of women outlined in *The Subjection* would fulfill an important function, one that could add to the theoretical background of his version of utilitarianism and provide the moral motivation needed for any practical application of his moral theory.

Thus the worst-case scenario is that the construction and maintenance of his utilitarian theory and its potential social policies cannot be separated from Mill's own view of the role of women and the connection of this role to the growth and maintenance of the British Empire. In other words, it is not simply that Mill's feminism in *The Subjection of Women* may be open to question, but that we now may want to ask whether his utilitarian theory itself has potentially antifeminist elements.

One can certainly dismiss these possibilities by claiming that my interpretation of Mill's utilitarianism, one that emphasizes an ethics of character rather than a straightforward ethics of action, is the problem here, not Mill's utilitarianism itself. This may indeed be the case; however, we are then still left with my initial question of whether Mill can truly be considered a feminist based on the relationship we find in *The Subjection* between women's moral role and the need for Englishmen to be of a certain character to run the Empire.

Closing Comments

It is clear that neither Bentham nor James Mill offers empowerment for women. However, an examination of commentators' analyses of their works allows us insights into the ways that mainstream approaches to the history of philosophy, and their accompanying patrimonial picture of philosophy, confine discussions of the feminism of Bentham and Mill and may ultimately restrict our construction of a feminist canon. Conversely, the use of the empowerment question offers an analysis of John Stuart Mill's *Subjection* that throws new light on his supposed feminism and allows us to ask whether he deserves a place in that same feminist canon.

Finally, an examination of the work of canonical utilitarians is helpful in understanding the relationship between utilitarianism and feminism, the minor theme in this book. Although I originally chose nineteenth-century feminist utilitarians simply because they constituted a small, connected group, I came to discover that utilitarianism needs to be appropriately politicized if it is to be part of the feminist project, and when I say appropriately politicized I mean what I am calling "empowerment utilitarianism." Indeed, my concern with John Stuart Mill's utilitarianism is the possibility that it may contain hidden, antifeminist elements; in other words, that it is not empowering to women.

We saw with Wheeler and Thompson that a theoretically "pure" (i.e., unpoliticized) utilitarianism ultimately fails their feminist enterprise. In contrast we saw with Beecher that her more politicized utilitarianism formed the theoretical glue for a philosophical system that would lead to the mental, moral, social, and economic empowerment of women, even though the type of politicized utilitarianism and empowerment Beecher is offering may seem regressive or hyper-conservative to the modern reader.

When we turn to modern interpretations of historical utilitarian figures, we can see that Boralevi, in framing utilitarianism as the philosophical and ideological foundation for feminism, is able to maintain the separation of the two and thus the purity of utilitarian theorizing. If utilitarian theory is kept pure in this way, then it is easy to apply either of the mainstream approaches to the history of philosophy to interpretations of canonical utilitarianism; however, as I have argued, this kind of interpretation is not particularly fruitful.

It is with an examination of the philosophy of Wright that we can see how a theoretically "impure" utilitarianism, one that is both politicized and synthetic, can underpin a properly feminist philosophy, albeit an early and rudimentary incarnation. Key to Wright's success is the ethical and political consciousness of our connectivity to others, one that plays out in her ethics, epistemology, metaphysics, and the structure of her philosophical system itself. As I have already suggested, Wright offers us an example of how an alternative to the patrimonial picture might look, and it is now time to leave the discussion of the relationship between utilitarianism and feminism and return to the main discussion of the book: considerations for a feminist history of philosophy.

Notes

1. After much heart-searching, I decided not to include a discussion of Harriet Taylor Mill, specifically her 1851 work, *The Enfranchisement of Women*, for two main reasons. First, and primarily, much has been written on Taylor, whereas my primary focus is to recapture forgotten or neglected nineteenth-century feminist utilitarian philosophers. Second, even though Taylor is now a recognized influence on John Stuart Mill, *The Enfranchisement* is significantly more progressive than *The Subjection*, and I did not want to get involved in a tangential attempt to explain the differences between their views, in particular Taylor's claim that married women should be given the right to work and Mill's view that marriage itself was a suitable profession for women.

2. Again, thanks to Gracia for elucidating this problem for me. See Gracia 1991.

3. The identification of feminist thought in historical texts is not necessarily anachronistic if it is appropriate for its period.

4. See also Jose 2000.

5. Jose's discussion of Mill occurs within a larger discussion of what he calls the "patrilineal" account of the history of feminist political thought. Jose is concerned with the tendency to locate the sources of feminist political theory within already established canonical theories, such as "liberal feminism." He claims that the origins of this tendency comes from "a number of radical nineteenth-century men philosophers . . . who appear to have defended women's political rights, or at least provided frames of analysis that entailed women's political rights" (2004, 2). Jose challenges this narrative of the formation of feminist political theory by arguing that "it rests on a derivation or genealogy that remains squarely within the logic of malestream political theory" (3). He focuses on a particular trope that has been "decisive in assessing the genealogical significance of these particular

men philosophers for the development of feminist political thought"; the trope in question is the use of women's emancipation as an indicator of social and political progress more generally (3). Jose argues that this trope is only superficially a mark of progress; instead, it "reproduced the masculinist signification and symbolism that each of these theorists took for granted. . . . Rather than opening out a space in which feminist political theory could be seen as significant in its own right, this trope served to reinforce the patrilineal descent of feminist political theory" (3–4). In essence, while the trope is *about* women, it does not allow women to be speaking subjects, to be part of the making of political theory. And thus we are handed an account of the history of feminist thought emerging "just like Pallas Athena, the offspring of already existing malestream political theory" (4–5). Jose's point about political theory is a crucial one; however, I think it needs to be framed against the more general background of the question of how we do the history of philosophy. Jose offers us a description of a problematic account of the origins of feminist theory, but he offers us little explanation as to *why* there is a tendency to accept this account on the part of both feminist and nonfeminists alike. As I said earlier, there is a "patrimonial" picture of philosophy or intellectual thought at play here.

6. The influences on John Stuart Mill have been well documented; see, for example, the work of Susan Moller Okin (1988). Okin does not locate these influences in any one place. She sees, among others, influences of Bentham and his circle, English and French socialists, and Harriet Taylor. She notes that the evidence points to Mill having formed his beliefs on gender equality prior to meeting Taylor, and that his connections with Mill made him see the realities of women's situation and increased his commitment to its alleviation.

7. For example, Julia Annas (1977) argues that Mill's work is a confused mixture of radical arguments and reformist arguments, while Keith Burgess-Jackson (1995) argues that Mill is a radical feminist.

8. Varouxakis (1998) states that Mill's concept of state of civilization and its relation to national character is not always clear.

9. According to Varouxakis (1988, 50), Mill did not offer a strict definition of the English national character. Sometimes Mill separated it from the Welsh and the Scottish characters, and sometimes he saw them as covered by his view of the English national character. Given that this type of view is still surprisingly prevalent in England, this is not that troublesome.

10. The connections between utilitarianism and English rule in India have already been made; see, for example, Stokes 1959.

CONCLUSION AND NEXT STEPS

This work was initiated by my interest in recapturing, evaluating, and interpreting forgotten or neglected historical works of feminist philosophy. In other areas of philosophy, such as ethics or epistemology, feminist philosophers have challenged the maleness and gender biases of the Western intellectual tradition; however, there has been relatively less time spent on examining the maleness and gender bias in how the Western philosophical canon *itself* has been constructed. It is true, but somewhat obvious, that women and feminists have been left out of the canon because of gender bias or sexism; what is less obvious is how women and feminist philosophers have been left out of the canon (or canons) because of the traditional or mainstream philosophical methodologies themselves, which have been employed to examine historical works and construct our histories. Moreover, as I aimed to show in the previous chapter, it may be that mainstream methodologies have led to "false positives" when we have tried to build our own feminist canons.

I am not claiming that these mainstream methodologies cannot produce interesting readings of texts and theories for feminists, nor am I arguing that these methodologies in themselves are sexist or gender biased; indeed, they appear to be "empty" of value. The problem I find is that when they are used each on their own, and against a particular philosophical framework, the patrimonial model of philosophy, these mainstream methodologies are not well suited for the recovery or examination of historical works of feminist philosophy. The interpretive lens I offer instead does still contain both historical and philosophical elements, and perhaps this should not be surprising, as navigating the relationship between feminist philosophy and mainstream philosophy is tricky: too close and the feminist philosophy loses its critical edge, too far and feminist philosophy may become irrelevant or struggle to be accepted as philosophy. The crucial difference, however, is that my guiding interpretive question—"Does it empower women?"—is asked against a different picture of philosophy and philosophical knowledge.

I hold that we should spend time considering our methodologies for the history of philosophy, and this is not simply for the sake of theoretical thoroughness. There is a sense that the history of philosophy requires a level of responsibility to historical authors to interpret their works in the best way we can. This is especially true in the case of philosophies, like historical feminist philosophy, that aimed to promote real political, social, and moral change for other humans—these philosophies were not simply an intellectual exercise, so it should not become merely an intellectual exercise on our part. This notion of responsibility need not run foul of debates about the "ownership" of a text. The issue is not whether the text can be open to multiple interpretations or whether there is one interpretation—the authorial interpretation— which the interpreter is responsible to uncover. Instead, this notion of responsibility is about self-reflection on our role as interpreters, an acknowledgment of the political beliefs and goals we bring to our interpretation, a recognition of the political and ethical consequences of our interpretation, and—above all in the case of historical feminist philosophers—a responsibility to give a charitable but critical analysis of their work. In sum, this notion of interpretive responsibility is not just about interpretive appropriateness; it can also bring new insights to texts and new perspectives on meta-questions about interpretation itself.

Yet this emphasis on interpretive responsibility and its corollary, the political and personal connections between interpreter and text or author, is not a methodology, new or otherwise, nor am I claiming this is the case. In fact, as I have tried to make clear throughout this book, I am not offering a new methodology in any full-blown sense for feminist history of philosophy, and I have aimed to bring this out by describing what I am doing as an interpretive lens or perspective rather than an approach or methodology. This notion of lens or perspective allows me to identify characteristics or features of a feminist history of philosophy without the more problematic claim that I am offering a new methodology. Even though the interpretive lens I am proposing differs from the two mainstream methodologies in its goals and understanding of the role of the interpreter, the empowerment question still draws from or is a version of both methodologies. If we do want to offer a new methodology for feminist history of philosophy, it cannot simply be a replacement for the two traditional models. As I have argued, simply to offer a replacement model would be to remain within the patrimonial picture of philosophy, as this would be to buy into the picture of philosophy as a series of battles or opposing positions with one viewpoint as the winner and the other as the loser.

Instead, I have made the claim that work in feminist history of philosophy is best done against a different picture of philosophy *itself*, and I have offered one possible example of how that different picture might look, drawn from the work of the philosophers I have examined. This alternative picture reflects work done in feminist epistemology with its notion of a situated knower, a knower—in the case of the history of philosophy—who could be the author, audience, or interpreter. Within this alternative picture of philosophy, it may be possible to keep the traditional approaches of the historical and the philosophical; however, we may also find that we want to explore new approaches or new ways of combining the two traditional approaches. Whatever approach we decide to take to a feminist history of philosophy, it is clear that we must first identify and recognize features or characteristics of feminist interpretation of historical texts.

A comparison with the social sciences might be helpful at this stage. Sandra Harding (1998, 2–3) distinguishes between a research method ("a technique for [or way of proceeding in] gathering evidence"); a methodology ("a theory and analysis of how research does or should proceed"); and an epistemology, a theory of knowledge that asks questions, for example, about who can know and what can they know. Ultimately, most of my arguments about feminist history of philosophy, and the identification of characteristics of what I am calling a feminist interpretive perspective or lens, take place at the epistemological rather than the methodological level, and I hold that we need to give priority to the epistemological questions raised in doing feminist history of philosophy. Yet, as Harding states, these three different elements in social sciences are intertwined, and it is clear in the history of philosophy that feminist epistemological considerations feed into critiques of mainstream methodologies and vice versa.

Although there are obvious and distinct differences between social science research and research in the history of philosophy, it is possible to learn from the former and draw useful connections between the two. In examining feminist work in the social sciences, Harding has argued that the best research goes beyond simply adding women by recognizing their research or their contributions to the public world, or by offering analyses of women as victims of male dominance. However, Harding does not suggest that we should look for a distinctive feminist method of research in the social sciences, as she claims that this search in fact "mystifies what have been the most interesting aspects of feminist research processes" (1). Instead, Harding identifies three methodological and epistemological features of feminist research, rather than actual methods, that produce the best research, although she does not claim that these three features are the only possible ones.

The first feature is that the importance of women's lived experiences is recognized, although it must be acknowledged that this is not a universalized experience, as women's lived experiences will differ depending on race, class, and so forth. The projects that grow out of these experiences are driven by research questions about social change and emancipation: "The questions an oppressed group wants answered are rarely requests for so-called pure truth" (8). If inquiry begins with women's (politicized) experiences, then research becomes designed for women accordingly, as opposed to being for men or for "humans" (meaning men). This shift in purpose is the second feature of feminist research identified by Harding. The final feature of the best feminist research is the location of the researcher in the same critical place as the subject: "Thus the researcher appears to us not as an invisible, anonymous voice of authority, but as a real, historical individual with concrete, specific desires and interests" (9). This is a recognition that "the cultural beliefs and behaviors of feminist researchers shape the results of their analysis" no less than androcentric researchers.

There are some clear and useful similarities between feminist social science research, as depicted by Harding, and the interpretive lens for feminist history of philosophy I am proposing, in particular, notions of empowerment, audience, connection/collaboration, ethical and political responsibility, and the authority to speak (for oneself or for others). The empowerment question allows us to begin from women's experiences (including those of the text's author), and asking this question within a historicized context allows for analyses of these experiences that recognize difference (e.g., social class in Beecher or John Stuart Mill). The empowerment question is itself a politicized inquiry; while it may share similarities with the philosophical approach, it is asking a question on behalf of an oppressed group that is not a search for "pure" truth. Finally, even though this question is asked on behalf of a historical, oppressed group (in this particular case, nineteenth-century English and American women), the interpreter "participates" in the investigation in some way: he or she is not the detached, disinterested knower. In a similar way to research in the social sciences, the researcher and subject are not separate;

moreover, there is a consciously chosen political and ethical underlay to research, whether it be research of social science or interpretation of historical texts.

Throughout I have asked the empowerment question of the works I have studied. This question is an alternative to asking the two mainstream questions of "What did x say?" and "Is it true?" Obviously, the latter two questions are shorthand for fully worked out methodologies. Can the same be said for my alternative empowerment question? Currently not, nor has producing an alternative feminist methodology been my goal; however, I do not see this as a failure on my part. I am more interested in identifying the characteristics of a different perspective or lens through which we examine the works of historical feminist philosophers. A development of this perspective or lens is less about establishing a new, independent feminist approach to or methodology within the history of philosophy, and far more about identifying the features that would make an interpretation both feminist and rich. I am certainly asking meta-questions about the history of philosophy, but they are more questions that lead to consciousness about our political and ethical responsibilities as interpreters and less about creating a new methodology, at least in any traditional sense of the word.

What I aim to do now is to offer some guidelines for exploring the work of historical feminist philosophers drawn from my examination of the works of Wheeler and Thompson, Beecher, Wright, and the male utilitarian canon through the lens of the empowerment question. Even though I am not claiming that the empowerment question stands in for a new methodology, I am claiming that it is a useful perspective or lens through which to examine works of historical feminist philosophy, although it need not be the only lens available to feminist historians. At its starkest, as in the case of my interpretation of John Stuart Mill's *Subjection of Women*, asking the empowerment question allows us to see that—despite Mill's personal goodwill toward women—his work may not qualify as truly feminist. Again, the notion of political responsibility comes up here; while we should not hold Mill to unrealistic or anachronistic standards, we must also be prepared to scrutinize the work of even our most cherished forefathers and foremothers. In the case of Wheeler and Thompson, the empowerment question allows us to see both their theoretical strengths and their failures, whereas it allows us to claim Catharine Beecher not only as a philosopher but also as a feminist philosopher.

The empowerment question can be asked on multiple levels, but this is not to say that every level will fit all texts. On an initial—historical or textual—

level, we simply ask whether a historical text or theory would lead to the empowerment of women of that particular era. If we are lucky, as in the case of Wheeler and Thompson or Beecher, then the philosopher will give us an account of the concrete, quotidian lives of his or her female contemporaries and we will be in an immediate position to judge the impact of his or her theorizing on these lives. If not, then we will need to do historical research to build a picture of these lives before we can make such judgments. Crucially, as we can see from the analysis of Mill's *Subjection*, we should not restrict ourselves to research just on women, but we should recognize the ways that class, race, nationality, and so forth intersect with gender.

We can also ask the empowerment question at a historical level in relation to the author's own goals of empowering women, and we can do so without running up against the philosophical problem of authorial intent. In the particular texts I have examined I have made claims about authorial goals of empowerment based on whether the text or theory is overtly or explicitly politicized. Beecher seems aware that her theory is not politically neutral, whereas Wright seems to delight in her lack of neutrality. Thompson justifies his writing of the *Appeal* by claiming that he has learned about gender inequality from Wheeler and he is essentially rehearsing her ideas, and again, Wheeler and Thompson are open about their lack of political neutrality. Mill, on the other hand, offers an argument that is at times openly political and at other times based on supposedly value-neutral empirical evidence about women, evidence that typically reflects the cultural biases of his era.

Where Mill also fails—and Thompson, Beecher, and Wright succeed—is that Mill does not understand the potential problems in speaking for an oppressed group—women—from his position of gender, race, and class privilege. Thompson helps us understand the ethical and political importance of giving Wheeler her proper due. The arguments in the *Appeal* would remain the same regardless of authorship, but its overall message would have failed if Thompson had taken the credit. Thompson has recognized—and this is part of his criticism of James Mill—that we are accountable for the ethical and political results of our theorizing. Thompson understands that in speaking for others we are accountable and responsible for what we say. Moreover, he anticipates by almost two centuries the modern work of Linda Alcoff (1991–92) on speaking for marginalized others, in that he recognizes that if we wish to speak for his female contemporaries we must ask whether it will bring them empowerment. Indeed, part of the *Appeal* is devoted to rallying women to their own cause, although, as I have argued, there are flaws with the way this call to empowerment is put into practice.

It can be claimed that both Beecher and Wright implicitly recognize the need to position themselves so that they are not speaking as privileged outsiders. Beecher positions herself for her female audience so that she is speaking to female "friends" and colleagues about shared experiences and goals. Wright also claims that her sex and social situation position her to speak for women, black Americans, and the poor, and further, that her philosophical view of knowledge and truth itself provides justification for her speaking out about inequality and the need for empowerment through education. Although we should not ask for anachronistic philosophizing by our historical figures on speaking for oppressed others, the empowerment question asked at a textual level may lead to discussion by modern interpreters of a philosopher's recognition that it is more powerful or justified to discuss empowerment from the epistemic or political location of the disempowered group.

At its heart, stripped of complicated modern theorizing about ownership, interpretation of historical texts itself is speaking for others, and it is here that we ask the empowerment question at a more transhistorical level. We should recognize that recapturing the work of a historically marginalized group— historical women philosophers—intersects with work done by feminist philosophers (e.g., Alcoff) on the problems of speaking for others, specifically, marginalized groups. While there are many distinct and important differences between these two different sets of theorizing—the most obvious being that what we say about or on behalf of historical women philosophers can have no effect on them—there are shared elements, most significantly what Alcoff (1991–92) calls the need for speaking to always carry with it accountability and responsibility for what one says. If we do not self-reflect on our role as interpreters/speakers, then we may end up re-silencing the figures we hope to recapture, especially as these figures have been neglected or forgotten and thus there are rarely competing or alternative interpretations of these individuals.

Alcoff says that if we wish to speak for marginalized others, and here she is talking of our contemporary others, we must ask whether it will bring them empowerment. What is interesting is that, in some ways, I have ended up drawing a similar conclusion about interpreting works of historical feminist philosophy: reading such philosophy is reading for empowerment. Having said this, I want to be careful not to be too glib in drawing comparisons between silenced contemporary marginalized groups and historical feminist philosophers. Among the many differences, a central difference is that "speaking for" contemporary marginalized groups can serve to maintain oppression and have a very real material effect on the lives of actual people.

The empowerment I have looked for, and found, in these historical texts comes in part from the claiming of authority, epistemic, political, and ethical, both for the authors themselves and also on behalf of their female contemporaries, and—in the case of Beecher and Wright—would lead to empowerment for their contemporaries. Wheeler is the epistemic authority for the *Appeal*, even though the theoretical framework of Wheeler and Thompson's utilitarianism ultimately fails to provide empowerment. Beecher claims an epistemic and ethical authority for herself and for her female contemporaries that is the foundation for her vision of women's role as "heaven-appointed" educators for moral and social progress, a position that—for Beecher—is empowering. Wright claims epistemic, political, and ethical authority for herself and other women. This authority finds its theoretical justification in Wright's philosophy, one that is not only inclusive of marginalized groups but requires their equality and contributions for social and moral progress: in other words, their empowerment. For both Beecher and Wright, female authority and empowerment is deserved and justified; it is not inherited due to an unearned privilege or right.

In asking the empowerment question of historical texts the interpreter is engaged in what I want to call connectivity, a relation that bears some similarities with the ways feminist researchers in the social sciences locate themselves on the same critical plane as their "subjects." Obviously, unlike feminist social science research, the feminist historian of philosophy cannot collaborate or engage in a dialogue with their subjects, as they are not dealing with living subjects. However, we must acknowledge a shift in the relation between philosophical researcher and subject/text. It is difficult to call this collaboration, but I do want to emphasize that there is connectivity here of some kind. Wright can help us understand this notion of connectivity with her delineation of an ethically and politically self-aware knower who is linked to a community of like-minded others by shared political goals and a shared sense of responsibility to the society they wish to reform.

The patrimonial picture of philosophy encourages us to be adversarial, to critique, to find flaws, to pull apart. While we should not necessarily reject an adversarial model of philosophy, we should not make the mistake of thinking it is the *only* model; we should find different ways of engaging with texts, albeit critically. This has been done in interesting ways outside the Anglo-American tradition—Luce Irigaray would be a prime example here—but less often within it. The patrimonial picture idealizes distance and purity, thus enabling an adversarial model for doing philosophy and for framing the history of philosophy as a series of battles or opposing positions. On the patrimonial picture, our relationship with the text/author reflects the ideal of the traditional "knower" in that this relationship is distant, neutral, and "pure" in the sense that it is untainted by personal connection: the good interpreter is anonymous and invisible. This "good" interpreter is the worthy inheritor of a text, work, idea, or position. This follows for both mainstream approaches. For the philosophical approach, the focus is on universal problems, positions, or truths; by definition these universal entities should not involve a historically located, concrete interpreter. For the historical approach, historical accuracy is also jeopardized by the presence of a historically located, concrete interpreter.

Instead, we should begin by acknowledging our experiences of interpretation and why we are drawn toward interpreting historical works. Yes, historians of philosophy of all stripes are attracted by the "puzzle-solving" element, but we should not close our eyes to our personal attachment to the figures we study. Those of us who have worked on a philosopher, especially one unstudied by others, can grow quite possessive of him or her or fall into talking of the figure as if he or she were our living friend. Less extreme, the work of Annette Baier on Hume or Martha Nussbaum on Aristotle owes its intellectual richness to the sense of personal connection with the historical figure that runs throughout, even though this stance may not be consciously adopted.

Once we have recognized that interpretation is not neutral or distant, we are better able to make a shift in viewing a feminist interpretive relationship to a text or historical figure as one of connection or collaboration, based on similar goals. This shift is accompanied by a recognition of the political foundation, and thus the potential consequences, of our interpretation. In addition, the trope of connection or collaboration helps us understand the sense in which interpretation is a form of speaking for others, as both require a sense of ethical and political consciousness and responsibility. Finally, this political and ethical consciousness of the interpreter and his or her subsequent interpretation includes an explicit recognition of the background picture of philosophy at play in the interpretation.

Making historicized feminism or gender central to interpretation is a political act; the feminist interpretive project is not just for knowledge for its own sake. However, this enterprise—as I have described it—still may seem to reflect mainstream approaches: the empowerment question is a universal (albeit interested) question and is grounded within a historical context. Still, the empowerment question differs in significant ways. What is crucial to notice is that the empowerment question is placed within a framework of ethical responsibility and political consciousness. We must have an awareness of implicit commitments or implied conclusions about knowledge. Who can know? How can they know? How do they express what they know? How do we as interpreters express this knowledge? This is primarily about how we approach the text, but it also leads to self-reflection about the relationship between the interpreter and the text.

Asking the empowerment question of a historical text produces a shift away from the evaluative categories employed by mainstream philosophy. As we saw with Wheeler and Thompson, the empowerment question allows for more nuanced categories of evaluation beyond success or failure, or "getting it right." Such judgments in themselves may not be problematic, although there is always potential for a slippery slope on the philosophical approach when, for example, Aristotle is judged by modern philosophical standards and found wanting. Obviously, the historical approach eschews evaluative judgments that are determinations of philosophical worth or interest. The empowerment question, on the other hand, can allow for praiseworthy attempts, novel approaches, or insightful analyses, evaluations that are more in keeping with our interpretive responsibility to give a charitable but critical analysis of historical texts. Thus the empowerment question can allow us to see why Wheeler and Thompson's *Appeal* would be an important text in any alternative feminist canon we might want to build, despite their ultimate "failure" to offer empowerment for women and the lack of theoretical finesse in their utilitarianism. Wheeler and Thompson offer a disturbing and poignant account of the lives of their contemporaries and a call for radical social change that cannot fail to stir the blood of their reader.

This type of effect on the audience is clearly not an acceptable category of evaluation on either mainstream approach, as both require a distancing of the philosophical reader or audience, a move that is directly connected to the traditional picture of the philosophical knower as independent, solitary, and unconnected emotionally to objects of knowledge. However, Wheeler and Thompson, Beecher, and Wright, albeit in different ways, are all attempting to speak directly to their audience, and this audience is composed of real people. Wheeler and Thompson as well as Wright call to women and like-minded men to bring about change, while Beecher speaks at times "privately" to her female readers as though they were friends. In contrast, Mill writes for a universalized or abstract audience that is in fact an audience of white, privileged males. If we allow for a different picture of the philosophical knower/interpreter, however, a picture on which the interpreter is self-reflective and responsible both to the texts and the goals of feminist philosophy, then we can judge a text for its political connectivity with its audience (historical or modern) or even its potential for audience empowerment, as in the case of Beecher or Wright.

A shift in evaluation of texts also allows us to see that we can build our own canons in our own ways; canon construction need not be modeled on the mainstream or traditional ways of the past. Given that the feminist philosophical project aims to bring about social and political change, it may initially appear that recovering the history of feminist philosophy is of little value to our contemporary feminist philosophical enterprise beyond the identification of our historical foremothers as a counterpoint to the traditional patrimonial histories of philosophy. These are questions that are asked of mainstream philosophy: What is the value of the history of philosophy for philosophy and what is the relationship of the two? Is the former essential, important, or irrelevant for the latter? (Wilson 1992, 6).

Certainly, few contemporary feminist works draw on the thought of these foremothers; indeed, it is hard to see how we could benefit from theories that are often so grounded in their historical and cultural context as to be sometimes mere intellectual curiosities. Either the narrative is one of the rare author who preempted contemporary thoughts or one where we shudder at the past horrors women faced and congratulate ourselves on the changes that have occurred. However, we need to be careful here and not fall back into the mainstream conceptualization of the "value" and "lack of value" of past theories and texts, which finds it basis in the philosophical approach: theories and texts that appear to be part of our contemporary discourse and those that are not.

The notions of family resemblance and empowerment allow us to circumnavigate the value/no value dichotomy. On the patrimonial picture, philosophical ideas and positions are passed from philosophical father to philosophical son. If philosophy is "inherited" in this way, then it is consistent to ask about the value of historical texts for contemporary philosophizing. However, the empowerment question does not lead us to search for abstract philosophical "truths" that can be separated from their originator and thus passed on; instead we are drawn to ask whether a text or theory places women and a commitment to their liberation and fulfillment at its center, and whether it can allow for women to claim both political empowerment and the right to knowledge. Wheeler and Thompson, Beecher, and Wright all call in their different ways for empowerment for women; as we have seen, the relative strengths and weaknesses of these different calls are grounded on how much women are to claim this empowerment for themselves.

A text or theory that allows for women to claim empowerment for themselves cannot be separated from its historical location, which I would claim holds true for all historical feminist philosophical texts. But such a text or theory need not be confined to its historical time period in that we can make connections between texts and theories, based on the goal of empowerment, in a manner similar to the notion of Wittgensteinian family resemblance. If we employ the notion of family resemblance, then the value/no value dichotomy can be replaced with a continuum of family resemblances. At one end of the continuum we will find work we praise for its political commitment but that shares little with modern theorizing. At the other end of the continuum we will find work that bears distinct resemblances to modern theorizing; indeed, it may even be work we want to use to inform our own scholarship.

These notions of family resemblance and empowerment also allow us to see how the lines normally drawn between historical author, historical audience, modern interpreter, and modern theorist become blurred. The historical feminist philosophical author is writing for his or her particular audience and is responsible, epistemologically, ethically, and politically, to this community of knowers to foster their own empowerment through ideas for political change and knowledge (or access to knowledge). The modern interpreter and the modern theorist are responsible to the historical author to transmit or use his or her work without bias or misunderstanding, and they are responsible to their own community of knowers to further the goals of the feminist project.

Throughout this work, I have aimed to draw attention to the need for self-consciousness about the political and ethical dimensions of our theorizing. This is something we can also learn in different ways from the philosophers I study, and it is a worldview that is a corollary to the characterization of feminist philosophy with which I am working. It is this proposition about our ethical and political awareness—and thus accountability—that I am claiming should lie at the heart of any proposed feminist history of philosophy.

References

Alanen, Lilli, and Charlotte Witt, eds. 2004. *Feminist Reflections on the History of Philosophy*. Dordrecht: Kluwer Academic Publishers.

Alcoff, Linda. 1991–92. "The Problem of Speaking for Others." *Cultural Critique* 20 (Winter): 5–32.

Annas, Julia. 1977. "Mill and *The Subjection of Women*." *Philosophy* 52:179–94.

Baier, Annette C. 1987. "Hume, the Women's Moral Theorist?" In *Women and Moral Theory*, edited by Eva Feder Kittay and Diana T. Meyers, 37–55. Savage, Md.: Rowman and Littlefield.

Ball, Terence. 1980. "Utilitarianism, Feminism, and the Franchise: James Mill and His Critics." *History of Political Thought* 1 (1): 91–115.

———. 1993a. "Bentham No Feminist: A Reply to Boralevi." In *Jeremy Bentham: Critical Assessments*, 4 vols., edited by Bhikhu Parekh, 4:255–57. New York: Routledge.

———. 1993b. "Was Bentham a Feminist?" In *Jeremy Bentham: Critical Assessments*, 4 vols., edited by Bhikhu Parekh, 4:230–38. New York: Routledge.

Baym, Nina. 1993. *Women's Fiction: A Guide to Novels by and about Women in America, 1820–70*. Urbana: University of Illinois Press.

Bederman, Gail. 2005. "Revisiting Nashoba." *American Literary History* 17 (3): 438–59.

Beecher, Catharine. 1827. "Female Education." *American Journal of Education* 2 (4–5).

———. 1829. *Suggestions Respecting Improvements in Education, Presented to the Trustees of the Hartford Female Seminary, and Published at Their Request*. Hartford: Packer and Butler.

———. 1831. *The Elements of Mental and Moral Philosophy, Founded upon Experience, Reason, and the Bible*. Hartford: Peter B. Gleason.

———. 1835. *An Essay on the Education of Female Teachers*. New York: Van Nostrand and Dwight.

———. 1836. *Letters on the Difficulties of Religion*. Hartford: Belknap and Hammersley.

———. 1837. *An Essay on Slavery and Abolitionism, with Reference to the Duty of American Females*. Philadelphia: Henry Perkins.

———. 1838. *The Moral Instructor*. Cincinnati: Truman and Smith.

———. 1839. "An Essay on Cause and Effect in Connection with the Difference of Fatalism and Free Will." *Biblical Repository* 2 (4): 381–408.

———. 1841. *Treatise on Domestic Economy*. Boston: Marsh, Capen, Lyon, and Webb.

———. 1842. *Letters to Persons Who Are Engaged in Domestic Service*. New York: Leavitt and Trow.

———. 1845. *The Duty of American Women to Their Country*. New York: Harper and Brothers.

———. 1846a. *An Address to the Protestant Clergy of the United States*. New York: Harper and Brothers.

———. 1846b. *The Evils Suffered by American Women and American Children: The Causes and the Remedy*. New York: Harper and Brothers.

————. 1850a. *Miss Beecher's Domestic Receipt-Book: Designed as a Supplement to Her Treatise on Domestic Economy.* New York: Harper and Brothers.

————. 1850b. *Truth Stranger Than Fiction.* New York: Mark H. Newman and Company.

————. 1851. *The True Remedy for the Wrongs of Woman; with a History of an Enterprise Having That for Its Object.* Boston: Phillips, Sampson, and Company.

————. 1855. *Letters to the People on Health and Happiness.* New York: Harper and Brothers.

————. 1856. *Physiology and Calisthenics.* New York: Harper and Brothers.

————. 1857. *Common Sense Applied to Religion; or, The Bible and the People.* New York: Harper and Brothers.

————. 186?. *Industrial and Domestic Science.* New York.

————. 1860. *An Appeal to the People on Behalf of Their Rights as Authorized Interpreters of the Bible.* New York: Harper and Brothers.

————. 1864. *Religious Training of Children in the School, the Family, and the Church.* New York: Harper and Brothers.

————. 1869. *Something for Women Better Than the Ballot.* New York: D. Appleton and Company.

————. 1871. *Principles of Domestic Science: As Applied to the Duties and Pleasures of Home: A Text-Book for the Use of Young Ladies in Schools, Seminaries, and Colleges.* New York: J. B. Ford and Company.

————. 1872. *Woman's Profession as Mother and Educator with Views in Opposition to Woman Suffrage.* Philadelphia, Boston: G. Maclean; New York: Maclean, Gibson and Company.

————. 1873. *Miss Beecher's Housekeeper and Healthkeeper, Containing Five Hundred Recipes for Economical and Healthful Cooks.* New York: Harper and Brothers.

————. 1874. *Educational Reminiscences and Suggestions.* New York: J. B. Ford and Company.

Beecher, Catharine, and Harriet Beecher Stowe. 1869. *American Woman's Home: or, Principles of Domestic Science, Being a Guide to the Formation and Maintenance of Economical, Healthful, Beautiful, and Christian Homes.* New York: J. B. Ford and Company.

Bentham, Jeremy. 177?. "Proposal for the Restraining of the Male Sex from the Exercise of Certain Trades: In Favour of Purity of Manners, and of the Employment of the Female: Staymakers, Hairdressers." University College, London, Collection Box 149, 97, stray sheet.

————. 1780. *An Introduction to the Principles of Morals and Legislation.* London: T. Payne and Son.

Boralevi, Lea Campos. 1984. *Bentham and the Oppressed.* Berlin: Walter de Gruyter.

————. 1987. "Utilitarianism and Feminism." In *Women in Western Political Philosophy: Kant to Nietzsche,* edited by Ellen Kennedy and Susan Mendus, 159–78. Brighton: Wheatsheaf.

————. 1993. "In Defence of a Myth." In *Jeremy Bentham: Critical Assessments,* 4 vols., edited by Parekh Bhikhu, 4:239–54. New York: Routledge. Originally published in *The Bentham Newsletter* 4 (May 1980): 33–46.

Borchard, Ruth. 1957. *John Stuart Mill: The Man.* London: Watts.

Boyer, Paul S. 1971. "Frances Wright." In *Notable American Women, 1607–1950: A Biographical Dictionary,* 3 vols., edited by Edward James and Janet T. James, 3:675–80. Cambridge: Harvard University Press.

Brucker, Johann Jakob. 1742–1744. *Historia Critica Philosophiae (Critical History of Philosophy).* 3 vols. Leipzig.

Burgess-Jackson, Keith. 1995. "John Stuart Mill: Radical Feminist." *Social Theory and Practice* 21 (3): 369–96.

Child, Lydia Maria. 1829. *The Frugal Housewife: Dedicated to Those Who Are Not Afraid of Economy.* Boston: Marsh and Capen/Carter and Hendee.

Code, Lorraine. 1991. *What Can She Know? Feminist Theory and the Construction of Knowledge.* Ithaca: Cornell University Press.

Collingwood, R. G. 1939. *An Autobiography.* New York: Oxford University Press.

Connors, Robert J. 1999. "Frances Wright: First Female Civic Rhetor in America." *College English* 62 (1): 30–57.

Cummins, Maria Susanna. 1854. *The Lamplighter.* Boston: John P. Jewett and Company.

Dooley, Dolores. 1996. *Equality in Community: Sexual Equality in the Writings of William Thompson and Anna Doyle Wheeler.* Cork: Cork University Press.

Eckhardt, Celia Morris. 1984. *Fanny Wright: Rebel in America.* Cambridge: Harvard University Press.

Freeland, Cynthia. 2000. "Feminism and Ideology in Ancient Philosophy." *Apeiron* 33 (4): 365–406.

Garber, Daniel. 2000. *Descartes Embodied: Reading Cartesian Philosophy through Cartesian Science.* Cambridge: Cambridge University Press.

Ginzberg, Lori D. 1994. "'The Hearts of Your Readers Will Shudder': Fanny Wright, Infidelity, and American Freethought." *American Quarterly* 46 (2): 195–226.

Gracia, Jorge J. E. 1991. *Philosophy and Its History: Issues in Philosophical Historiography.* Albany: State University of New York Press.

Graham, Gordon. 1982. "Can There Be History of Philosophy?" *History and Theory* 21 (1): 37–52.

Hall, Mark David. 2000. "Catharine Beecher: America's First Female Philosopher and Theologian." *Fides et Historia* 32 (1): 65–80.

Harding, Sandra. 1998. *Feminism and Methodology: Social Science Issues.* Bloomington: Indiana University Press.

Harrison, Stephen. 1995. "Poetry, Philosophy, and Letter-Writing." In *Ethics and Rhetoric: Classical Essays for Donald Russell on His Seventy-Fifth Birthday*, edited by Doreen C. Innes, Harry Hine, and Christopher Pelling, 47–61. Oxford: Oxford University Press.

Hayek, F. A. 1951. *John Stuart Mill and Harriet Taylor: Their Correspondence and Subsequent Marriage.* London: Routledge and Kegan Paul.

Jackson, Helen Hunt. 1873. *Bits of Talk About Home Matters.* Boston: Roberts Brothers.

Jaggar, Alison. 1991. "Feminist Ethics: Projects, Problems, Prospects." In *Feminist Ethics*, edited by Claudia Card, 78–106. Lawrence: University Press of Kansas.

Jose, Jim. 2000. "Contesting Patrilineal Descent in Political Theory: James Mill and Nineteenth-Century Feminism." *Hypatia* 15 (1): 151–74.

———. 2004. "No More Like Pallas Athena: Displacing Patrilineal Accounts of Modern Feminist Political Theory." *Hypatia* 19 (4): 4–22.

Kolmerton, Carol. 1990. *Women in Utopia: The Ideology of Gender in the American Owenite Communities.* Bloomington: Indiana University Press.

Leavitt, Sarah A. 2002. *From Catharine Beecher to Martha Stewart: A Cultural History of Domestic Advice.* Chapel Hill: University of North Carolina Press.

MacIntyre, Alasdair. 1984. "The Relationship of Philosophy to Its Past." In *Philosophy in History: Essays on the Historiography of Philosophy*, edited by Richard Rorty, J. B. Schneewind, and Quentin Skinner, 31–48. Cambridge: Cambridge University Press.

Mack, Mary. 1962. *Jeremy Bentham: An Odyssey of Ideas, 1748–1792.* London: Heinemann.

McFadden, Margaret. 1996. "Anna Doyle Wheeler (1785–1848): Philosopher, Socialist, Feminist." In *Hypatia's Daughters: Fifteen Hundred Years of Women Philosophers*, edited by Linda Lopez McAlister, 204–14. Bloomington: Indiana University Press.

Mill, James. 1817. *The History of British India.* 3 vols. London: Baldwin, Cradock, and Joy.

———. 1820. "Government." Supplement to the *Encyclopaedia Britannica*. London: J. Innes (1816–23).

Mill, John Stuart. 1863. *Utilitarianism*. London: Parker, Son, and Bourn.

———. 1869. *The Subjection of Women*. London: Longmans, Green, Reader, and Dyer.

———. 1969a. "Bentham" [1833]. In *Essays on Ethics, Religion, and Society*. Vol. 10 of *The Collected Works of John Stuart Mill*, edited by John M. Robson, 75–116. Toronto: University of Toronto Press.

———. 1969b. "Coleridge" [1840]. In *Essays on Ethics, Religion, and Society*. Vol. 10 of *The Collected Works of John Stuart Mill*, edited by John M. Robson, 117–64. Toronto: University of Toronto Press.

———. 1973. *A System of Logic* [1843]. In *A System of Logic Ratiocinative and Inductive Part II, Being a Connected View of the Principles of Evidence and the Methods of Scientific Investigation* (Books IV–VI and Appendices). Vol. 8 of *The Collected Works of John Stuart Mill*, edited by John M. Robson. Toronto: University of Toronto Press.

———. 1977. "Considerations on Representative Government" [1861]. In *Essays on Politics and Society Part 2*. Vol. 19 of *The Collected Works of John Stuart Mill*, edited by John M. Robson, 371–578. Toronto: University of Toronto Press.

———. 1981. "Autobiography." In *Autobiography and Literary Essays*. Vol. 1 of *The Collected Works of John Stuart Mill*, edited by John M. Robson, 1–290. Toronto: University of Toronto Press.

———. 1982. "England and Ireland." In *Essays on England, Ireland, and the Empire*. Vol. 6 of *The Collected Works of John Stuart Mill*, edited by John M. Robson, 505–32. Toronto: University of Toronto Press.

———. 1984. "On Marriage" [1832–33?]. In *Essays on Equality, Law, and Education*. Vol. 21 of *The Collected Works of John Stuart Mill*, edited by John M. Robson, 35–50. Toronto: University of Toronto Press.

Morales, Maria H., ed. 2004. *Mill's "The Subjection of Women": Critical Essays*. Lanham, Md.: Rowman and Littlefield.

Moulton, Janice. 1983. "A Paradigm of Philosophy: The Adversary Method." In *Discovering Reality: Feminist Perspectives on Epistemology, Metaphysics, Methodology, and Philosophy of Science*, edited by Sandra Harding and Merrill Hintikka, 11–25. Dordrecht: Reidel.

Offen, Karen. 2000. *European Feminisms, 1700–1950: A Political History*. Stanford: Stanford University Press.

Okin, Susan Moller. 1988. "Editor's Introduction." In John Stuart Mill, *The Subjection of Women*, edited by Susan Moller Okin, iv–xiv. Indianapolis: Hackett.

Pankhurst, Richard. 1954. *William Thompson (1775–1833): Britain's Pioneer Socialist, Feminist, and Co-operator*. London: Pluto Press.

Passmore, John. 1965. "The Idea of a History of Philosophy." *History and Theory*, Beiheft 5:1–32.

Perkins, A. J. G., and Theresa Wolfson. 1939. *Frances Wright, Free Enquirer: The Study of a Temperament*. New York: Harper.

Rée, Jonathan. 1978. *Philosophy and Its Past*. Brighton: Harvester Press.

Rorty, Richard, J. B. Schneewind, and Quentin Skinner. 1984. Introduction to *Philosophy in History: Essays on the Historiography of Philosophy*, edited by Richard Rorty, J. B. Schneewind, and Quentin Skinner, 1–14. Cambridge: Cambridge University Press.

Shanley, Mary Lyndon. 1998. "The Subjection of Women." In *The Cambridge Companion to Mill*, edited by John Skorupski, 396–422. Cambridge: Cambridge University Press.

Sklar, Kathryn Kish. 1973. *Catharine Beecher: A Study in American Domesticity*. New Haven: Yale University Press.

Smart, Paul. 1992. "National Character, Social Progress, and the Spirit of Achievement."
    History of European Ideas 15 (4–6): 527–34.
St. John, Michael Packe. 1954. *The Life of John Stuart Mill*. New York: Macmillan, 1954.
Stokes, Eric. 1959. *English Utilitarians and India*. Oxford: Clarendon Press.
Taylor, Barbara. 1984. *Eve and the New Jerusalem: Socialism and Feminism in the Nineteenth
    Century*. London: Virago.
Thompson, William, and Anna Doyle Wheeler. 1825. *Appeal of One Half the Human Race,
    Women, against the Pretensions of the Other Half, Men, to Retain Them in Political,
    and thence in Civil and Domestic Slavery*. London: Longman.
Tonkovich, Nicole. 1997. *Domesticity with a Difference: The Nonfiction of Catharine Beecher,
    Sarah J. Hale, Fanny Fern, and Margaret Fuller*. Jackson: University Press of
    Mississippi.
Travis, Molly. 1993. "Frances Wright: The Other Woman of Early American Feminism."
    Women's Studies 22 (3): 389–97.
Varouxakis, Georgios. 1998. "National Character in John Stuart Mill's Thought." *History of
    European Ideas* 24 (6): 375–91.
Waithe, Mary Ellen. 1991. *Modern Women Philosophers, 1600–1900*. Vol. 3 of *A History of
    Women Philosophers*. Dordrecht: Kluwer.
Waterman, William Randall. 1967. *Frances Wright*. New York: AMS Press.
Wilson, Margaret. 1992. "History of Philosophy in Philosophy Today and the Case of
    Sensible Qualities." *Philosophical Review* 101 (1): 191–243.
Witt, Charlotte. 2007. "Feminist History of Philosophy. *Stanford Encyclopedia of Philosophy*.
    http://plato.stanford.edu/entries/feminism-femhist/.
Wright, Frances. 1819. *Altorf*. Philadelphia: M. Carey.
———. 1821. *Views of Society and Manners in America*. London: Longman, Hurst, Rees,
    Orme, and Brown.
———. 1822. *A Few Days in Athens*. London: Longman, Hurst, Rees, Orme, and Brown.
———. 1825. "Plan for the Gradual Abolition of Slavery without Danger of Loss to the
    Citizens of the South." *The Genius of Universal Emancipation* (October 15): 58–59.
———. 1828. "Explanatory Notes on Nashoba." *New Harmony Gazette*, January 30,
    February 6, February 13.
———. 1829. *Course of Popular Lectures; with 3 Addresses on Various Public Occasions, and
    a Reply to the Charges against the French Reformers of 1789*. London: James Watson.
———. 1844. *Biography, Notes, and Political Letters of Frances Wright D'Arusmont*. Dundee:
    J. Myles.

Index

....